ALL ABOUT ICES, JELLIES, AND CREAMS

The growing concern about the importance of pure and proper ingredients in ice cream and the rediscovery of the joys of jellies and gelatin desserts of all kinds has prompted the reissue of this rare classic text. Written by the authors specifically to remind readers of the unique and inimitable delights that are only to be achieved by using fresh fruits and juices, syrups, liqueurs and creams, it shows what a delicious variety of iced treats were once widely available, and can still be made quickly and easily today. The books begins with an exceptional selection of 'water ices' as sorbets were once known - lime, tangerine, apple, mille fleur, pistachio, white raspberry, muscat and many more. Sorbets are increasingly popular, both for their clear taste and the fact that they are fat free. Then comes a section on granitas of a very sophisticated kind - roman punch, rum punch and a sensational dry sherry granita. Section II starts wth cream ices of both kinds - those that use cream and those that have a custard base. Among the enticements on offer are raspberry and red currant ice cream, green tea ice cream and a luscious almond praline cream ice. Iced souffles come next including caramel and the aptly-named souffle des anges, a heavenly confection of maraschino and orange-flower. Bombes feature next, with instructions on how to prepare such forgotten delights as Pompadour Bombe (coffee cream, strawberry cream, lemon water ice, tangerine water ice) and the irresistible Harlequin Bombe (green chartreuse cream and orange water ice). From the cold charms of ices the book moves on to the cool blandishments of jelly. The maraschino, cassis and rose jellies, elegant vanilla and coffee jellies and wonderful fresh fruit jellies to while the summer away - grape, cherry, peach, apricot and white currant. Next come the jellied creams, justly beloved by the Victorians - succulent nectarine cream, cantaloupe melon cream, mirabel cream, mulberry cream, greengage cream and many more. Then come the liqueur creams - chartreuse both green and yellow, pink maraschino cream, chestnut and caramel creams perfect for winter and regal Victoria cream studded with jewel-like glace fruits. The book continues with a section on jams, preserves and compotes, concluding with a section on wine cups and fruit beverages including refreshing cherryade, mille fruitade and the ravishing Chianti cup - a holiday in a glass. Full directions are given for all recipes, and there is a detailed index. Affordable home ice cream making machines are now widely available, and for the creams and jellies, no equipment is required except for a fridge. So buy this book, and rediscover the lost world of ices, jellies and creams.

All About Ices, Jellies, and Creams

HENRY G. HARRIS

S. P. BORELLA

LONDON AND NEW YORK

First published in 2002 by
Kegan Paul International

This edition first published in 2010 by
Routledge
2 Park Square, Milton Park, Abingdon, Oxfordshire OX14 4RN

Simultaneously published in the USA and Canada
by Routledge
711 Third Avenue, New York, NY 10017, USA

First issued in paperback 2016

Routledge is an imprint of the Taylor & Francis Group, an informa business

© Kegan Paul, 2002

Transferred to Digital Printing 2010

All rights reserved. No part of this book may be reprinted or reproduced or utilised in any form or by any electronic, mechanical, or other means, now known or hereafter invented, including photocopying and recording, or in any information storage or retrieval system, without permission in writing from the publishers.

British Library Cataloguing in Publication Data
A catalogue record for this book is available from the British Library

ISBN 13: 978-1-138-96571-3 (pbk)
ISBN 13:978-0-7103-0724-8 (hbk)

Publisher's Note
The publisher has gone to great lengths to ensure the quality of this reprint but points out that some imperfections in the original copies may be apparent. The publisher has made every effort to contact original copyright holders and would welcome correspondence from those they have been unable to trace.

DEDICATION.

To

T. Percy Lewis, Esq.,

(of Malvern),

Our

Very dear Friend and Colleague,

who shares our ideals, and dreams our dreams,

This Book is Dedicated.

"Do we sleep, do we dream, or is visions about?

Is our trade education a failure,

    Or is Confectionery played out."?

        (With Apologies to the late Bret Harte.)

A FOREWORD.

It is a very unsatisfactory reflection in an age when progress generally is evidenced on all sides and a widespread information reaches nearly all classes, that so many confectioners, if they do not actively assist in the consistent depreciation of the quality of their products, at least passively acquiesce. Ices have suffered greatly in this way, and all kinds of sweetened flavoured farinaceous substances taken the place of the proper ingredients. An examination of the so-called cream ices, or "ice-cream," to use the general, but inaccurate title, made by the vast majority of sellers would clearly demonstrate the fact. Of course, there are fine ices still made by confectioners, but only by a small minority, the bulk of the high-class trade being in the hands of the large hotels and restaurants.

To assist in an awakening, and lest it be forgotten that fruit juices and cream are still available and are outside and beyond imitation, the Section devoted to the making of ices has been written, and it is earnestly hoped, may have an influence for good with thinking men.

A high standard for Jellies and Moulded Creams is equally important, and will, if maintained, justify itself by results.

Good and suitable Jams are an essential in every confectionery workshop, and can be made by each user at a lower price than he can obtain a corresponding quality elsewhere. The difference of advantageous buying by the wholesaler, although considerable, does not represent his necessary profit.

The preservation of fruits, especially those bottled in water or light syrup, is almost equally important, and can be undertaken at a time when most confectioners are not very busy, and time can well and profitably be devoted to the work.

Every formula in the various sections has been carefully balanced and tested; nothing has been taken for granted: and nothing included unless it was within the actual experience of the writers.

A word as to nomenclature.—An attempt has been made in part to adhere, as far as possible, to properly descriptive titles. Exceptions to this rule occur in the case of well-known (even if inaccurate) titles which have occasionally been retained. The titles of the moment ("a la," this or that) which appear on so many menus have been ignored. An example of this type, which is an exception to the "given to-day and forgotten to-morrow" rule, is "Peches a la Melba," for which one of the really great chefs—M. Escoffier—is responsible. It is composed of two portions of vanilla cream ice, between which is sandwiched a layer of halves of peaches masked in raspberry conserve or sweetened and reduced raspberry juice. Good as this dish is, its title is complimentary, not descriptive.

Nothing will ever prevent this method of naming dishes, and there is no reason why it should not continue—except its multiplied confusion.

Our desire is to be helpful—not only to individuals, but to our trade as a whole. It is, however, to the younger members that we hope chiefly to appeal, for with them lies the trade's future. Those older ones, deeply set in their wicked ways, are largely past praying for. Even a few of these may perhaps be converted, and "there is more joy over one sinner that repenteth than over ninety and nine just men."

HENRY G. HARRIS.
S. P. BORELLA.

ALL ABOUT ICES, JELLIES, CREAMS, & CONSERVES.

ICES.

This important department of the catering business is one that does not as a rule receive the attention it deserves. Proper appliances and utensils are necessary to obtain good results, and it should be the aim of every confectioner to send out better ices than any of his competitors. In almost every town or district it will be found that the confectioner whose ices are the most highly esteemed is the one to whom the best orders naturally gravitate. Low prices may attract some of the less desirable, but consistent quality—and the term covers condition and finished workmanship as well as richness—is bound to tell in the long run. Such a reputation, once firmly established, is of the greatest value in securing future orders, not only for the ices themselves, but for all the other things that usually accompany them.

The appliances necessary for the ice-making department will, of course, depend entirely upon the quantity that has to be produced. If only an occasional pint or quart is required, it would be unwise to provide an extensive plant; if, on the contrary, a large business can be done, either as a daily shop trade, an outdoor trade, or both combined, the larger quantity can be more economically produced and far more satisfactorily in a properly equipped department. As an example: to freeze a small quantity of cream or water ice, the comparatively small quantity of ice needed can be chipped into small pieces with the ice pricker, although it is a wasteful and laborious method; if large quantities are needed a proper ice breaker will do the work in a fraction of the time without waste: the former is the more usual method even in cases where the latter method is justified. Occasionally where large quantities have to be broken, and the pricker method is too slow, a large wooden mortar and pestle are used, and ice is even broken on the floor, either in a sack or open, and smashed with a mallet or other instrument. All these methods are to be deprecated, chiefly on account of wastefulness, but also because of the bad results and the dreadful mess. In breaking ice by any of the hand methods there is always a large percentage of very small pieces which dissolve into water before they can be utilised, and are consequently lost. By using the machine, the ice is bitten off by the teeth in pieces approximately the same size, and the maximum results are obtainable.

ICE.

Whilst upon the subject of the ice itself, a slight comparison of the relative values of naturally frozen and artificially produced ice will not be out of place.

The naturally frozen ice is far more valuable for freezing purposes than that produced artificially by any of the anhydrous ammonia methods. The difference in the temperature of the two products can be easily demonstrated by burying a sensitive thermometer in a hole in the middle of a block of each kind. An easier method of arriving at the same result and one more likely to commend itself to the mind of the practical man, is to obtain two cubes of the same dimensions,—one of the natural and one of the artificial—wrap each in a blanket and set, not too near one another, in a cool cellar, and test the time taken for each to dissolve entirely. We venture to think that the result will be surprising

All about Ices.

and conclusive. The difference in time taken will approximately demonstrate the difference in value for freezing purposes. Where ice is needed for adding to drinks of various sorts, it is conceivable that the artificial ice *may* be made from the purer water, although it does not necessarily follow that it is so.

SALT.

This can readily be obtained from most salt merchants. In its best form it is of large coarse grain, nearly white, and should be almost free from moisture. Usually it contains a too large percentage of water, in which condition it is more profitable to the vendors. Samples should be carefully chosen, as it is inadvisable to pay somewhere in the neighbourhood of 2s. per cwt. for water, when it can be avoided. The difference between 10 per cent. and 25 per cent. of water in freezing salt makes a perceptible difference in the actual cost; so dry, or comparatively dry, parcels should be insisted upon.

FREEZERS.

There are many forms of these, many types being advertised, all of them claiming to be the best. If one is to believe all that is said of them, they all use the minimum amount of ice, with comparatively little labour, and give the best possible results.

The freezers available for the confectioner's use may be roughly divided into three types.

No. 1.—The old-fashioned pewter type with straight sides, with a bottom, flat in the centre, and curving upwards to meet the sides. This type is operated by hand, a wooden-handled spattle with a flat spooned-shaped head in pewter being its component part. The cover fits tightly, and has a heavy rounded handle, which is often used to spin the freezer in the tub. This type is the most generally used, and is in many respects the most useful, especially for small quantities.

No. 2.—The various forms of the American type, two forms of which are shown, made of sheet copper or iron, and tinned or galvanised. These are operated by cog wheels attached to the lid, which has some form of attachment to the freezer itself. They

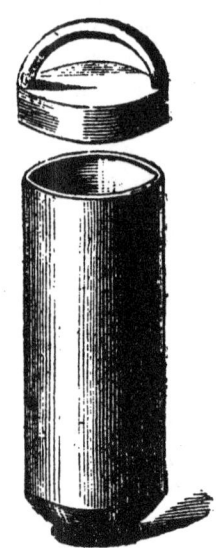

No. 1.

are driven by a handle at the side (the larger sizes having power attachment), and have either stationary or movable beaters inside, which beat and churn the mixture whilst freezing proceeds. This type gives its best results with water and custard ices, where cream is not used, as they are apt to churn cream up to the point where disintegration of its component parts sets in. All ices need thorough spattling, but none really need churning, although some will stand it without hurt.

One point about these inner beaters is worth noting. As the mixture freezes on the revolving cylinder and forms a coating it is necessary to remove it, not only to blend it

No. 2.

Freezers.

with the less frozen centre, but to allow that centre in its turn to be frozen. The beaters are supposed to do this, one side of the frame sometimes having a thin slip of wood running parallel with the side of the freezer and sliding in a slotted frame. If the wooden lath were fitted tightly against the side of the freezer it would effectively scrape the sides, but very little resistance would either break the lath, or stop the freezer. It is therefore given a certain amount of play, with the result that the shell of frozen matter, as it gradually hardens and thickens on the freezer's sides, drives it just as far away from the sides as the amount of play allows, and it ceases to be effective. The harder that shell becomes, the more difficult it is to remove and to blend it with the balance of the mixture. It therefore becomes more and more necessary as the

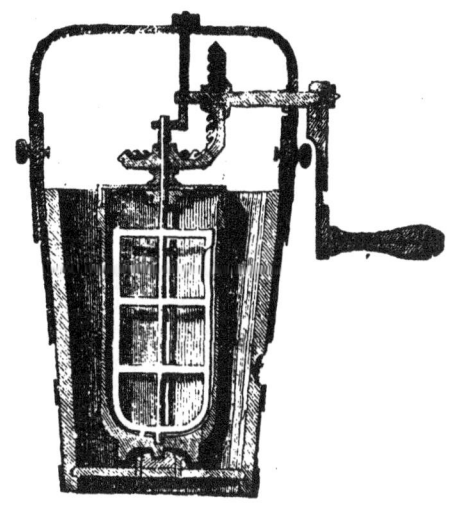

No. 2A.

freezing proceeds to remove the lid and cut away the shell, thus creating the very difficulty that this type of freezer is supposed to avoid.

No. 2A shows the interior of the freezer fitted with a solid frame, which is stronger, but open to the same objection of non-clearance.

No. 3.—The Kirchoff and a simpler French machine are alike in principle but distinct in form, the former having many advantages over the latter. The form of the Kirchoff freezer is almost ideal. It lends itself not only to perfect, but very rapid freezing, as, when it is running centrifugal force spreads the matter to be frozen in a thin sheet over the greater portion of its inner surface. The container is made of very hard white metal. Its form is that of a sphere, indented at the bottom, and open at the top. The indentation at the bottom carries a gun-metal centre, which runs on a cone-shaped pin, securely fixed in the bottom of the tub. From the centre of the inside, and moulded to follow the shape of the outside indentation, stands an upright rod, which in its turn runs up to the side bearings, and holds the container rigidly upright whilst running. This movement gives the minimum amount of friction, and whether the machine is driven by hand or power, the power needed is small.

THE KIRCHOFF FREEZER.
No. 3.

In this machine every point appears to have been well thought out, and every detail cared for. The outer or tub portion is made of small pieces of hard wood and felt, pressed together with pitch or other adhesive matter in a frame or mould, and afterwards faced up inside and out. The result is an almost perfect non-conductor, that enables the operator to make the most of the ice used.

All about Ices.

The simpler type of French machine, No. 3A, runs in the same way as the Kirchoff, but is slighter in construction, with just a shallow stave tub; and the sides of the container being ordinary straight upstanding, it can only be driven at a slow speed, or centrifugal force would drive the liquid contents over the sides.

No. 3A.

CONSERVATORS.

The usual plan is to repack the tub in which the ice was frozen with fresh ice and a little salt, and send up to the sale shop—if intended for such a purpose—in the ordinary pewter freezer.

There is, however, no place so good for storing the finished ices, whether for sale in the shop or for sending out for balls or other functions, as the Kirchoff porcelain containers. These are white, and of the ordinary cylindrical form. They can be packed in exactly the same way as the pewter variety, are cheaper and cleaner, but breakable.

If for shop use, then the Kirchoff Conservator not only economically preserves the ices, its body being built exactly as that of the freezer, but it is a handsome piece of furniture. One, two, three or more freezers can be set up in it with the minimum amount of ice and the certainty of remaining the entire day in perfect condition.

It must be understood that the writers have no interest in this or any other form of ice machine, and are honestly expressing their opinion only as to relative values. These machines were first introduced to this country from Vienna, by Mr. Carl Reichert, and are now to be obtained of most dealers in confectioners' utensils.

There are many other forms of freezing utensils, some of them largely advertised, that freeze by conducted cold, simply being immersed in ice and salt or some form of freezing composition. These are all open to the objection that spattling is impossible, with the result that smooth, fluffy ices cannot be produced. In freezing by this plan there is always a partial separation of the constituents used, the watery portions freezing first, thus producing, especially with water ices, a semi-granular mass.

Whenever it is possible the ice-making department should be quite distinct from the bakery and confectionery portion of the establishment. A comparatively small room can be so arranged that all utensils and appliances can have proper positions apportioned to them that will greatly facilitate the work and insure, with ordinary care, its being turned out not only better, but quicker and with less labour than if it is done amongst the everyday work, in a temperature that of necessity must be higher than desirable.

In such a room as that suggested the floor should be of either stone slabs or concrete. Bricks well laid will answer as well, but there is a good deal of wear on the floor, and bricks are apt to get chipped and broken. Whatever be the substance used, the floor should have one or two channels cut towards a gully, and there should be a slight slope in the same direction.

It is usual in Continental establishments for the workmen who make the ices to wear wooden

Freezers.

clogs, but no such indignity is ever suggested for free Britishers, who would far rather get wet footed, and lay the foundation of future rheumatism than so condescend. Therefore as an alternative protection wooden gratings are proposed round the machines and where otherwise needed. There should be a few strong shelves to carry moulds when not in use. Racks in skeleton form, where freezing pots, whether of pewter or porcelain, can be set at an angle after washing and drying, and also racks to carry lids and covers, which must always be kept perfectly clean and dry.

There must be an ice box, large enough to hold at least one day's supply. This box should be lead lined, and have a draw-off tap to run away water when necessary. Alongside should be another box or bin for salt. Both these bins or boxes should have sloping lids, so that they cannot be used as tables, otherwise whenever the lids have to be opened many things will need to be shifted.

One or two or more large single ice prickers will be needed, and these should have a definite place when not in use. The largest size is suggested, not only because they will do the work more quickly, but because they will be unsuitable for toothpicks or forks.

Tubs, whether used to actually freeze the ices in pewter freezers, or for packing and sending out the finished goods, should be made of stout oak staves, well banded together with iron hoops, and each one should have a $\frac{3}{4}$ in. hole near the bottom on one side that can be corked whilst in use, and when desired opened to draw away water. Whether these tubs are plain or painted matters little (except that the painted ones last the longer), so long as they are kept clean, and when not in use occasionally well wetted to prevent shrinkage and leaking. These tubs should also have their proper place apportioned to them, arranged in such a way that they are attractive rather than unsightly.

A fair-sized working table, with a marble slab at one end and a drawer or two underneath to hold necessary tools, is a great convenience, if used only for their legitimate purpose.

Over the table a narrow shelf or two to carry small bottles of colours and syrups, and under the shelves racks for knives, spoons, etc., and proper places elsewhere for hanging spattles when not in use, and strong pins for hanging brass or copper and hair sieves and whisks, will go a long way to complete the arrangements.

A lock-up cupboard is a convenience, but not a necessity if the room itself can be locked.

A number of china basins or pans will, of course, be necessary; but copper bowls for whisking can generally be borrowed from the confectionery department. If jellies and creams are to be made, they should be moulded in the same room, but it is best to keep the moulds in a dryer place, and to make the jelly in the warmer kitchen.

No provision has here been made for custard making for ices, as it is not advisable to have a stove in this room. Custards, like jellies, are best made in the kitchen, where all appliances should be found.

If a large freezing machine is used it is best driven with a small motor, if electric current is available, in which case an ice-breaking machine can be driven the same way. The illustrations show only small hand-driven machines.

A number of ice caves would be needed if ices, iced puddings, and iced souffles are to be sent out ready for table, and in the case of the two former save a good deal of labour and permit of the ices being turned out of their moulds, dished in the ice-house, and carried by a messenger instead of some competent person having to attend each order.

There are many makes of these useful little conveniences, but all of them involve the same principle—*i.e.*, a small chamber the surrounding walls of which are hollow, ready for filling with ice and salt. They should be painted or enamelled, as the outside coating will largely help to conserve the freezing mixture.

All about Ices.

If nicely enamelled and the owner's name writ large, they form a good advertising medium.

FREEZING OF ICES.

No matter how well made the ice mixtures may be, unless they are frozen in the proper way they will not be satisfactory. The first thing of importance is the proper setting up of the actual freezer, and whether this be of the ordinary old-fashioned pewter type for hand turning, or the Kirchoff or any other machine, the method will be practically the same. The ice should be broken in small pieces and mixed with one-sixth its weight of freezing salt. This should be well packed round the freezing vessel, and driven into a compact mass with a long wooden driver. The top of the tub may be covered in with a heavy wooden lid, fitting an inch or more inside from the top, with a hole or holes to allow the top of the freezer or freezers to come through, if desired, but this is not a necessity. An expert worker will prefer to work without this cover, but an inexpert man may find it helpful. This applies only to the old-fashioned method of freezing by hand.

In all cases the setting up of the freezers should be completed before placing the mixture to be frozen inside them. This should be done to avoid the possibility of any of the ice or salt getting inside amongst the mixture and spoiling it. After setting up, the inside of the freezer should always be carefully wiped out with a clean cloth, and the lid, which has, of course, been used as a cover, carefully washed to remove any salt that may have accumulated.

Now pour in the previously prepared cream or water mixture, put on the lid, which should fit tightly, and spin the freezer round and round for about five minutes. This can be done with both hands, catching the handle whilst still spinning, and reversing the movement. The freezing will not commence until a certain quantity of water has formed at the base of the ice and salt, so if this does not form readily it is well to pour a little water over the ice to give it a start.

As soon as the mixture begins to form a casing on the sides of the freezer use the spattle, scrape the casing off, and mix it with the unfrozen portion. Continue turning and scraping alternately, and as soon as the mixture is about half frozen keep the lid off, twist the freezer with fingers and thumb of the one hand, and with the other hand use the spattle vigorously. Upon the proper spattling of the ice will greatly depend the degree of smoothness obtained, so do not spare labour.

It is usual with the old-fashioned freezer to have a wooden-handled and pewter-bladed spattle, but one made entirely of hard white wood is preferable, especially if the blade is rounded to fit the form of the freezer at one side and flat at the other, the edges of both sides and bottom being tapered sharply.

When the freezing is completed, if the ice is to remain in the same freezer for serving, remove the cork from the tub, withdraw the water, and repack with ice and salt, but using rather less salt than at first. Sprinkle a little salt over the top of the ice to form a casing, and keep the whole covered with a damp cloth—until required to be used.

It is always advisable to raise the finished ice in the freezer a little higher in the centre than at the sides, so that any slight separation of saccharine matter, sometimes occurring in very rich water ices, may find its way to the sides of the freezer, instead of collecting in the centre, where it stands no chance of again freezing. If, on the other hand, the ice is to be transferred to moulds, or porcelain freezers for sending out, or to the conservator for the sale shop, these should be properly set up, ready to receive their quota, and the original tub will not need re-setting up. Instructions for moulding ices will appear in the proper place

SECTION 1.—WATER ICES.

Water ices, when properly made and frozen, should be as smooth and creamy in texture as cream ices, but will not, of course, have the fluffiness that should distinguish the latter. This necessary smoothness will entirely depend upon two things—firstly the saccharine strength of the mixture, and secondly the method of freezing. Should the quantity of sugar used in the mixture be too small the mixture will freeze too readily and be snowy in character. On the other hand, should there be too much sugar, it will be difficult, if not impossible, to freeze properly. As sugar varies considerably in saccharine strength, the formulæ given can only be approximately accurate, and must be finally determined by testing with a saccharometer, a handy little instrument that, when floated in a liquid body, will sink according to the density of the floating medium. When testing, if the density is too great water must be added; if not great enough, then simple syrup must be added to adjust as required. Whilst, of course, for ices intended to be used for small decorative fruit moulds on the one hand, or for Neapolitan moulds on the other, there will need to be slight differences of saccharine strength, for all ordinary purposes a standard is best established of 21 deg. of strength. This can be modified as necessity requires. In choosing a saccharometer, it is advisable to select one as short as possible, as it can then be used in the actual mixing bowl, instead of having to ladle out some of the mixture into a deeper vessel, in which there is depth sufficient for the instrument to float.

Sugar should never be used in the dry state for making water ices, but should always be made into a syrup, clarified and bottled for use. It can be made when required, but time will be saved by preparing beforehand, with the additional advantage of having your syrup cold for use.

The best strength is the simple syrup of the British Pharmacopœia, which is made as follows. Good loaf or crushed sugar is absolutely essential.

SIMPLE SYRUP.

12 lbs. loaf sugar.   4 quarts water.

Place the sugar in a clean copper-egg-bowl, pour on the water; let it stand for half an hour, giving it an occasional stir with a wooden spattle. Set on the stove and gradually bring to the boil, skimming off any scum that rises to the top. When it reaches the boil, by which time the sugar will be thoroughly dissolved, strain through a fine hair sieve into a large pan or basin. When cold fill into large fruit bottles, and store in a cool, dry place for use. If made in large quantities it is not necessary to bottle it, provided a proper vessel is kept for storing, but it is very essential that perfect cleanliness of both utensils and syrup be maintained. It is not advisable to prepare more than a week's supply at one time.

LEMON WATER ICE.

To make one quart use
8 good juicy lemons.
1 pint simple syrup.
Water, quantum sufficit to make the whole 21 deg. by saccharometer.

With a razing-knife take off the outer yellow rind of four of the lemons into a basin. Cut and squeeze the lemons into the basin; add the syrup and sufficient water to bring the saccharine strength to 21 deg. Let all stand for half an hour, and then strain through a hair sieve, and freeze as directed.

All about Ices.

LIME WATER.

14 West India limes.
1 pint simple syrup.
Water, quantum suff.
Grated rind from 8 of the limes.

Grate the outer rind from eight of the limes, put it in a basin, cut and squeeze the limes into the basin, add the syrup, and water sufficient to bring all to 21 deg. by the saccharometer. Let the whole stand for at least half an hour, then strain through a hair sieve, and freeze as directed.

This fruit has a flavour quite distinct from that of lemons, and is by many epicures preferred to the better known fruit. The fruit must, however, be quite fresh and soft. When the skins are dry and hard they cannot be grated easily, and the juice has an accentuated flavour that is not desirable. Above all must the lime juice of commerce be avoided. It is not at all suitable for ice-making, having a well-developed flavour of mould. There are one or two reputable houses who actually bottle the juice of limes, but the bulk of so-called "lime juice" is simply the juice of lemons squeezed from the fruit that afterwards becomes lemon-peel.

CEDRATI WATER.

This ice can only be satisfactorily made when fresh ripe citrons can be obtained. The zest of this fruit, whilst strong and of an acrid bitterness if too freely used, is distinctive in character, and, when delicately used, delicious. For making one quart of ice use only two small cubes of sugar, and rub each of the six sides on the fruit until saturated with the oil from the small vesicles of the skin. Then take

8 lemons.
1 pint simple syrup.
The 2 cubes of sugar.
2 tablespoonfuls pale brandy
Water, quantum suff.
A slight tint of green colour.

Place the two cubes of saturated sugar in the basin, cut and squeeze the lemons on to the sugar; add the syrup, the brandy, and sufficient water to bring the whole to 21 deg. by the saccharometer. Work down a little green paste colour quite smooth, and add enough to give the whole a very pale green tint. Stir gently until the sugar cubes are dissolved, and then strain through a fine hair sieve, and freeze as directed.

The shade here intended is only a suggestion of green, not a definite colour. If so used it will be delightfully delicate in appearance, and the ice itself will be equally delicate in flavour.

The natural colour of a ripe citron, which is a rather deeper yellow than that of a lemon, is not, of course, aimed at.

ORANGE WATER.

6 ripe sweet oranges.
2 lemons.
1 pint of simple syrup.
Water, quantum suff.
Razed zest of 3 of the oranges.

Mix as for lemon water, adding water to bring to 21 deg. of saccharine strength. Add a few drops of liquid egg-colour and just a touch of liquid carmine if the zest does not give a sufficiently deep tint.

The use of a razing knife has been advised to obtain the zest of oranges and lemons, so it is as well to explain what is meant, as well as the method of using.

The ordinary method of obtaining the zest of these fruits is to use a piece of a broken sugar loaf, and rub the fruit on the sugar until the rough, porous surface has absorbed the

Water Ices.

oil in the minute cells in the outer yellow portion of the skin. For many purposes this is entirely the best method, as it gives quickly a very pungent flavour, as well as a rich colour. It is, however, a rather laborious task, and it also means adding sugar to the mixture when it is not always needed. Again, it is very seldom that sugar loaves are used in the ordinary shop, so the razing knife comes in as a useful labour saver.

This knife has a short blade about $\frac{3}{8}$ in. wide and $\frac{1}{8}$ in. thick, and at the extreme end are five perforations with cutting edges on each side. These cutting edges, when drawn sharply without much pressure across or along the fruit, cut through the outer skin, removing it in fine threads. As these threads carry the divided oil vessels, by soaking in the juice and syrup, the desired flavour is obtained. This useful little knife costs one shilling of any French cooks' supply house, and is well worth its price.

Another useful tool is a wooden lemon squeezer, or rather, gouge. This is made of boxwood, and with moderate care will last for many seasons. It will more quickly and effectively bring away the juice and break up the juice cells than most of the more expensive appliances. The cost of this also is about one shilling, and it will save its cost many times over during its lifetime.

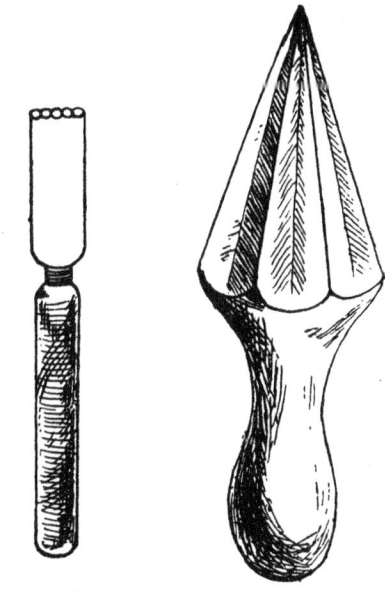

RAZING KNIFE.   LEMON PULPER.

TANGERINE ORANGE WATER.

8 tangerine oranges.
2 sweet oranges.
1 lemon.
1 pint simple syrup.
Water, quantum suff.

Take the zest from one sweet orange and lightly cut off the zest from the whole of the tangerines with the razing knife, into a basin. Cut the oranges, the tangerines, and the lemon across the sections, as in this way they are more easily broken up, and squeeze out the juice with the wooden gouge. This must be done very gently with the tangerines, or they will be liable to leave the skins in pieces, instead of being thoroughly broken up. The number given here must depend a little upon the size of the fruit. If very small more must be used. The quantity of juice obtained should be about half a pint. Add the syrup and water to make 21 deg. of strength. Let the whole soak for half an hour to become impregnated with the flavour of the zest. Then strain through a hair sieve, and freeze as directed.

If the zest does not give a sufficiently deep colour, a few drops of liquid egg-yellow and a drop of liquid carmine may be added. These must, however, be used with great discretion.

ORANGE CURACOA WATER.

Make a quart of tangerine ice as above, but before adding the water mix in half a gill of orange curacoa, then add the necessary water to make the strength by the saccharometer 22 deg., and freeze as directed. This ice will be slightly softer when frozen than

All about Ices.

the plain tangerine water, and the extra richness is intentional, as in the softer body the flavour of the liqueur will be emphasised.

MILLE FRUIT WATER.

Make a quart of lemon water ice, mixing it to 20 deg. only. Freeze it as smooth as possible, spattling even more than usual, as it is not quite so rich. When quite solid stir into it ½ lb. of glacé and other fruits, cut small, half an hour previously, and set in a basin with half a gill of maraschino poured over them. The choice of fruits is somewhat at discretion, and regard should be had to contrasts of colour. Bright cherries, angelica, apricot, greengage, green almonds, figs, etc., amongst the glacé fruits, and banana, pine apple, apricot for the fresh fruit.

The reason for steeping these fruits in the liqueur is to prevent them freezing into hard, tasteless pieces and to retain their lusciousness.

When the fruit and liqueur is added the ice will run down, and must be re-frozen, using the spattle tenderly so as not to break up the fruit.

By the time the fruit and liqueur is blended the ice will be almost 22 deg., so the reason for keeping it below the usual strength in the first place will be apparent.

This ice is especially suitable for moulding or for filling into small soufflé cases, but not for serving from a freezer or conservator for counter use, as, owing to its extra saccharine strength and the presence of particles of soft fruits, it is liable to become slightly disintegrated in the freezer, and it cannot be constantly handled without breaking up the fruits and spoiling its beautiful appearance.

MILLE FLEUR WATER.

Make one quart of lemon water ice, adding water to make it barely 21 deg. by the saccharometer, and before straining add

- 1 drop attar of roses.
- 4 drops essence of violets.
- 1 drop oil of neroli or 1 dessertspoonful orange flower water.
- 1 teaspoonful green chartreuse.
- 4 long petals of white chrysanthemum.

and just tint a very pale pink with liquid carmine. Let it stand half an hour, and then strain through a hair sieve, and freeze as directed. Great care must be exercised, both in accurately measuring the flavouring matters and in the tinting with carmine, or the delicacy of this epicurean ice will be lost.

Measuring bottles to drop single drops can be bought for a few pence at any good-class chemist's, and are well worth the small outlay.

MUSCAT WATER ICE.

- 1½ oz. dried elder flowers, or 3 ozs. if quite freshly picked.
- 4 lemons (juice only).
- 1 pint simple syrup.
- ¼ pint boiling water.
- 1 wineglassful of Malaga (white wine).
- Water quantum suff. to reduce to 21 deg. by the saccharometer.

The quantity of dried elder flowers must vary according to its strength. It varies considerably in different seasons, so that the palate must be the final judge. The flavouring should be delicate, and suggest the refined taste of the Muscat grape. The best wine to use is Muscatto d'Asti, but it is so seldom available that Malaga is here substituted.

Put the elder flowers, free from stalk, into a small jug, pour on the boiling water, cover up the jug, and stand in a warm place to steep for about half an hour. Set a muslin

Water Ices.

cloth over another basin, hold it stretched rather loosely and pour the infusion, flowers and all, into the cloth. Gather up the two ends and twist in opposite directions, so that the whole of the infusion is squeezed into the basin.

Sqeeze the lemons into another basin, add the syrup, and strain free from pulp. Add the wine and enough of the infusion of elder flowers to give a little stronger flavour than needed. The flavour will not appear so much in evidence after freezing as before. Add water as required to reach 21 deg. by saccharometer. Freeze as directed. Whilst freezing, tint a very pale yellowish-green.

RASPBERRY WATER ICE.

This ice is never quite satisfactory unless it is made from the fresh fruit or properly made syrup (see fruits for ices), and it is advised that it be only made when freshly-picked fruit or syrup is available.

- 1½ lb. freshly-picked raspberries.
- A handful of white currants, picked from stalks.
- 1 pint simple syrup.
- Water, quantum suff. to reduce to 21 deg. by the saccharometer

Place the raspberries, free from stalks, and the picked currants in a copper sugar-boiler with a gill of water. Put on the stove, and boil gently until the fruit is broken up. Then pass through a fine hair sieve, pressing gently with the back of a wooden spoon. Avoid passing the actual pulp or pips of the fruit. Add a pint of simple syrup, and water as required to reduce to 21 deg. by the saccharometer. Freeze as directed.

The addition of white currants will give a little necessary acidity to the mixture, and will slightly reduce the rather high colour of the raspberries. There will be no flavour of currants, the proportions being insufficient to affect the stronger flavour of the raspberries.

RASPBERRY AND RED CURRANT WATER ICE.

- ¾ lb. fine fresh raspberries, free from hulls.
- 1 pint simple syrup.
- ¾ lb. fine red currants, after picking from stalk.
- Water sufficient to reduce to 21 deg. by the saccharometer.

Boil and pass exactly as for raspberry water. Add the syrup, and reduce with water to the 21st degree. Freeze as directed.

WHITE RASPBERRY WATER ICE

This is quite a distinctive ice, very delicate in both flavour and appearance if properly made.

- 1½ lb. fine white raspberries, free from hulls.
- A handful of fine white currants, picked from stalks.
- 1 pint simple syrup.
- Liquid carmine, one or two drops only.
- Water sufficient to reduce to 21 deg. by the saccharometer.

Boil and pass exactly as for raspberry water. Add the syrup and sufficient water to reduce to 21 deg. Then stir in one or two drops only of liquid carmine to give a blush-rose tint only. Freeze as directed

All about Ices.

RED CURRANT WATER ICE.

1¼ lb. red currants
 (before picking).
¼ lb. red Kentish cherries.

1 pint simple syrup.
Water sufficient to reduce to 21
 deg. by the saccharometer.

Set the cherries, the picked red currants, and ¼ pint of water in a small sugar-boiler and reduce to pulp over the fire. Then pass through a fine hair sieve, pressing lightly with the back of a wooden spoon. Be careful that you do not rub too hard. You require all the juice, but not the pulp or pips. Add the syrup and enough wat to reduce to 21 deg., and freeze as directed.

WHITE CURRANT WATER ICE.

1½ lb. white currants
(before picking).
1 pint simple syrup.

1 tablespoonful yellow Chartreuse.
Water sufficient to reduce to 21
 deg. by the saccharometer.

Put the picked currants with a gill of water in a small copper sugar-boiler, and reduce over the fire to pulp. Pass through a fine hair sieve, gently pressing with the back of a wooden spoon to squeeze out every drop of juice, but not passing the pulp or pips. Add the syrup and chartreuse, and sufficient water to reduce to 21 deg. of saccharine strength. Freeze as directed, great care being given to the spattling to ensure a smooth body.

BLACK CURRANT WATER ICE.

1 lb. black currants (fine large fruit),
 (before picking.)
¼ lb. red currants.

1 pint simple syrup.
Water sufficient to reduce to 21
 deg. by the saccharometer.

Red currants are used here to slightly reduce the depth of colour, and in these proportions there will be no apparent diminution of flavour. Set the black and red currants with one gill of water in a copper sugar boiler, and reduce to pulp on the fire. Pass through a fine hair sieve, using only slight pressure with the back of a wooden spoon to squeeze through the whole of the juice. Add the syrup and sufficient water to reduce to 21 deg. of saccharine strength, and freeze as directed, spattling thoroughly.

STRAWBERRY WATER ICE.

1½ lb. strawberries (free from hulls).
1 pint simple syrup.
The juice of one lemon.

1 teaspoonful of fine Jamaica rum
Water sufficient to reduce to 21
 deg. by the saccharometer.

The best strawberries of all are the small wild "Scarletts," but these are seldom obtainable, unless ordered specially for preserving. Failing "Scarletts" the most satisfactory are small or medium-sized "Paxtons," fully ripe. Many people prefer "Royal Sovereigns," on account of their delicacy of flavour, but they are somewhat thin and wanting in body, although possessing a little more acidity. The distinguishing delicacy of the "Royal Sovereigns," whilst marked as a dessert fruit, largely disappears in freezing, whilst the thinness is accentuated. Pass the fruit through a fine hair sieve, being careful not to rub sufficiently hard to pass the pips. Add the syrup, the strained juice of the lemon, the rum, and sufficient water to reduce to 21 deg. of saccharine strength. Freeze as directed, spattling thoroughly. The small quantity of rum will appreciably accentuate the flavour of the fruit, but it must be fine Jamaica. Crude Demerara must not be used.

Water Ices.

CHERRY WATER ICE.

1½ lb. cherries,
  (after picking).
1 pint simple syrup.

Juice of 2 lemons.
Water sufficient to reduce to 21
  deg. by the saccharometer.

The best cherries for ice making are the pale red acid variety, known respectively as "Kentish," "Flemish," or "May Duke." The latter term is a perversion of "Medoc," the district of France whence these cherries originally came. All of these are easily broken down, retain their bright colour and fine flavour, and are mostly acid enough to use without the addition of lemon juice, if not too ripe. Their condition, however, must decide whether or not juice is necessary.

Pound the cherries a few at a time in a clean marble mortar, breaking up the stones, and with a card or horn scoop out into a copper sugar-boiler. When all are pounded add a gill of water, and simmer over the fire until well pulped Pass through a fine hair sieve with care, so that the broken stones do not cut the sieve. Add the syrup, the strained juice of the lemons (if used), and sufficient water to reduce to 21 deg. of saccharine strength.

It may be necessary to add a few drops of liquid carmine should the colour not be sufficiently bright, but this will largely depend upon the kind and condition of the cherries used. Confectioners must therefore be guided by their own judgment in this matter. Freeze as directed, spattling thoroughly.

MORELLA CHERRY WATER ICE.

1¼ lb. fresh Morella cherries,
  (fully ripe).
1 pint simple syrup.

1 dessertspoonful fine pale brandy.
Water sufficient to reduce to 21
  deg. by the saccharometer.

Pound the cherries in the mortar, add the gill of water, and scald on the fire. These will very readily break down, and will not need so long to pulp as the ordinary fruit. The stones must be well broken, so that the short time on the fire will bring out the noyeau flavour of the kernels. The main reason for less heating is to avoid the undue darkening of the fruit. The tint is very deep, and much heat is likely to turn the shade of deep lake to brown.

Pass through the hair sieve, add the syrup and brandy, and sufficient water to bring to 21 deg. of saccharine strength. Colour should not be needed, and will not be if the scalding has been carefully done. Freeze as directed, spattling thoroughly.

APRICOT WATER ICE.

This ice has the best flavour when made from ripe fresh fruits. These are, however, seldom obtainable in this country in the required condition, so it is advised that either fine Californian pulp be used, or a good brand of apricots in syrup. The proportions given below are for the fruit in syrup. Should pulp be used, it will be necessary to reduce the quantity of fruit and increase the sugar proportionately.

1 can of apricots in syrup (a nominal 2½).
¾ pint of simple syrup.
Juice of 1 lemon.

1 dessertspoonful of noyeau (liqueur).
Water sufficient to reduce to 21
  deg. by the saccharometer.

All about Ices.

Turn out the fruit, syrup and all, into a basin, and break it up by pressure. Pass through a fine hair sieve by pressure with the hand. Add the syrup, the strained juice of the lemon, the liqueur, and mix all together with a wooden spoon. Then add water gradually until reduced to the proper saccharine strength. Freeze as directed, and spattle thoroughly.

PEACH WATER ICE.

Fine peaches can be obtained here, but they usually cost a fine price, so it is advised to have the white Freestone Californian fruit in syrup. Carefully avoid the dark yellow cling stone sorts. Many of them have good flavour, but the fruit is too hard and does not pulp easily.

1 can white Freestone peaches in syrup (nominal 2½).
¾ pint of simple syrup.
Juice of 1 lemon.

1 dessertspoonful of noyeau (liqueur).
Water sufficient to reduce to 21 deg. by the saccharometer.
Two or three drops of liquid carmine

Mix and freeze exactly as for apricot, spattling thoroughly. The colour to be added should only be sufficient to give the most delicate tint of pink, or its beauty will be entirely spoiled.

APPLE WATER ICE.

It is necessary to be very careful to select the proper kind or kinds of apples for this purpose, or you will have either flavourless or badly-coloured ice. The pulp must be white, and must render down easily. The most suitable kinds for this purpose are Wellingtons, Suffields, or Keswicks. These are all very white in flesh, and easily break down. The Wellingtons are the best of the three, and are much more acid than either of the others. Their flavour is good, but rather thin. Blenheims are far finer in flavour, and if under-ripe are a good colour.

2 lbs. of apples (peeled and cored).
½ pint of water.
1 pint of simple syrup.
Juice of two lemons (unless acid apples are used).

Small wineglassful pale brandy.
Few drops green colour.
Water sufficient to reduce to 21 deg. by the saccharometer.

Peel, quarter, and core the apples, and as they are peeled throw them into a pan of cold water to prevent them changing colour. When cut, place in copper sugar-boiler (untinned), add the water, and reduce by heat to pulp, preferably in a bainmarie. This will evaporate some of the water, and leave a margin to accurately reduce to the proper strength afterwards. Pass the pulp by pressure with the back of a wooden spoon through a fine hair sieve into a good-sized basin, add the strained lemon juice (if used), the syrup, and brandy, and reduce carefully with water to 21 deg. of saccharine strength. Tint a very pale shade of green, which will be very delicate if the colour of the pulp has been conserved. Freeze as directed, paying great attention to spattling.

Unless great care has been taken, the resulting ice will be dingy and unattractive It can with care be made both attractive in appearance and delicious in flavour.

Water Ices.

PEAR WATER ICE.

There are many sorts of pears suitable for this very delicate ice, if fresh fruit is desired to be used and is available. The list will include Williams's Bon Chrétien, Marie Louise, Jargonelle, Calabash, Bishop's Thumbs, and many other of the soft, white-pulped fruits in their different seasons. These can all be pulped and frozen without rendering down by heat, and should be quite white enough to take a delicate tint of yellow or green. The most luscious of, or one of the most luscious, autumn pears is a new one named "Conference." This has a delicate pink pulp that is distinctive both in colour and flavour.

Should any of the stewing pears be used, as they will discolour a little in cooking, they will need to be tinted pink. Most of these will give a stronger flavour than the raw fruits, but a less delicate one. The easiest and simplest way is to use the canned Bartlett pears. These are very delicate in flavour, but rather thin, and as they are quite white, will take any pale tint satisfactorily. Green is advised as the best, but it should be only suggested. The proportions here given are for the Bartlett pears, but will serve accurately for the other varieties if used free from rind and cores.

1 can of Bartlett pears (nominal $2\frac{1}{2}$).	Juice of one lemon.
Syrup in the can.	2 tablespoonfuls of fine pale brandy.
$\frac{1}{2}$ pint of simple syrup.	Water sufficient to reduce to 21 deg. by the saccharometer.

Turn the fruit and syrup from the can into a basin, squeeze it to break it up, and then rub through a fine hair sieve into another basin. Add the simple syrup, the strained lemon juice, the brandy, and the necessary water to reduce to 21 deg. of saccharine strength. Tint delicately with a little green colour, and freeze as directed, spattling thoroughly.

PINEAPPLE WATER ICE.

This ice is somewhat difficult to get with a full flavour of the fresh fruit, and unless very good fresh fruit is available, it is advised to use a really good brand of the canned variety. Of these the Singapore fruits are most suitable, and "Bastians" among the best.

1 can of Singapore pineapple (and juice).	Water sufficient to reduce to 21 deg. by the saccharometer.
1 pint of simple syrup.	Tint with yellow colour and a drop of liquid carmine.
Juice of one lemon.	
1 tablespooful of noyeau (liqueur).	

Open the can carefully, so that the juice is not spilled. Set the pine to drain on a hair sieve standing over a basin. When fairly dry, cut up in slices and pound fine in a clean marble mortar. Lift the pounded pulp into the basin, add the juice, the syrup, and the juice of the lemon, let it stand for half an hour after mixing, then pass through the hair sieve, rubbing well, so that all the juice is pressed well through, leaving the fibrous matter on the sieve. Add the noyeau, and water sufficient to reduce to 21 deg. of saccharine strength. Colour to a pale orange tint, and freeze as directed, spattling thoroughly.

SHADDOCK WATER ICE.

This fruit, that is well known by various names—grape fruit, forbidden fruit, etc.— has some of the characteristics of oranges, lemons, and citron. It is as large as a small citron, the colour of a lemon, and the shape of an orange. Its vesicular construction is exactly the same as that of lemons, but the cellular walls are thicker and carry less juice.

All about Ices.

Its flavour is thinner than either the orange or lemon, it has not the saccharine body of the former nor the acidity of the latter. It has more of both, however, than the citron, and a curious delicate pungency of its own. It is a great favourite with many people, but the taste is generally an acquired one, and of slow growth. The zest gives practically the same flavour as that of a pale unripe orange. Treated as below, it will produce an ice that, whilst few would recognise the fruit, many epicures would be delighted with.

 5 large shaddocks.
 1 ripe orange.
 1 pint of simple syrup.
 1 tablespoonful fine pale brandy.
 1 dessertspoonful Jamaica rum.
 1 dessertspoonful maraschino.
 Water sufficient to reduce to 21 deg. by the saccharometer.
 Tint of yellow colour.

With the razing-knife cut away the zest of the shaddocks and the orange, cutting in very small thin pieces into a basin. Pour on the spirits and liquor and steep for half an hour. Cut and sqeeze the juice from the shaddocks and orange, add the syrup, and when the zest has steeped as directed, mix all together, stir well, and let stand for another quarter of an hour. Add water to reduce to 21 deg. of saccharine strength, and strain through a fine hair sieve. Add a few drops of yellow colour and freeze as directed, spattling thoroughly.

MELON WATER ICE.

There are quite a number of melons that can be used to make this ice, but they must be of the highly-flavoured varieties. All the orange-fleshed, the green-fleshed, and one or two of the fine white-fleshed, especially the Cantaloup, are suitable. One of the orange-fleshed, the "Rock," gives good results, and is lower in price than the finer hothouse fruits. The common Spanish yellow and green smooth-skinned melons are useless, being thin in flavour and without perfume. The real water melon, the one with smooth, deep green skin, pink sponge-like flesh, and chocolate-coloured seeds, is entirely useless for ice-making, although an ever-recurring joy to a hungry negro.

 1 melon, not less than 1½ lbs. in weight.
 2 lemons, juice only.
 1 pint simple syrup.
 1 dessertspoonful orange flower water (triple).
 1 dessertspoonful Jamaica rum.
 Water sufficient to reduce to 21 deg. by the saccharometer.

Cut the melon in half and scoop out the pulp with a silver or silver-plated spoon, after carefully removing the seeds. Pass the pulp through a fine hair sieve into a basin, cut and squeeze the lemons, also passing through the sieve, add the syrup, the orange flower water, the rum, and reduce with water to 21 deg. of saccharine strength. Should the melon used be orange-fleshed, add a few drops of yellow colour and one spot of liquid carmine. Should it be either green or white fleshed, tint with just a suspicion of green colour. Freeze as directed, spattling thoroughly.

ORLEANS PLUM WATER ICE.

 1 lb. Early Orleans plums.
 4 ozs. loaf sugar.
 ¾ pint simple syrup.
 ½ pint water (with fruit).
 1 teaspoonful fine Jamaica rum.
 Water sufficient to reduce to 21 deg. by the saccharometer.

This plum is one of the earliest of the cooking varieties, and has quite a distinctive flavour, as well as a beautifully bright colour when pulped. It is sharply acid, and lends itself to the making of a really exquisite water ice.

Water Ices.

Pick off the stalks and cut the fruit in halves with a plated or silver knife. Put them in an untinned copper sugar-boiler with half a pint of water. Set on the fire, and gently reduce to pulp, allowing the pulp to simmer for a few minutes, so that some portion of the flavour of the stone kernels may be extracted. When fully pulped add the loaf sugar, and boil gently until the sugar is dissolved. Pass the pulp through a fine hair sieve into a basin, add the syrup, the rum, and sufficient water to reduce to 21 deg. of saccharine strength. Freeze as directed, spattling thoroughly.

VICTORIA PLUM WATER ICE.

- 1 lb. ripe Victoria plums.
- 4 ozs. loaf sugar.
- ¾ pint simple syrup.
- 1 lemon (juice only).
- ½ pint water.
- 1 tablespoonful pale brandy.
- Few drops of liquid carmine.
- Water sufficient to reduce to 21 deg. by the saccharometer.

This ice can be prepared exactly as for Orleans plum, except that as the pulp will be very much paler in colour it will be advisable to use a few drops of liquid carmine. This, of course, should be used with discretion, as the ice must not be anything like as bright in colour as the Orleans plum. Freeze as directed, spattling thoroughly. A better flavour will be given to this ice if the stones are removed and pounded in a marble mortar and added to the fruit and boiled with it. Great care will need to be used in passing, so that the broken stones do not cut the hair sieve.

GREENGAGE WATER ICE

- 1 lb. greengages.
- ¼ lb. lump sugar.
- ¾ pint simple syrup.
- 1 lemon (juice only).
- ½ pint water (with fruit).
- Teaspoonful of noyeau (liqueur).
- Water sufficient to reduce to 21 deg. by the saccharometer.

There are many varieties of gages suitable for this work, but in our opinion none are so suitable as the "Reine Claude." When these are fully ripe they have almost as fine a flavour as wall fruit, and they have the great advantage of retaining their pale green colour during the ripening longer than most other varieties. Unripe fruit will, of course, give the best-coloured ice and the greatest acidity, but what is gained in colour is lost in richness of flavour. If, therefore, fully ripe fruit be used, and the resulting colour is not satisfactory, a few drops of well rubbed down vegetable green colour may be added with advantage. Great care, however, must be exercised to avoid overdoing the colour, and it is advised that it be added when the ice is partially frozen.

Split the fruit with a silver or plated knife, remove the stones, pound them in a marble mortar, and lift into a small copper sugar-boiler. Add the halves of fruit and the half-pint of water, place on the stove, and reduce to a pulp. When quite reduced add the sugar, and simmer gently until the sugar is entirely dissolved. Add the syrup, and water sufficient to reduce to 21 deg. of saccharine strength. Pass carefully through a fine hair sieve. Add the noyeau last of all, so that none of the liqueur is wasted by remaining with the unpassable portions. When the mixture is cold it must again be tested with the saccharometer, as the density will increase slightly by cooling, and if above 21 deg. adjust by the addition of a little water. Freeze as directed, spattling thoroughly, and carefully tint if desired when partially frozen.

All about Ices.

DAMSON WATER ICE.

1 lb. damsons (very ripe).
¼ lb. lump sugar.
¾ pint simple syrup.
½ pint water (with fruit).
1 dessertspoonful pale brandy.
Water sufficient to reduce to 21 deg. by the saccharometer.

Thoroughly wash the fruit in cold water, and drain on a hair sieve. Set them in a copper sugar-boiler with the half-pint of water, and reduce by heat to pulp, stirring occasionally with a wooden spattle to prevent burning, which this acid fruit is very apt to do. When fully pulped, add the sugar, and gently simmer until the sugar is dissolved, stirring frequently. Add the syrup, and water to reduce to 21 deg. of saccharine strength, and pass with pressure through a fine hair sieve into a basin. Allow the mixture to stand until cold, then stir in the brandy, and again test with the saccharometer, and if necessary adjust with water to the proper degree of saccharine density. Colour will not be necessary, as the fruit will give a beautiful rich tint. Freeze as directed, spattling thoroughly. This ice is very seldom made, and is not sufficiently known. Its rich flavour and acid astringency should make it a great favourite if carefully made.

MULBERRY WATER ICE.

¾ lb. ripe mulberries (red).
¼ lb. ripe raspberries (preferably white).
1 pint simple syrup.
1 lemon (juice only).
1 dessertspoonful pale brandy.
Water sufficient to reduce to 21 deg. by the saccharometer.

The reason for advising the use of white raspberries in this mixture is to reduce the depth of the colour in the mulberries. Put both fruits in a basin and crush with the hand. Place a fine hair sieve over another basin, and pass the pulped fruit by pressure through the sieve. Cut and squeeze the lemon, passing the juice through the sieve, and then pour the syrup also through the sieve, so that all available juice of fruit is carried with it. Mix all well together, and add the necessary water to reduce to 21 deg. of saccharine strength. Last of all add the brandy and mix. The whole of the mixing should be done either with a plated spoon or a perfectly clean wooden spattle. Freeze as directed, spattling thoroughly.

CRANBERRY WATER ICE.

1 lb. fine red Michigan cranberries.
2 oranges (juice only).
¼ lb. loaf sugar.
¾ pint of simple syrup.
½ pint water (with fruit).
1 tablespoonful of orange curacoa.
Water sufficient to reduce to 21 deg. by the saccharometer.

The Michigan cranberries are the fruit to be seen in most fruiterers' shops during the winter and spring season. These are the size of small cherries. They are very light, as their inner structure is cellular. They readily break down into pulp by heat, have a bright rich red colour, are delicately acid and astringent in flavour, and are largely used as a corrective sauce with rich meats. They are very reasonable in price, and would be as popular with the masses as they are with the epicures were they better known.

Well wash the fruit to remove any dust, drain on a hair sieve, set in a copper sugar-boiler with the half-pint of water, and pulp by heat. When thoroughly broken down, add the sugar, and gently simmer until it is dissolved. Add the syrup, and water to reduce to the proper saccharine strength, and pass through a fine hair sieve into a basin. Well

Water Ices.

mix with a plated spoon, and then cut and squeeze the oranges through the sieve into the mixture. When cold, add the curacoa, again well mix, and test with the saccharometer, and if necessary adjust to 21 deg. with water or syrup. No colour will be needed, as the fruit will give a very pretty red tint, toned down by the orange juice. Freeze as directed, spattling thoroughly.

BANANA WATER ICE.

This is at best a somewhat insipid ice, but it is occasionally asked for when bananas happen to be scarce and dear, so it is here included, although not recommended. Whenever it does happen to be made, Canary bananas should be chosen, as they are preferable to the large coarse Jamaican variety that have latterly flooded the market. There is another distinct type, with red skins and pulp, grown in Madeira, Florida, and the West Indies, that is sometimes, although inaccurately, called a "plantain." That is smaller and much better flavoured, and gives altogether better results. It is, however, seldom obtainable here.

- 8 small Canary bananas.
- 2 lemons (juice only).
- 1 pint of simple syrup.
- 1 dessertspoonful orange flower water (triple).
- 1 dessertspoonful orange Curacoa.
- Water sufficient to reduce to 21 deg. by the saccharometer.
- Few drops of yellow colour.

Peel the bananas and pound in a marble mortar to a smooth pulp, lift out into a basin, add the syrup, the lemon juice, and mix well together. Pass the whole through a fine hair sieve into another basin, add the orange flower water and the curacoa, and then reduce gradually with water until the proper degree of saccharine strength is reached. Freeze as directed, spattling thoroughly, adding a little yellow colour whilst the freezing proceeds.

MIRABELLE WATER ICE.

This plum, the true Prunus Mirabelanum, is one of the most delicately flavoured of all the cooking plums. It grows freely in France, Italy, Belgium, Spain, and less freely in Germany and Holland. In the latter countries, as well as England, a variety of the same fruit, called the cherry plum, is more general. The true Mirabelle is bright yellow in both flesh and skin, the cherry plum being yellow in flesh, but a bright red on the outside. The true Mirabelle is slightly oval in shape, and very small. The cherry plum is larger and spherical. Use the Mirabelle plum as follows :—

- 1¼ lb. ripe Mirabelle plums.
- ¼ pint of water.
- ¼ lb. of sugar.
- ¾ pint of simple syrup.
- 1 teaspoonful of noyeau.
- Water to reduce to 21 degrees by the saccharometer.
- Little yellow colour.

Pound the Mirabelles in a clean marble mortar, breaking up the stones and kernels; lift out with a horn scoop into a small copper sugar-boiler, add the water, and by heat reduce to a smooth pulp; add the sugar, and simmer gently until the sugar is dissolved. Pour into a basin, add the syrup, and water sufficient to reduce to the proper saccharine strength, and pass through a fine hair sieve into another basin, and when cold add the noyeau and again test with the saccharometer, and if necessary add a little syrup or water to adjust to the proper degree. The reason for adding the water whilst warm is that the mixture is more easily passed, but as the density of the whole will be slightly increased

All about Ices.

when cold, it is advisable to test the second time. Freeze as directed, spattling thoroughly, and adding a few drops of liquid yellow colour to obtain the desired tint, *i.e.*, a pale apricot colour.

During the seasons when fresh fruit is not available this delicate ice can be equally well made from Mirabelles bottled in light syrup or water, using the syrup or juice and adjusting to the proper saccharine strength.

NECTARINE WATER ICE.

This ice is very seldom made, but the fruit is the most delicate and distinctive of all the peach types, and the ice deserves to be better known, especially amongst those moulded and served in small fruit shape, which will be dealt with when the moulding and serving of ices are hereafter described.

- 1 lb. fresh ripe nectarines.
- Juice of one lemon.
- 1 pint of simple syrup.
- 1 dessertspoonful of Kirsch.
- Water to reduce to 21 degrees by the saccharometer.
- Few drops of liquid carmine.

Split the nectarines in halves with a silver or plated knife, remove the stones, and pound them in a clean marble mortar. Place the halves of fruit in a basin and squeeze them to pulp. Add the pounded stones, the syrup, and half a pint of water, and let the whole steep for half an hour. Pass through a fine hair sieve, and add the necessary water to reduce to 21 deg. of saccharine strength, then add the Kirsch and sufficient liquid carmine to give a pale pink colour. Unless you are in the habit of frequently making these tinted water ices, it is best to add the colour when freezing, as the freezing will perceptibly decrease the depth of the colour, and if coloured whilst the liquid is unfrozen allowance must be made for the lightening of the tint. Freeze as directed, spattling very thoroughly.

POMEGRANATE WATER ICE.

For those persons who like pomegranates made into ices it is the kind of ice that that sort of person likes. One moiety of the present collaboration is that sort of person, and considers the ice really good; the other moiety is not, and thinks and says unprintable things about it. The first moiety maintains that there are many with tastes similar to his own; the second moiety regrets it, but admits it may possibly be true.

To make this ice, take:—

- 6 large ripe pomegranates (or more).
- Juice of one lemon.
- Zest and juice of two oranges.
- 1 pint of simple syrup.
- 1 tablespoonful of curacoa.
- Water to reduce to 21 degrees by the saccharometer.
- Few drops of liquid carmine.

Split the pomegranates, and with a plated spoon scrape out the seeds and pulp into a 'sin. Rub well between the hands to break down the pulp vessels, add the lemon ju   the zest and juice of oranges, the syrup, and half a pint of water, and allow to ste.   for half an hour. Pass through a fine hair sieve, rubbing the seeds well with the hand, to be certain that none of the pulp vessels remain unbroken. Add the curacoa and reduce with water to the proper saccharine strength. Should the fruit be small or unripe a larger number will be required to give the necessary strength; this, however, must be left to the judgment of the operator, the fruit varying so much in the quantity of juice extractable. Tint the whole with a few drops of liquid carmine, and freeze as directed, spattling thoroughly.

Water Ices.

A more effective method of extracting the juice is to put the seeds in a copper sugar boiler, with half pint of water, and simmer for a few minutes, but the seeds are apt to give an unpleasant bitterness. Pounding the seeds and pulp in a mortar is a plan sometimes followed; this also gives bitterness, and accentuates the earthy taste of the juice; so simple rubbing and steeping, even if more fruit has to be used, is advised as the best method.

CASSIS WATER ICE.

Cassis is a cordial obtained by fermenting the juice of black currants, and adding clarified syrup and brandy. It is largely used as a summer drink, with iced water, and less largely as a liqueur. Although its foundation flavour is easily recognisable, it is quite distinct from fresh fruit, and makes a deliciously-flavoured water ice. Its chief drawback is its colour, a deep purplish red, which is apt to develop into an ugly purple if left long in a pewter freezer. It should therefore be stored as soon as possible after freezing in a china freezer, unless it is intended to be moulded or packed in soufflé cases:—

½ pint French cassis.
Juice of two lemons.
4 ozs. of red currant jelly.

½ pint of simple syrup.
Water to reduce to 21 degrees by the saccharometer.

Put the red currant jelly in a basin, add a little syrup gradually, and mix with a silver or plated spoon until free from lumps and quite smooth. Pour in the remainder of the syrup, the cassis, the strained juice of the lemons, and water to reduce to the proper saccharine strength. Freeze as directed, spattling thoroughly, and remove from the freezer as quickly as possible into previously prepared moulds, cases, or china freezer.

ORGEAT WATER ICE.

This ice, like the beverage of the same name, is a great favourite in France, Belgium, Italy, and Spain, but is seldom made in this country. It deserves to be better known than it is. Use

¼ lb. Sicily almonds (blanched)
1 pint simple syrup.
1 teaspoonful of noyeau.

1 tablespoonful of orange flower water (triple).
Water sufficient to reduce to 21 deg. by the saccharometer.

Pound the almonds in a clean marble mortar, adding the orange flower water, and a little water as needed to prevent the almonds oiling. When quite fine and smooth, lift out into a basin, add half a pint of cold water, and let steep for half an hour, stirring occasionally. Then add the syrup. Mix well, and pass through a fine hair sieve. Stir in the noyeau, and any more water that may be necessary to reduce to the proper saccharine strength. If properly made, the liquid will be as white as milk, and of most delicate flavour. Freeze as directed, spattling thoroughly.

GINGER WATER ICE.

½ lb. jar Chyloong preserved ginger.
½ pint syrup from the jar.
½ pint simple syrup.

Juice of four lemons.
Water sufficient to reduce to 21 deg. by the saccharometer

Drain the pieces of ginger on a hair sieve, allowing the syrup to run through into a basin. Pour the syrup into a pint measure, and make up to a pint with simple syrup. Pound the ginger to a pulp in a clean marble mortar, lift out with a horn scoop into the

All about Ices.

basin, add the syrup gradually, and mix thoroughly. Put in the lemon juice, and pass the whole through a fine hair sieve with hand pressure, leaving only the fibrous matter behind. Add sufficient water to reduce to 21 degrees by the saccharometer, and freeze as directed, spattling thoroughly.

CHAMPAGNE WATER ICE.

1 pint bottle of champagne.
4 lemons, juice and zest.
1 orange, juice and zest.
2 ozs. brown sugar candy.
Simple syrup to make it up to 21 degrees by the saccharometer.

Remove the zest from the orange and lemons, cut and squeeze them on to the zest in a basin, beat up the sugar candy as fine as possible, and add it with half a pint of simple syrup to the orange and lemon juice. Let it stand for half an hour, so that the zest may give the syrup a good flavour and the sugar candy dissolve. See that the freezer is set up and ready to freeze the ice at once, then open the champagne and pour in and well mix, and at once add sufficient syrup to bring the mixture up to 21 degrees of saccharine strength. Pour at once into the freezer and freeze as directed, as quickly as possible, spattling thoroughly.

It is desirable that no time should be lost in freezing this ice as soon as it is mixed, so that as much of the carbonic acid gas may be conserved as possible. Well made, this is a delicious ice; badly made, it is flat.

PERRY WATER ICE.

If really good perry, well matured in bottle, be used, a very delicious water ice can be made by the following formula, and it is certain to be appreciated by those with a sufficiently refined palate to recognise the nuances of flavouring. But the perry must be good. If the bottles have been stood on their side in the wine-bin, as they should be, a very slight white sediment will be seen on the under side. If the bottle be gently turned over until the sediment is on the upper part, and the cork drawn in that position, the whole of the perry can be decanted without disturbing the sediment.

1 pint bottle of old perry
3 lemons, zest and juice.
1 fresh peach or 2 oranges (zest of 1 only).
2 ozs. brown sugar candy.
Simple syrup to bring up to 21 deg. by the saccharometer.

If the fresh peach be available, peel and halve it with a silver or plated knife. Remove the stone, crack it, crush the kernel, and put it in a basin. Squeeze the halves of the peaches to pulp, and put into the basin. Crush the sugar candy fine and add to the crushed kernel. Take the zest of the lemon and add that with the juice. If the oranges are used instead of the peach, take the zest of one and the juice of the two, and add to the zest in the basin. Pour in half a pint of simple syrup, and let the whole steep for half an hour. Strain through a fine hair sieve, decant the perry and add to the strained juices, and at once bring up to 21 degrees of saccharine strength by adding the small quantity of simple syrup necessary. Freeze immediately as directed, spattling thoroughly, taste the ice, and look pleased and grateful.

PUNCH WATER ICE.

Punch, except in the frozen or semi-frozen form, is largely out of date.

4 lemons (zest of 2).
2 oranges (zest of 1).
1 wineglassful Jamaica rum (proof).
½ wineglassful pale brandy.
½ wineglassful orange curacoa.
1 pint simple syrup.
Water to reduce to 21 deg. by the saccharometer.

Water Ices.

Remove the zest from the orange and lemons, put it in a basin with the squeezed juice of both, add the syrup, and let it steep for half an hour. Strain through a fine hair sieve, add the rum, brandy, and curacoa, and sufficient water to reduce to 21 degrees of saccharine strength. Freeze as directed, spattling thoroughly.

MARASCHINO WATER ICE.

6 lemons.	½ wineglassful of kirsch.
Zest of 3 of them.	¾ of a pint of simple syrup.
1½ wineglassfuls of maraschino.	Water to reduce to 19 deg. by the saccharometer.

Take the zest from three of the lemons and put it in a basin, cut and squeeze the lemons on top of the zest, add the syrup, and stand on one side to steep for half an hour. Strain through a fine hair sieve, add the maraschino and kirsch, and water sufficient to reduce to 19 degrees of saccharine strength. Freeze as directed, spattling thoroughly.

This beautiful water ice is generally frozen its natural colour, but its delicacy of appearance is enhanced if one or two drops of liquid carmine be added. The desired tint is not pink, but the suggestion of pink only.

PISTACHIO WATER ICE.

4 ozs. fine green pistachio nuts (blanched).	1 tablespoonful of maraschino.
4 ozs. fine Sicily almonds (blanched).	1 dessertspoonful of kirsch.
½ pint of water.	1 tablespoonful of orange-flower water (triple).
1 pint of simple syrup.	Water to reduce to 21 deg. by the saccharometer.

Carefully blanch both pistachio nuts and almonds, and pound them in a clean marble mortar, adding the orange-flower water, and, if necessary, a little of the water, to prevent them oiling. When the nuts are reduced to a fine smooth puree lift them out of the mortar with a horn scoop into a basin. Scrape the pestle quite free from pulp, putting every particle in the basin. Add the half-pint of water and stir all together until quite milky. Add the syrup. Put on one side for half an hour. Have ready another basin, and spread a clean, fine muslin cloth over its top. Let both ends be held, pour in the melange, and holding one end of the cloth yourself, let an assistant take the other, and then twist the ends of the cloth together from left to right. This will bring the straining portion of the cloth so tightly together that the whole of the liquid will be squeezed through, leaving only the fibrous portion behind. Well mix in the maraschino and kirsch, and add any water required to reduce the whole to 21 degrees of saccharine strength. The pistachio nuts, if a good colour, will give a very pale tint of green to the mixture, which should be distinctly milky in appearance. Freeze as directed, spattling very thoroughly.

It will be noticed that wherever liqueurs are used as the chief flavouring there is an appreciable difference recommended in the saccharine strength. This is because alcohol increases the difficulty of freezing, and this has to be met by a reduction of saccharine strength. In pistachio water ice this law appears to be ignored. In reality it is entirely adhered to. The method of measuring saccharine strength is simply one of density, and as the extracted oil of the nuts gives an appreciable density before the addition of the syrup, this has to be met by an additional density afterwards. Therefore, in spite of the addition of liqueur to this ice, it is still necessary to make it register 21 degrees before freezing if the desired smoothness is to be obtained.

All about Ices.

ELDERBERRY WATER ICE.

¾ lb. ripe elderberries (free from stalk).
¼ pint of water with fruit.
1 pint of simple syrup.
1 dessertspoonful of rum.
1 dessertspoonful of orange-flower water (triple).
Juice of two lemons.
Water to reduce to 21 deg. of saccharine strength.

Place the elderberries with the quarter-pint of water in a small copper sugar-boiler, and gently reduce by heat to a pulp; add the syrup, and pass through a fine hair sieve. Cut and squeeze the lemons, passing the juice through the sieve. When cold, add the rum and orange-flower water, and sufficient water to reduce to 21 degrees by the saccharometer. If the elderberries are a good colour they will give a sufficiently deep tint to the ice; if not a few drops of liquid carmine may be necessary. Freeze as directed, spattling thoroughly. This ice must not be allowed to stand in a pewter freezer, or it will rapidly turn to a very ugly purple.

MELON PEAR WATER ICE.

This very curious water ice was made by one of the writers for the first time lately. The fruit itself, which is not generally known to the trade, is a semi-tropical one. In shape it is an irregular ellipse, about the size of a lemon. Its skin is smooth, hard, and strong, and about ¼ in. thick. When ripe it is a pale yellow, and the skin on the calyx end becomes slightly less opaque. The flesh when ripe varies from a pale pink to a pale orange, and resembles in structure both melon and pear. Its flavour is its most curious feature. It suggests melon, cucumber, persimmon, and scarlet runner beans—a most extraordinary combination. It is, however, intensely refreshing, and it cleans the palate in a wonderful degree. When unripe it is very nasty, tasting exactly like a combination of raw turnips and French beans.

It is unlikely to be generally popular, although it has its admirers as a dessert fruit. It was one of these for whom the ice was made, and was ordered again and again as long as the fruit was obtainable. It is here included as a curiosity exactly as it was made.

8 large size melon pears (fully ripe).
¾ of a pint of simple syrup.
Juice of three lemons.
Zest of one.
1 tablespoonful of rum.
Water to reduce to 21 deg. by the saccharometer.
Two or three drops of liquid carmine.

Split the fruit in halves lengthways. Scoop out the pulp with a silver or plated spoon into a basin. Take off the zest of one lemon into the basin, cut and squeeze the juice of three lemons on the pulp, add the rum, and stand aside for half an hour; then pass by pressure through a fine hair sieve, adding the syrup, a little at a time, to assist the passing. Reduce with water to 21 degrees of saccharine strength. Tint very slightly with two or three drops of liquid carmine. Freeze as directed, spattling thoroughly. This ice was served, moulded in small melon shapes, at dessert.

GRANITA OR GRANITO

Under this name quite a number of demi-glacé are classed. The term is one that accurately describes the condition of the various confections. It simply implies granular form, and is the original Italian word. The French equivalent is "granite." There is another title common to both countries—"sorbet" in French, "sorbetti" in Italian, which is the equivalent of our word "sherbet." It is difficult to define the differences

Water Ices.

between the concoctions, or to say when one ceases to be one and becomes the other. It is sometimes claimed that the "granito" is the less solid body, and the "sorbet" the more solid. This does not appear to be a very common-sense view. It would be better to reverse them and make the "sorbet" the more liquid. It has always seemed to the writers that a sensible basis of division would be to class those forms in which effervescent liquids are used to reduce the base as "sorbets," and retain the term "granite" or "granito" for those that are still. However, a very strong argument against this course rests on the fact that one or two of the oldest and best-known "granito" are always lowered with champagne. In the face of this difficulty the plan adopted here will be to adhere to the earlier Italian title to describe all the demi-glacés in which an essential feature is a granular one.

All granitos, when properly made, have a frozen base foundation, to which is added the liqueur and wine portion of the mixture at the proper time. This proper time is just before serving, so that the granular and creamy condition of the granito is at its best. This will be better understood when the process of preparation has been carefully studied. The general conception of granitos is that they are simply half-frozen ices. It is desired that the following formulæ and description may help to dissipate that conception and interest confectioners in accurate methods.

ROMAN PUNCH GRANITO.

This is the best known, as far as its name goes, of all the granito family, but no two confectioners in Britain appear to entirely agree as to its composition. The most impossible combinations are recommended—rum, brandy, green tea, black tea, cinnamon, nutmeg, pineapple, ginger—in addition to the three really necessary and harmonious alcoholic items. The formula here appended is the simple one known and used in the days when Roman punch granito was famous among epicures. Its base is a lemon water ice as follows :—

    10 lemons.
    Zest of three.
    1 pint of simple syrup.
    Water to reduce to 21 deg. by the saccharometer.

After freezing.

    3 whites of eggs.
    ¼ pint of simple syrup.
    ½ pint of kirsch.
    ¼ pint maraschino.
    1 pint of champagne.

Make and freeze this ice exactly as for lemon water, spattling it very thoroughly. Before starting to freeze it put half a pint of simple syrup in a small copper sugar-boiler, and quickly boil it up to the feather degree (36 degrees of density by the saccharometer). Have ready at the same time three whites of egg beaten up to a solid mass, and as soon as the sugar is ready pour it gradually on the whites, whisking vigorously the while. Continue beating until the meringue is nearly cold. When quite cold and the lemon ice well frozen, gradually add the meringue to the ice and spattle it thoroughly. When ready to serve, mix in the kirsch and maraschino, and last of all the pint bottle of champagne, poured in the moment the cork is drawn, and gently but quickly blended. Serve at once.

RUM PUNCH GRANITO.

For the base.

    5 lemons.
    Zest of all.
    5 oranges.
    Zest of four.
    ¾ pint of simple syrup.
    Water to reduce to 21 degs. by the saccharometer.

All about Ices.

After freezing.

3 whites of eggs.
½ pint of simple syrup, boiled to the feather.
¼ pint of Jamaica rum.
¼ pint of orange curacoa.
1 pint bottle of chablis

Take off the zest of the lemons and oranges into a basin, cut them and squeeze the juice on to the zest, add the syrup, and stand on one side to steep for half an hour. Strain through a hair sieve, and add sufficient water to reduce to 21 degrees of saccharine strength. Freeze as directed, spattling thoroughly. Put the syrup in a small copper stew-pan and boil up to the feather degree. Beat the whites to a firm snow, and pour in the hot sugar, beating the whole into a firm meringue. Beat until nearly cold. When quite cold, add the meringue to the frozen ice, and beat it well in with the spattle. Add the rum and curacoa, mix thoroughly, and last of all add the chablis and again well mix. Serve at once in small tall glasses or tiny tumblers.

MARASCHINO GRANITO.

Ice base.

6 lemons.
Zest of all.
⅔ pint of simple syrup.
Water to reduce to 20 deg. by the saccharometer.

After freezing.

2 whites of eggs.
⅓ pint of simple syrup, boiled to the feather.
1 gill (¼ pint) of maraschino.
1 pint bottle of dry Sillery or Saumur.

Take off the zest of the lemons into a basin, squeeze the juice on the zest, add the syrup, and steep for half an hour. Strain through a fine hair sieve, and add water sufficient to reduce to 20 degrees of saccharine strength. Freeze as directed, spattling thoroughly. Boil the syrup up to the feather degree. Beat the whites to a strong snow; pour on the hot sugar gradually, beating vigorously the while. Beat until nearly cold, and when quite cold stir into the frozen base, mixing it thoroughly. Add the maraschino, mixing it well in with the creamy mass, and at the last moment, before serving, open the small bottle of Sillery or Saumur and pour into the mass, mixing the whole thoroughly, but carefully. Serve at once.

QUIRINALE GRANITO

Ice base.

1 lb. fresh morella cherries.
¾ pint of simple syrup.
Juice of 2 lemons.
Water to reduce to 18 deg. by the saccharometer.

After freezing.

3 whites of eggs.
½ pint of simple syrup, boiled to the feather.
1 gill (¼ pint) of maraschino.
1 pint flask of muscato d'Asti (Italian sweet white wine).

Strip the cherries from the stalks, and pound a few at a time in a clean marble mortar, breaking up the stones. Scoop out the pulp and juice with a horn scoop into a small copper sugar-boiler, and reduce by heat to a thin pulp. Add the syrup, and after well mixing let stand until cold Pass through a fine hair sieve, squeezing the lemons so that the juice is also strained. Add sufficient water to reduce to 18 degrees of saccharine strength, and freeze as directed, spattling very thoroughly. Boil the half-pint of syrup up

Water Ices.

to the feather degree. Beat the whites up to a strong snow; pour on the hot sugar gradually, beating vigorously the while. Continue beating until nearly cold, and when quite cold beat the meringue well into the frozen base. Add the maraschino and thoroughly well mix, and just before serving pour in and well blend the pint of Muscato d'Asti. Serve in small red tumblers.

This is an exquisite granito if carefully made. Should fresh morella cherries not be available, those bottled in syrup or water can be used, but a great deal of the delicacy of both flavour and colour will be lost. Muscato d'Asti is one of the sweet dessert wines of Italy. It is a soft amber in colour, and delicious in aroma and flavour. It is not so well known in this country as the more celebrated Lacrima Christi, but it deserves to be even better known.

GRANITO LOMBARD.

Ice for base.

8 oranges, or 6 oranges and 2 lemons.
Zest of 4 oranges.
$\frac{3}{4}$ pint of simple syrup
Water to reduce to 18 deg. by the saccharometer.

After freezing.

3 whites of eggs.
$\frac{1}{2}$ pint of simple syrup, boiled to the feather.
1 gill ($\frac{1}{4}$ pint) of orange curacoa.
1 pint bottle of Cedrati water, or old bottled perry.

Take off the zest of the oranges into a basin, cut the fruit, and squeeze the juice on the zest. Add the syrup, and allow the whole to steep for half an hour. Strain through a fine hair sieve, and add sufficient water to reduce to 18 degrees of saccharine strength. Freeze as directed, spattling thoroughly.

Boil the half-pint of syrup to the feather degree. Beat the whites into a firm snow, and pour the hot sugar on the whites, beating vigorously the while. Beat until nearly cold, and when quite cold add to the frozen base and mix thoroughly. Add and well mix in the curacoa, and just before serving pour in the cedrati water or the perry, and thoroughly but carefully blend. Serve in small tumblers. Cedrati water is prepared from the soft ripe pulp of the citron, and is as universally drank in Italy as lemonade is in this country. It is not, however, easily obtainable here, so old bottled perry is given as an alternative. The resulting flavour will be entirely different, but both are good. If perry be used the bottle should be taken from the storage bin after lying on its side, and be gently turned half round before opening. Perry long in bottle deposits a white sediment, which must not be disturbed. The half turn will bring this sediment into the uncovered space in the bottle, and the cork can be drawn and the wine poured away without disturbing it.

GRANITO FLORENTINE.

Ice base.

6 lemons.
Zest of 3 lemons.
$\frac{2}{3}$ pint of simple syrup.
Water to reduce to 18 deg. by the saccharometer.
2 drops o ottar of roses.
8 drops essence of violets.
2 drops of oil of neroli, or 1 tablespoonful of orange-flower water (triple).

After freezing.

3 whites.
6 ozs. of castor sugar.
1 gill ($\frac{1}{4}$ pint) of green chartreuse.
1 pint bottle of Haut Sauterne.

All about Ices.

Take off the zest of three lemons into a basin, cut the fruit, and squeeze the juice on the zest. Add the syrup, and allow the whole to stand for half an hour. Strain through a fine hair sieve, add the water necessary to reduce to 18 degrees of saccharine strength, and then using, if possible, a "dropping bottle," add the floral flavours and well mix. Be most careful not to add more than the quantity given, or the delicacy will be lost. Freeze as directed, spattling thoroughly. Beat up the whites to a firm snow, and beat the sugar thoroughly well into it, adding a little at a time. When quite solid add the meringue to the frozen base and beat it well in. Add the chartreuse a little at a time, and thoroughly well amalgamate. Last of all, and just before serving, pour in the sauterne slowly, and blend all together in a creamy mass. Serve in small green tumblers.

This granito is quite new, but it is so distinctive and delicate that it is certain of instant appreciation if properly made.

STRAWBERRY GRANITO.

For the base.

1½ lb. of hulled strawberries.
1 pint of simple syrup.
Juice of 2 lemons.

Water to reduce to 20 degrees by the saccharometer.

After freezing.

3 whites of eggs.
½ pint of simple syrup, boiled to a feather.

1 tablespoonful of rum (old Jamaica).
1 pint bottle of chablis.
Few drops of liquid carmine.

The best strawberries for this granito are the small wild Scarletts. Failing these, any good variety will answer the purpose—Paxton, Royal Sovereign, British Queen, Doctor Hogg, etc., etc. The kind of fruit used must govern the quantity of carmine necessary, the deeper coloured ones, like Paxton or Doctor Hogg, of course, needing less than the paler varieties. It is advised that if the very delicately flavoured Sovereigns or British Queens be used, that the quantity of lemon-juice be slightly reduced, as both of these have rather more natural acid than the more fully bodied but less delicate fruits.

After hulling the fruit squeeze it by hand through a hair sieve sufficiently fine to keep back the seeds. Add the strained lemon-juice and the syrup, and sufficient water to reduce to 20 degrees of saccharine strength. Tint with carmine. Freeze as directed, spattling thoroughly. Let it rest, well packed in ice and salt, until slightly snowy in character.

Boil the half-pint of simple syrup to the feather, beat the whites of eggs into a stiff snow, pour on the hot sugar, beating vigorously the while, and continue beating until the meringue is nearly cold. When quite cold, add to the base, and well mix with the spattle. Just before serving add the rum, and last of all the pint bottle of chablis. Mix well and serve at once.

RASPBERRY GRANITO.

For the base.

1¼ lb. of fine ripe raspberries.
1 pint of simple syrup.
Juice of 2 lemons.

Water to reduce to 20 degrees by the saccharometer.

After freezing.

3 whites of eggs.
6 ozs. of castor sugar.

1 gill (¼ pint) of kirsch.
1 pint bottle of dry sparkling sillery

Water Ices.

The raspberries must be perfectly fresh and dry. Carefully hull them and pass by pressure through a very fine sieve, so that the seeds do not pass. Add the strained juice of the lemons and the simple syrup, passing this through the sieve so that all the juice is carried with it. Add sufficient water to reduce to 20 degrees of saccharine strength. No colouring will be needed. Freeze as directed, spattling thoroughly, and afterwards allow to stand, well set up with ice and salt, until slightly snowy. Beat up the whites of eggs to a stiff snow, and beat in the castor sugar gradually and thoroughly into a fine meringue. Work this into the frozen base and blend well together. Just before serving add the kirsch, mixing well, and last of all the pint bottle of dry sillery, mixing only sufficiently to blend thoroughly. Serve at once.

CLARET GRANITO.
For the base.

Juice of 5 lemons.
Zest of 3 lemons.
Juice of 3 oranges.
Zest of 2 oranges.

1 pint of simple syrup.
Water to reduce to 20 degrees by the saccharometer.

After freezing.

Whites of 2 eggs.
4 ozs. of castor sugar.
½ gill (⅛ of a pint) of orange curacoa.

½ gill of pale brandy.
1 pint (imperial) of claret.

Remove the zest from lemons and oranges into a basin. Squeeze the juice of both on the zest, add the syrup, and let stand for half an hour to absorb the flavour of the zest. Strain through a hair sieve, and add water to reduce to 20 degrees by the saccharometer. Freeze as directed, spattling thoroughly, and, packed well in ice and salt, let it stand until slightly snowy. Beat up the whites to a firm snow, and gradually beat the sugar in to make a firm meringue. Add this to the frozen base, and blend well together with the spattle. Just before serving add the curacoa and brandy and blend well. Last of all work in the claret, and serve in small red tumblers. The quantity of claret here given (one pint) equals two-thirds of an ordinary-sized bottle. It is not necessary to use an expensive vintage wine, but it is necessary to avoid the red ink at 10s. 6d. per dozen, usually considered good enough for this work.

SHERRY GRANITO.
For the base.

Juice of 6 lemons.
Zest of 3 lemons.
1 Tangerine orange.
Peel of 1 Tangerine orange.

¾ of a pint of simple syrup.
Water to reduce to 20 degrees by the saccharometer.

After freezing.

½ gill (⅛ of a pint) of mandarine (liqueur)
1 pint of pale dry sherry.

Strip the peel from the Tangerine orange, divide it into small pieces, and place in a basin. Add to this the zest of the three lemons and the juice of both orange and lemons. Pour in the simple syrup and steep for half an hour to extract the flavour from zest. Strain through a fine hair sieve, and add sufficient cold water to reduce to 20 degrees of saccharine strength. Freeze as directed, spattling thoroughly, and let stand, well packed in ice and salt, to become a little snowy. When ready to serve add the mandarine and well blend. Last of all pour in one imperial pint of sherry, and mix all together. Serve at once. Here also old vintage wine would be wasted, but it is well to remember that poor sherry is—well, poor sherry, and almost as objectionable as poor relations.

All about Ices.

MOSELLE GRANITO

For the base.

Juice of 6 lemons.
Zest of 3 lemons.
¾ of a pint of simple syrup.

Water to reduce to 20 degrees by the saccharometer.

After freezing.

4 ozs. of castor sugar.
2 whites of eggs.

1 gill (¼ pint) of kirsch.
1 pint bottle of sparkling moselle.

Take off the zest of the three lemons and put in a basin. Squeeze the juice on the zest, add the syrup, and let steep for half an hour. Strain through a fine hair sieve, and add sufficient cold water to reduce to 20 degrees of saccharine strength. Freeze as directed, spattling thoroughly. Beat up the whites to a stiff snow, adding the sugar gradually and beating to a firm meringue. When ready to serve beat the meringue well into the frozen base, stir in the kirsch, and well mix, and last of all pour in the pint bottle of sparkling moselle, and stir no more than is necessary to blend. Serve at once in small tall glasses.

CIDER GRANITO.

For the base.

Juice of 6 lemons.
Zest of 6 lemons.
¾ of a pint of simple syrup.

Water to reduce to 20 degrees by the saccharometer.

Afte freezing.

2 whites of eggs.
4 ozs. of castor sugar.

1 gill (¼ pint) of pale brandy.
1 pint bottle of old cider.

Put the rest and juice of the lemons in a basin with the syrup to steep for half an hour to absorb the flavour from the zest. Strain through a fine hair sieve, and add sufficient cold water to reduce to 20 degrees of saccharine strength. Freeze as directed, spattling thoroughly. Beat up the whites to a firm snow, adding the sugar gradually and beating to a firm meringue. Add this to the frozen base and well mix with the spattle. When ready to serve pour in the brandy and well blend, and last of all pour in the cider, and mix only sufficiently to blend. Serve at once in tiny tumblers.

It is essential that the cider be of good quality, dry, and at least four years in bottle. It should be as bright as champagne. This granito is very inexpensive, but delicious when carefully made.

CREME DE MENTHE GRANITO.

For the base.

Juice of 6 lemons.
Zest of 2 lemons.
2 ripe peaches.

¾ of a pint of simple syrup.
Water to reduce to 20 degrees by the saccharometer.

After freezing.

2 whites of eggs.
4 ozs. of castor sugar.
1 tablespoonful of pale brandy.

1 gill (¼ pint) of crême de menthe (liqueur).
1 pint bottle of chablis or barsac

Place the zest and juice of the lemons together in a basin, with the syrup and pulp of the peaches, and let steep for half an hour. Strain through a fine hair sieve, and add sufficient cold water to reduce to 20 degrees of saccharine strength. Freeze as directed,

Water Ices.

and let stand, well packed in ice and salt, to become slightly snowy. Beat the whites of eggs with he castor sugar to a firm meringue, and well blend with the frozen base. Just before serving add the crême de menthe and brandy, and well blend. Last of all pour in the chablis, and mix thoroughly. Serve in small green glasses.

MILLE FRUIT GRANITO.

For the base.

Juice of 3 lemons.
Zest of 2 lemons.
Juice of 2 oranges.
Zest of 1 orange.
4 ozs. of strawberries.
2 ozs. of raspberries.

1 fresh peach.
1 tablespoonful of orange-flower water (triple).
¾ of a pint of simple syrup.
Water to reduce to 20 degrees by the saccharometer.

After freezing.

1 tablespoonful of kirsch.
1　,,　　,,　　prunella
1　,,　　,,　　orange curacoa.

1 tablespoonful of mandarine.
1 pint bottle of sauterne.

Place the zest and juice of the lemons and oranges in a basin, add the syrup and orange-flower water, and steep for half an hour. Pass through a fine hair sivee, then squeeze and pass the strawberries, raspberries, and peach through the same sieve. Add sufficient water to reduce to 20 degrees of saccharine strength. Freeze as directed, spattling thoroughly. Just before serving add the liqueurs and well blend, and last of all the bottle of sauterne. Mix all thoroughly together, and serve at once in very small tumblers. The sauterne should be good, but whilst avoiding low grade, it is not necessary to use Chateau Yquem.

SECTION II.—CREAM ICES.

STRAWBERRY CREAM ICE.

The best cream for ice-making is single cream, skimmed before the milk has rested sufficiently long to throw the whole of the cream to the surface. Roughly skimmed, a proportion of milk generally helped to make this thinner than the more carefully skimmed. This cream was not so rich, but sweeter than double cream. Single cream was sometimes the second skimming, and was then thinner without being sweeter. Separators now do the work more quickly than by the old-time method, and may be safely trusted to effect the separation thoroughly, leaving the cream of one grade only, subject only to the quality of the milk from which it is obtained. The single cream of to-day is therefore likely to be afterwards thinned down with milk, and as the price is seldom reduced proportionately, it is advisable to do the thinning down oneself. In the following formulæ thick cream will be given, with the proper proportion of new milk to reduce it to the desired richness. The proportion of strawberries used must depend a little upon the fruit, as this varies considerably in both flavour and percentage of juice. Whilst a good general rule is one pint of juice to one pint of double cream and one pint of milk, the fruit which gives the largest percentage of juice has often the least flavour. This points to more fruit being necessary, thus upsetting the guiding rule, and at the same time reducing the saccharine strength of the mixture. It is advisable, therefore, to choose fruit that is full in flavour and fairly juicy, but with good body. Scarletts are best of all, and it is upon their use that the rule is based. Royal Sovereigns are very delicate, but not so full-flavoured as Paxtons or Doctor Hoggs, and are more watery than either. If Royal Sovereigns are used lemon-juice will not be necessary, but with the less acid fruit it is advisable to use a little. The quantity of sugar also must vary with the percentage of water in the fruit, and as it is practically impossible to test the saccharine strength with the saccharometer owing to the varying density of the milk and cream, something must be left to the discretion of the confectioner. Should there be any difficulty in freezing, the addition of a little milk will overcome the trouble. Should the cream, on the other hand, show a tendency to freeze too hard, a little simple syrup will speedily correct it.

STRAWBERRY CREAM ICE.—No. 1 (FRESH FRUIT).

1¼ lb. of ripe strawberries (preferably Scarletts)
¾ lb. pulverised sugar
Juice of 1 lemon (if needed)
1 pint double cream
1 pint new milk
Few drops liquid carmine.

Pick the hulls from the fruit, and pass by rubbing through a fine hair sieve into a good-sized basin; avoid touching with metal of any sort. This should give a good pint of juice. Cut and squeeze the lemon (if used), and pass the juice through the sieve. Mix well with a spattle or wooden spoon. Add the sugar, which should be sifted free from lumps, and well mix. Pour in the cream (unbeaten), and mix well with the pulp and sugar. Then add the milk gradually, stirring gently, and last of all sufficient liquid carmine to give a delicate colour. Whilst it is necessary to remember that the freezing will take somewhat from the depth of colour, over-colouring should be avoided. The finished ice should be very pale and delicate.

Pour into a freezer, previously set up and freeze as directed, spattling thoroughly. If possible, as soon as frozen the ice should be either moulded or removed to a porcelain freezer, so that its delicacy of both colour and flavour may not be impaired by contact for any considerable time with the metal freezer.

Cream Ices.

STRAWBERRY CREAM ICE.— No. 2 (PRESERVED FRUIT).

The following formula will be for the season when fresh fruit is not available, and will consequently be prepared from strawberry syrup, which every confectioner making ices should prepare for his own use. Different methods for preserving this will be found under its proper heading amongst preserved fruits.

- 1⅛ pint strawberry syrup.
- 1 pint double cream.
- 1 pint new milk.
- Juice of 2 lemons.
- 1 teaspoonful Jamaica rum.
- Little liquid carmine.

Carefully strain the syrup through a hair sieve into a basin. Add the strained juice of the lemons and the rum, and mix. Pour in the cream (unbeaten) and mix, and add the milk gradually, stirring all with a wooden spoon. Tint to a delicate colour with liquid carmine, pour in the set-up freezer, and freeze as directed, spattling thoroughly. The same method of storing to conserve the colour as given in strawberry cream Ice No. 1 should be followed with this.

RASPBERRY CREAM ICE.—No. 1 (FRESH FRUIT).

- 1 lb. fresh raspberries (free from hulls).
- ¼ lb. ripe red currants (free from stalks).
- ¾ lb. pulverised sugar.
- 1 pint double cream.
- 1 pint new milk.
- Little liquid carmine (if necessary).

Pass the raspberries and red currants into a basin by rubbing through a very fine hair sieve, so that all the seeds and skins are kept back. Add the sugar and well mix. Mix the cream and milk together, and add just before passing into the freezer. If not sufficiently bright in colour, tint with a few drops of liquid carmine (not cochineal). The reason for not adding the milk and cream until the last moment is to avoid, as far as possible, the tendency to curdle by standing long in an acid mixture. Freeze as directed, spattling thoroughly, and if possible store as directed for strawberry cream.

RASPBERRY CREAM ICE.—No. 2 (PRESERVED FRUIT).

- 1 pint raspberry syrup.
- 1 pint double cream.
- 1 pint new milk.
- Little liquid carmine (if necessary).

This method, like the following one, is intended for the season when fresh fruit is unobtainable, and particulars for preparing the special syrup will be found under the proper heading amongst preserved fruits.

Carefully decant the syrup to avoid any sediment, and strain through a fine hair sieve into a basin. Add the cream and mix together, and then the milk gradually, stirring all well together with a wooden spoon. If necessary, add a few drops of liquid carmine to obtain the desired tint. Pour into a previously set-up freezer and freeze as directed, spattling thoroughly. If possible, store as soon as frozen in a porcelain freezer, unless the ice is intended to be moulded, otherwise the colour will be liable to turn to a very unpleasant purple.

RASPBERRY CREAM ICE.—No. 3 (PRESERVED FRUIT).

- 1 bottle (1½ pint) raspberries, in water.
- ¾ lb. pulverised sugar.
- 1¼ pint double cream.
- ½ pint new milk.
- Little liquid carmine (if necessary).

Instead of the 1½ pint bottle of raspberries in water, one-litre bottle of raspberries in syrup can be used, in which case the sugar proportionately to the thickness of the syrup can be reduced.

All about Ices.

Pass the raspberries through a fine hair sieve into a basin, keeping back the seeds. Add the sugar, and well mix together with a wooden spoon. Pour in the cream (unbeaten) and blend, and gradually add the milk. Last of all tint with a few drops of liquid carmine, pour into a previously set-up freezer, and freeze as directed, spattling thoroughly. Store if possible as soon as frozen in a porcelain freezer to conserve the colour.

RASPBERRY AND RED CURRANT CREAM ICE (1).

¾ lb. fresh raspberries (picked).
¼ lb. ripe red currants, free from stalks).
¾ lb. fine castor sugar.
1 pint of double cream.
1 pint of fresh milk.
Few drops of liquid carmine.

After carefully picking the fruit free from hulls and stalks, pass through a fine hair sieve, add the sugar, and stir until dissolved. Mix the cream and milk together, and add at the last moment before pouring into the freezer, to minimise the tendency to curdle if allowed to stand long mixed before freezing. If needed, add a few drops of liquid carmine to brighten the colour. Freeze as directed, spattling thoroughly, and either mould at once or store in porcelain freezers to conserve the colour.

It is a very usual plan to reduce the fruit to pulp with the sugar by heat before passing through the hair sieve. This plan has the advantage of giving a little more body and depth of flavour, but it destroys the delicate fresh-fruit flavour, and is not here advocated except with preserved fruit, as in No. 2 below.

RASPBERRY AND RED CURRANT CREAM ICE (2).

1 bottle (1½ pints) of raspberries and red currants (in water).
10 ozs. of sugar.
1¼ pints of double cream.
½ pint of milk.
1 teaspoonful of kirsch.
Few drops of liquid carmine.

Put the contents of the bottle of fruit, water and all, in a small copper sugar-boiler, and reduce by heat to pulp. Add the sugar and simmer together for a few minutes. Pass through a fine hair sieve into a basin, and when quite cold add the kirsch, the cream and milk, previously mixed together. Colour with a few drops of liquid carmine, pour into the freezer at once, and freeze as directed, spattling thoroughly. Store, if possible, in a porcelain freezer, previously set up ready to receive it.

Bottled fruit in water is here given because it is most easily obtainable, but specially prepared raspberry syrup is preferable, for the preparation of which instructions will appear in the proper place amongst preserved fruits.

RASPBERRY AND RED CURRANT CREAM ICE (3).

1 pint raspberry syrup.
6 ozs. red currant jelly.
1 pint double cream.
1 pint new milk.
1 teaspoonful of kirsch.
Few drops of liquid carmine.

Carefully decant the syrup (to avoid using any sediment) into a basin; melt the red currant jelly and add to it with the kirsch. Stir in the cream and milk, previously mixed together, lightly colour with the liquid carmine, and pour at once into prepared freezer, and freeze as directed, spattling thoroughly. Store in a porcelain freezer to conserve the colour.

Cream Ices.

PINEAPPLE CREAM ICE.

- 1 can of Singapore pine.
- 12 ozs. of pulverised sugar
- Juice of 1 lemon.
- 1 dessertspoonful of kirsch.
- 1¼ pints of double cream.
- ½ pint of new milk.
- Little yellow colour and suspicion of liquid carmine.

Open the can carefully to avoid spilling the juice. Lift out the fruit and drain for a few minutes on a hair sieve over a basin. Cut the pine into small pieces and pound in a clean marble mortar. Lift out with a horn scoop into the basin, add the juice, mix all together, and let stand for half an hour. Pass through a hair sieve by pressure, so that nothing but the dry fibrous portion is retained on the sieve. Add the sugar, the kirsch, and the strained juice of the lemon to the pulp, and mix all together. Stir in the cream and milk, previously mixed together, and with a little yellow colour and carmine tint a pale orange. Pour at once into a prepared freezer, and freeze as directed, spattling thoroughly.

As the delicate flavour of the pineapple is very evanescent it is imperative that fine fruit of full flavour be used. Singapore brands are most suitable, and Bastians if possible.

There is another form of pineapple cream ice that is quite distinct from the above, being made from a custard base. This will be found in its proper place amongst the custard ices

APRICOT CREAM ICE (1).

- 1 lb. ripe fresh apricots.
- 12 ozs. fine castor sugar
- 1 teaspoonful of noyeau (liqueur).
- ¼ pint of water.
- 1 pint of double cream.
- ¾ pint of new milk.
- Little yellow colour and suspicion of carmine.

Split the fruit in halves and remove the stones. Crack these and remove the kernels. Blanch the kernels and crush them. Place the halves of apricots, the kernels, and the water in a small copper sugar-boiler, and reduce by heat to pulp. Add the sugar and simmer together for a few minutes. Pass by pressure through a hair sieve into a basin, and when cold add the liqueur and the cream and milk. A few drops of yellow colour and carmine will give the desired tint. Pour at once into a prepared freezer and freeze as directed, spattling thoroughly.

APRICOT CREAM ICE (2).

- 1 can apricots (No. 2 size).
- 8 ozs. fine castor sugar.
- 1 dessertspoonful of noyeau (liqueur)
- 1 pint of double cream.
- 1 pint new milk.
- Little yellow colour and suspicion of carmine.

In this case the kernels will not be available, so the extra noyeau is required. Put the fruit and syrup in a small copper sugar-boiler, and reduce by heat to pulp. Add the sugar and simmer together for a few minutes until the sugar is melted. Pass through a hair sieve, and when cold add the noyeau and the cream and milk, and tint to a pale yellow. Freeze as directed, spattling thoroughly.

All about Ices.

PEACH CREAM ICE.—No. 1 (DE LUXE).

6 large ripe hothouse peaches.
12 ozs. castor sugar.
Juice of 1 lemon.
1 dessertspoonful orange-flower water.

1 pint double cream.
1 pint fresh milk.
One or two drops of liquid carmine.

Split the peaches in two with a silver or plated knife, remove the stones, and pass the fruit through a fine hair sieve into a basin. Cut and squeeze the lemon, and pass the juice through the sieve and mix with the pulp. Add the sugar and stir until the crystals are dissolved. Crack the stones and pound the kernels in a small mortar, adding a little of the orange-flower water to prevent oiling. Lift out into a small basin, add the rest of the orange-flower water and a little of the milk, and let it stand for a short time for the liquid to extract the flavour from the pounded kernels, and then strain through the hair sieve into the sweetened pulp. Add the cream to the pulp and pour the balance of the milk through the sieve, so that any pulp adhering to the sieve, as well as any flavour remaining in the pounded kernels, may be utilised. One or two drops of liquid carmine may be added to suggest blush rose colour. Freeze as directed, spattling thoroughly, and either mould at once or store in porcelain freezer, to conserve the delicacy of both colour and flavour.

PEACH CREAM ICE.—No. 2.

1 can (No. 2½) white Freestone peaches.
8 ozs. castor sugar.
Juice of 1 lemon.
Juice of the peaches.
1 dessertspoonful orange-flower water.

1 dessertspoonful noyeau (liquid).
1 pint double cream.
⅔ pint fresh milk.
Few drops liquid carmine.

Lift the peaches from the can and pass them through a hair sieve into a basin, passing the syrup afterwards through the same sieve. Add the strained juice of the lemon and the sugar to this pulp, and stir until the sugar is thoroughly dissolved. Then add the orange-flower water, the noyeau, the cream and milk, and sufficient liquid carmine to suggest pink. Freeze as directed, spattling thoroughly.

ORLEANS PLUM CREAM ICE.

1¼ lb. early Orleans plums (ripe).
12 ozs. loaf sugar.
¾ pint fresh milk.

¼ pint water.
1 pint double cream.

Divide the fruit in halves with a silver or plated knife, and remove the stones. Pound these in a marble mortar, crushing the kernels quite fine. Remove into a basin and add the milk. Stir well, and let stand whilst you prepare the fruit. This must be put into a small copper sugar-boiler with the ¼ pint of water, and reduced to a pulp by heat. When quite pulped add the sugar, and simmer until entirely melted. Pass through a hair sieve into a basin, and stand on one side until quite cold. When ready gently stir in the cream and strain the flavoured milk through the hair sieve. Straining the milk will serve the double purpose of straining out the broken stones and crushed kernels and removing any pulp that may adhere to the sieve. Freeze as directed, spattling thoroughly.

If the fruit is thoroughly ripe the colour will be a brilliant red, but should the ice be too pale it can be tinted with liquid carmine, which is, however, generally unnecessary.

Cream Ices.

GREENGAGE CREAM ICE.

1¼ lb. fine ripe greengages.
12 ozs. loaf sugar.
¾ pint fresh milk.
¼ pint water.
1 pint double cream.

This can be made exactly as for Orleans plum ice, except that the colour must be a very pale green instead of red. Unripe gages will give a much prettier colour than fully ripe ones, but the flavour is not so full and rich. Wall gages, which are almost yellow when fully ripe, are by far the finest in flavour, but the resulting colour is not a pretty one. The fruit we prefer for this purpose is one called "Reine Claude," which is of fine flavour, and of good colour when fully ripe.

CHERRY CREAM ICE.—No. 1 (FRESH MEDOC).

1¼ lb. ripe cherries.
12 ozs. loaf sugar.
Few drops liquid carmine.
1 pint double cream.
1 pint fresh milk.

The best cherries for this cream ice are those variously known as Kentish, Flemish, or May Dukes, apparently so called because they do not make their first appearance before the end of June. May Duke is simply a perversion of Medoc, the district of France whence they originally reached us. The type is the bright red transparent variety, intensely acid even when ripe. The Morella cherry has many of the same qualities, but differs in both colour and flavour.

Strip the fruit from the stalks and pound a few at a time in a small clean marble mortar, breaking up both fruit and stones. Scoop out with a small horn scoop into a copper sugar-boiler, and reduce to pulp by heat. Add the sugar, and stirring gently, simmer until the whole of the sugar is melted. Let it stand until cold, and pass through a fine hair sieve with great care to avoid the broken stones cutting the sieve. Add the cream and milk, previously mixed together, tint with a few drops of liquid carmine, pour at once into the previously set up freezer, and freeze as directed, spattling thoroughly. When frozen, either mould at once or store in a porcelain freezer to conserve the colour.

CHERRY CREAM ICE.—No. 2 (FRESH MORELLA).

1¼ lb. Morella cherries.
12 ozs. loaf sugar.
1 pint double cream.
1 pint fresh milk.

This cream ice must be made and frozen exactly as cherry cream ice No. 1, except that as the fruit is much deeper in colour, it will not require the addition of carmine. In both cases the milk and cream must be mixed together and be gently stirred into the fruit and sugar just previously to pouring into the freezer, to avoid the tendency of the acid fruit to curdle them. When this has been allowed, generally through carelessness or ignorance, it is almost impossible to obtain smoothly-frozen ices.

CHERRY CREAM ICE.—No. 3 (PRESERVED CHERRIES).

1 bottle (1½ pint) specially prepared cherries.
12 ozs. castor sugar.
Juice of 1 lemon.
1 dessertspoonful kirsch.
1 pint double cream.
1 pint fresh milk.
Few drops liquid carmine.

All about Ices.

The specially preserved cherries are not the ordinary cherries in water, but fruit that has been put up on purpose for ice-making, instructions for which appear in the proper place amongst preserved fruits.

Pass the fruit through a fine hair sieve, care being taken not to cut the sieve with the pieces of stones. Add the castor sugar, the strained juice of the lemon, the kirsch, and when the sugar is entirely dissolved add the cream and milk previously mixed together; gently mix and tint to a pale red with liquid carmine. Freeze as directed, spattling thoroughly, and store in porcelain freezer to conserve the colour and flavour.

GREEN TEA CREAM ICE.

1 pint double cream.	1 oz. green tea.
1 pint new milk.	¼ pint boiling water.
10 ozs. castor sugar.	1 tablespoonful pale brandy.

"Gunpowder" or "Young Hyson" is the tea generally used for this purpose, but really fine "Darjeeling," although not so pungent, is far more delicate. It must, however, be fine, and if right quality is obtained, it will cost quite 4s. per lb. The extra cost per quart of the finished cream ice is, however, only about one penny, and is not worth considering where the quality is concerned. Place the tea in a small teapot or jug, and pour in the quarter-pint of boiling water upon it. Cover at once, and allow to stand for five minutes only, when the liquor should be carefully drained away from the leaves. Put the milk, cream, and sugar in a small tinned copper stewpan and place on the stove, and heat to just under boiling point. Remove at once, stir well to ensure the melting of the sugar. Add the strained tea, and when cold the brandy. Freeze as directed, spattling thoroughly, and when partly frozen, so that the colour can be judged, tint to a very delicate green. The delicacy of this ice is evanescent. It is therefore at its best when freshly frozen, and is never worth re-freezing.

COFFEE CREAM ICE (1).

1½ pint double cream.	10 ozs. sugar.
½ pint new milk	3 ozs. coffee (freshly roasted).
1 dessertspoonful pale brandy.	

Freshly roast the coffee, not too highly, and lightly crack it. It must not be ground. Put the cream, milk, sugar, and cracked coffee in a stewpan, and heat to just under the boil. Remove from the fire, let it stand for fifteen minutes, and then strain through muslin. When cold add the brandy and freeze as directed, spattling thoroughly. It should be a very pale, delicate colour. If preferred, the coffee can be ground, and a strong infusion prepared separately and added to the cream after scalding. Made with the infusion from the ground coffee, a darker cream will result, with a stronger but less delicate flavour.

Coffee cream ice can also be made from a custard base, and a formula for that variety will be found under the head of custard cream ices.

WHITE COFFEE CREAM ICE (2).

1½ pint double cream.	10 ozs. sugar.
½ pint new milk.	4 ozs. freshly-roasted coffee.
¼ oz. vanilla sugar.	

Scald the cream, milk, and sugar, and the moment it is removed from the fire throw the freshly-roasted coffee (whole) and the vanilla sugar into the cream. Cover it up until cold, and then strain through a fine hair sieve. Freeze as directed, spattling thoroughly, and you will have a perfectly white cream.

Cream Ices.

GREEN COFFEE CREAM ICE (3).

1½ pint double cream.
½ pint new milk.
10 ozs. sugar.
4 ozs. green coffee.
1 dessertspoonful pale brandy.
Very little green colour.

Half roast the coffee until of a pale golden colour; crack it while still hot and throw it into the scalded cream, milk, and sugar. Cover down at once and let it stand until cold, when it must be strained through a fine hair sieve or a muslin cloth, and add the pale brandy. Freeze as directed, spattling thoroughly, and when partly frozen tint to a pale yellowish green. The flavour of this cream ice will be quite distinct, and if well made will be appreciated by connoisseurs. The coffee recommened for ice-making is a mixture of Mocha and Plantation, or, and especially for the No. 3, fine Peaberry.

BROWN BREAD CREAM ICE.

1½ pint double cream.
½ pint new milk.
6 ozs. crumbs of brown bread.
10 ozs. sugar.
2 ozs. ground almonds.
2 tablespoonfuls kirsch.

The crumbs of brown bread should be passed through a ten-mesh sieve and be well dried and slightly browned on a sheet of paper on a wire in the oven, and set on one side to get cold. Scald the cream, milk, almonds, and sugar, but do not let it boil. When cold strain through a fine hair sieve and add the kirsch. Freeze as directed, spattling thoroughly, and when nearly frozen add the crumbs and beat well in with the spattle. It is intended that the crumbs shall retain some of their crispness, so if possible it is advisable to add them only a short time before serving.

Occasionally this ice is made by adding the crumbs before freezing, but the result is a nasty pasty mess that even brown bread faddists cannot enjoy. Even when properly made it is not generally liked, but there are many people who profess to like it. Apparently they like it "for their stomachs' sake." Perhaps there might be a meed of popularity for a "brimstone and treacle" cream ice in the spring and fall if it were properly boomed.

It will be noticed that in the last five formulæ it has been recommended to scald the cream and milk. The reason for this is that the ice may gain a little in body and richness, as the cream will not beat up so light whilst freezing after the scalding as if used raw. This also means greater smoothness, but a little less bulk.

BISCUIT GLACE.

This is a contentious subject, and a healthy fight might perhaps result in an authoritative ruling that would establish a universal standard. At present there is no generally accepted standard. Each confectioner is a law unto himself, and the law, usual under such circumstances, is like unto that of the Medes and Persians. Of course, when the law-maker has brains and skill the result is pretty sure to possess merit, although it be entirely distinct from another production equally meritorious. One world-famous house produces its "biscuit glacé" from scalded cream, flavoured and sweetened, and in which crushed macaroons have been macerated and afterwards strained from. This mixture is frozen in the usual way, and whipped raw cream stirred into it when nearly frozen. In another case, well dried broken almond macaroons are added to the cream base after freezing.

Some such method as this would appear to have given the original title, although a totally different product is to-day more general. A rich, light sponginess is desired, and more often than not some form of iced soufflé is sent to table as a "biscuit glacé."

All about Ices.

"Iced soufflé," when well made, are delicious confections, but they are not ices. Their light honeycombed texture is quite distinct from a spattled ice, even when their composition is practically the same. For the purpose, therefore, of adhering as far as possible to accuracy of nomenclature, the various forms of iced soufflé will be confined to their proper chapter, and only those confections that in our judgment are properly so entitled (we being also laws unto ourselves) will appear here as biscuit ices.

Whilst writing we have before us a menu card of a very extravagant dinner served lately at a mammoth hotel, and amongst the dessert two dishes figure prominently. They are "bisque glaze" and "Bomba a la Rochefort." This is nomenclature gone mad with a vengeance. The admixture of French and English and Italian and French is delicious. "Bisque" is the almost universal French term for soups made from shell-fish, and has no reference to biscuit; the English word "glaze" is too well known to need comment. "Bomba" is the Italian equivalent for the French "Bombe," and should never be used with the French à la Rochefort or à la anything else. "Bomba" or "Bombe" is only a variant of soufflé, which will be presently described.

BISCUIT GLACE VANILLA (1).

12 yolks of eggs.
4 whole eggs.
¾ of a pint of simple syrup.
1½ oz. of vanilla sugar.
2 tablespoonfuls of kirsch.
1½ pints of double cream.

Set the yolks and whole eggs in a small copper egg bowl with the simple syrup. Place this over a pan of hot water on the stove. Whisk well together, and, beating all the time, gradually raise it up to 140 deg. F., being careful to prevent its catching on sides or bottom of the pan. The bottom of the pan containing the mixture should be above the hot water, not resting in it. When sufficiently heated remove from the stove and beat until cold, when the mixture should resemble a well-beaten sponge batter. Add the kirsch and vanilla sugar to the cream and half whip it, and then gently mix into the beaten egg batter. At once pour into a previously set up freezer and freeze steadily and carefully, keeping the mixture free from the sides as fast as it freezes, but without too vigorous spattling. The spattle should be used sufficiently to ensure perfectly smooth blending, but no more. When frozen, the mass should be light and spongy, and should be at once moulded into the form in which it is intended to be served.

BISCUIT GLACE CARAMELLED (2).

10 yolks of eggs.
6 whole eggs.
¾ of a pint of simple syrup.
1 tablespoonful of pale brandy.
1½ pints of double cream.

Place one-third of the simple syrup in a small copper sugar-boiler and quickly boil down to caramel; 312 deg. will do. As soon as it reaches this degree (it will be a bright golden colour), add a tablespoonful of cream and stir gently together. As the cream takes the caramel colour add a little more gradually until you have used about a quarter of a pint, and when all is caramelled lift from the fire and gradually add enough cream to render the mass thin enough to be stirred in when cold to the balance of the cream, which will need to be half whipped with the brandy.

Beat up the yolks, whole eggs, and the rest of the syrup exactly as in No. 1, and, when cold, add the beaten cream, into which the caramelled cream has been mixed, stir together, and freeze and mould exactly as for No. 1.

Cream Ices.

BISCUIT GLACE MARASQUIN (3).

12 whole eggs.
¾ of a pint of simple syrup.
1 tablespoonful of kirsch.
3 tablespoonfuls of maraschino.
1¼ pints of double cream.
½ pint of new milk.

Beat up the eggs and syrup exactly as for No. 1, and when quite cold half whip the cream with the kirsch and maraschino, stir into it the milk, and gently blend with the beaten batter. Pour into the freezer and freeze and mould as directed for No. 1. This ice will be a little lighter and more spongy than the preceding ones, but not quite so rich.

BISCUIT GLACE MACAROON (4).

12 whole eggs.
¾ of a pint of simple syrup.
1 tablespoonful of kirsch or noyeau, (liqueur).
4 ozs. well-baked almond macaroons
1¼ pints of double cream.
½ pint of new milk.

Crush the macaroons and place them in a small basin. Scald a quarter of a pint of the cream and the half pint of milk, and pour over the crushed macaroons, and cover down so that they are thoroughly soaked. It will depend a little upon the condition of the macaroons as to whether this soaking will be sufficient; if it is not, a short boiling all together will properly reduce them. When fully soaked they should be passed by pressure through a fine hair sieve and allowed to cool thoroughly.

Beat up the eggs and syrup as for No. 1, and when cold half whip the balance of the cream and the kirsch or noyeau, whichever is used, and stir into the macaroon pulp, afterwards blending all with the egg batter. Freeze and mould as directed for No. 1.

CUSTARD ICES.

Cream ices made from a custard base form a very important section. They have greater body than those made by any other plan, and therefore retain their frozen condition for a longer time, all other conditions being equal. Custard is not, however, suitable for admixture with fruit juices and fruit syrups, with the single exception of pine apple, boiled almost into a conserve with sugar. A banana cream ice is sometimes made with a custard base, but it is a sickly mess, even when the sliced fruit is drenched in liqueurs.

The methods of making custards are varied, so perhaps a few lines on the different plans, with the reasons for each, will be interesting and clear the way for the definite and individual formulæ. The more common or cheap custards are made from milk, sugar, eggs, or yolks, and some farinaceous matter, such as cornflour, arrowroot, or other farina, flour being occasionally used as a thickening agent.

One great, but usual, mistake made is to cook the eggs and farinaceous matter the same length of time. All farina needs at least a few minutes' boiling, and eggs, whether yolks only or yolks and whites, should barely reach the boiling point. The points to avoid are rawness on the one hand and over-cooking on the other. Eggs or yolks raised to the proper temperature retain a little of their powers of expansion, and help to lighten the mass under manipulation with the spattle. It is a hopeless task to try and convert a sort of boiled omelette into a smooth fluffy cream ice.

Therefore if farinaceous matter is used at all (for cheap ices) the eggs should be beaten separately in a basin, and the well-boiled farinaceous mixture be poured upon them and well stirred meanwhile. In every case, whether the eggs are intended to be partially or entirely coagulated, we advise adding them last in this way, and, if necessary, returning to the fire for a few moments after.

All about Ices.

In the case of rich mixtures, free from farina, when the boiling cream and milk have been poured on the beaten eggs and returned to the fire, the observant workman can see instantly when to remove the custard. If the whisk is moved quickly with a circular movement, as long as the eggs are uncoagulated the stirred cream will swing round with the whisk, but the moment coagulation commences this movement will cease, and the pan should be instantly removed from the stove.

Many people use cornflour because they cannot make their custards smooth with eggs or yolks alone, apparently unaware that the sole reason for the trouble is that they cook the eggs too much. The only excuse for farinaceous assistance is to replace the due proportion of cream and eggs, where economy must be considered. In the three formulæ immediately following high-grade ices only will be considered, but afterwards a few of the more economical ones may be included.

VANILLA CREAM ICE (1).

1 pint of double cream.
1 pint of new milk.
7 ozs. of lump sugar.

12 yolks of eggs.
2 ozs. of vanilla sugar.
1 dessertspoonful of fine pale brandy.

Set the cream, milk, and sugar in a clean tin-lined copper stewpan, and put on the fire to boil. Stir occasionally to be certain that the sugar is dissolved by the time that boiling point is reached. Put the yolks of eggs into a basin, and beat them sufficiently to break down thoroughly. Just before the cream and milk come to the boil add the vanilla sugar and stir well in. Pour the boiling cream, etc., on the beaten yolks, stirring vigorously with the whisk. When cold pass through a fine hair sieve, add the brandy, and freeze as directed, spattling thoroughly.

This cream will be light and fluffy if well beaten with the spattle, but will still have its due meed of smoothness. It is intended for customers of knowledge, who will welcome the small black specks of vanilla.

VANILLA CREAM ICE (2).

1 pint of double cream.
1 pint of new milk.
8 ozs. lump sugar.
8 yolks of eggs.

1 oz. fine ground almonds.
4 small fillets of thinly cut lemon rind.
½ of a vanilla bean (split).
1 dessertspoonful of pale brandy.

Put the cream, milk, sugar, ground almonds, pieces of lemon rind, and the split half of a 6-in. vanilla bean into a tin-lined copper stewpan, and set to boil. Put the yolks of eggs in a basin and break well down with a whisk. Stir the cream, etc., occasionally, to dissolve the sugar, and when boiling pour on to the yolks, beating well with the whisk. Return the whole to the stewpan, place on the fire, and stir until the custard ceases to follow the movement of the whisk. Remove from fire instantly, and at once pass through a fine hair sieve. When cold add the brandy, pour into the previously-prepared freezer, and freeze as directed, spattling thoroughly.

This ice will not be quite so light as the first one, but will be of delicious flavour and smoothness if care has been taken to avoid over-cooking the yolks. Carefully save all pieces of vanilla used as above ; they can all be utilised, and instructions will be found as to their use. (See extract of vanilla.)

Cream Ices.

VANILLA CREAM ICE (3).

- 1 pint of double cream.
- 1 pint of new milk.
- 8 ozs. lump sugar.
- 1 oz. (liquid) essence of vanilla.
- 12 yolks of eggs.
- 1 oz. fine ground sweet almonds.

Boil the cream, milk, sugar, and almonds, and pour on to the beaten yolks, but do not return to the fire. Strain through a fine hair sieve to remove any fibrous matter from the almonds. Add the essence of vanilla when the custard is cold, and freeze as directed, spattling thoroughly. This cream will be as light and fluffy as No. 1, but will be free from the little black specks of the vanilla bean.

VANILLA CREAM ICE (4).

- 1 quart of new milk.
- ½ pint of double cream.
- 9 ozs. of lump sugar.
- 10 yolks of eggs.
- 2 ozs. of fresh butter.
- 1½ ozs. of arrowroot.
- 2 ozs. ground sweet almonds.
- 1½ ozs. (liquid) of vanilla essence.

Put nearly all the milk, the cream, sugar, butter, and ground almonds on to boil; break down the arrowroot in a small basin with the balance of the milk until quite smooth, and when the milk, cream, etc., comes to the boil pour in the liquid arrowroot and stir vigorously with the whisk. Cook thoroughly for at least two minutes, stirring to prevent burning. Beat up the yolks in a basin, and pour the boiling custard upon them, stirring them well all the time. Pass at once through a fine hair sieve to remove fibrous matter from the almonds, and when cold add the essence of vanilla, and freeze as directed, spattling thoroughly.

The above formula will give a smooth, firm ice of good flavour and moderate richness that will remain in good condition for a long time if properly frozen and spattled

VANILLA CREAM ICE (5).

- 1 quart of new milk.
- ½ pint of double cream.
- 8 ozs. lump sugar.
- 8 whole eggs.
- 2 ozs. fresh butter.
- 1½ ozs. arrowroot.
- 3 bay leaves.
- 2 ozs. of vanilla sugar.

Three small strips of thin lemon rind.

Boil the milk, cream, sugar, butter, lemon-peel, and bay-leaves together, reserving a small quantity of the milk to break down the arrowroot, which must be poured into the boiling mass, well stirred, and cooked for at least two minutes, being careful to avoid burning. Break the eggs into a basin and whisk until well broken up, then well whisk them into the custard and return to the fire for one minute, whisking well all the time. Do not allow the custard to come to the boil again, or the eggs will be too much cooked. Whilst the rawness must be removed, there must be a little spring left in them. Pass at once through a fine hair sieve after removing the bay-leaves and lemon-rind, and when cold freeze as directed, spattling thoroughly.

For a moderate-priced ice this will give entire satisfaction to those who do not object to the small black specks. It will be light and fluffy, and at the same time soft and smooth. It is economical for counter trade, as it bulks well in freezing. The bay-leaves will give a delicate flavour, almost equal to almonds.

All about Ices.

VANILLA SUGAR.

½ lb. fine vanilla beans.　　　　　　　　　12 lbs. lump sugar.

This is very easily made by pounding together in a clean marble mortar, beginning by pounding the vanilla with 2 lbs. of sugar as finely as possible, sifting, and returning what does not pass through a fine sieve to the mortar, adding 1 lb. more of sugar, and so on until the whole of the sugar has been used and the whole of the vanilla reduced to powder. Mix all the siftings together and store in tins or bottles for use.

EXTRACT OF VANILLA.

So-called essence of vanilla can be bought from any wholesale druggist or supply house, but is always relatively dear, and often has an admixture of cumarin, an extract from the Tonquin bean. This is a beautiful perfume, and is the foundation to the scent known as "New-mown Hay," but it is objectionable as a flavouring essence, and certainly is not vanilla.

There is no reason why each confectioner should not make his own extract, and be certain of obtaining the maximum quality at first cost.

Vanilla beans, or pods, come chiefly from Mexico, and are the seed vessels of an orchidacious plant. When fully ripe they are a brilliant red colour, and when cured are a more or less deep chocolate colour. They are generally sold in bundles of a hundred pods, and vary in price per pound according to length and condition. There are, of course, market fluctuations, but these apply to all commodities.

Whilst very small beans are apt to be immature, and if so should be avoided, even if low in price, those between 6 in. and 8 in. in length, if in good condition, are generally to be bought at a price that gives the best value to the confectioner.

When in good condition the beans should be mellow, not dry, bright, not dull-looking, and intensely pungent in aroma. Those that are coated with fine silky white crystals fetch the highest price, but are not necessarily the best value. The crystals are, of course, evidence of quality, being the crystallised exudation of the best part of the sap, but its presence outside is the result of temperature conditions chiefly. Therefore, although we like to see it, we object to pay more for its being there. The best way to make the extract from the beans is unquestionably to distil the macerated beans with a small still with condensing worm attached, but this is outside practical politics with most confectioners, and the following plan will answer well and give satisfactory results. Use

　　1 lb. of vanilla beans.　　　　　　　　1 pint of simple syrup.
　　2 quarts of spirit vini rect., 60 deg. o.p.　　1 pint of water (distilled)

Split the beans lengthways and divide into 1-in. lengths. Put in a four-quart bottle or jar, and pour on the spirits of wine. Shake well after corking, at intervals, for fourteen days, then add the simple syrup and shake occasionally during two days more. Drain the whole of the liquor away and put in another bottle. Add one pint of distilled water to the pieces of vanilla and shake well. Let it rest until next day, when again drain away the liquor, add it to the sweetened spirit, and pass the whole through a small jelly-bag until perfectly clear. Bottle and cork, and keep in the dark until required for use. It is best to fill into six one-pint bottles, so that only a small quantity need be in use at one time.

The pieces of vanilla can be carefully dried and used where directed for pounding and adding to chocolate praline, where every atom will serve a good purpose, either in biscuits, pastry, cream, or for praline centres for chocolates.

Cream Ices.

COFFEE CREAM ICE (CUSTARD).

1½ pints of milk.
1½ pints of double cream.
12 ozs. lump sugar.
12 yolks of eggs.

4 whole eggs.
Extract of coffee (quantum suff.).
1 teaspoonful extract of vanilla.
1 tablespoonful pale brandy.

Place the milk, one pint of the cream, and the sugar in a tin-lined stewpan to come to the boil, stirring occasionally to ensure the melting of the sugar. Beat up the eggs and yolks in a basin, and pour the boiling milk and cream upon them, stirring vigorously with the whisk until the first heat has lessened a little. Pass through a fine hair sieve, and when cold add sufficient of the extract of coffee until the desired flavour is obtained, and then mix in the vanilla and the brandy. Freeze as directed, spattling thoroughly, and when nearly frozen add the remaining half-pint of cream, half whipped, and beat well into the mixture. This will make a light, fluffy cream of delicious flavour and smoothness.

There are many brands of coffee extracts that will give good results, but there is none that is quite so good as an infusion made from good coffee freshly but not too highly roasted, very coarsely ground, and passed quite clear and bright. The choice of coffee must be left to the taste of the operator, but a blend of one-third Mocha and two-thirds fine Plantation is recommended for the purpose. In making infusions for ices it is well to concentrate them as much as possible, or the quantity needed to give the necessary flavour will reduce the richness of the mass. One pint of water to each 4 ozs. of coffee used will give about half a pint of rich extract. The coffee must not be boiled; it should be pressed firmly into a china percolator (the bottom of the percolating section having been previously covered with a piece of fine muslin), the presser remaining on the coffee, and the boiling water poured on top of it. The first passing should be returned to the top chamber until the liquid runs quite clear. The coffee itself will absorb nearly half the bulk of the water, but the portion running clear will be deliciously strong and of fine aroma.

CHOCOLATE CREAM ICE (1) (CUSTARD).

1 pint of new milk.
1 pint of double cream.
8 ozs. of sugar (lump).

8 yolks of eggs.
1 oz. ground sweet almonds
4 ozs. pure cocoa.

1 teaspoonful essence of vanilla.

Place the milk, cream, sugar, and ground almonds in a tin-lined stewpan, and set on the stove to just reach boiling point, stirring occasionally to dissolve the sugar. Beat the yolks in a basin to break them thoroughly, and pour the hot milk and cream on them, stirring well with the whisk. Return to the stove to slightly thicken, but not to boil, removing the moment the custard ceases to follow the swing round of the whisk. Pass at once through a fine hair sieve to be certain that no lumps are present and to remove the fibrous portion of the almonds.

Slowly melt the pure cocoa in a basin until quite liquid, but not hot; add a small quantity of the custard and well mix. Continue to add custard gradually until quite smooth, then thoroughly stir into the rest of the custard, and when nearly cold add the essence of vanilla. When cold freeze as directed, spattling thoroughly.

The above method will give a very rich and smooth cream, but it will be rather solid, as both cream and eggs, having been well scalded, will not bulk by spattling.

All about Ices.

CHOCOLATE CREAM ICE (2) (CUSTARD).

1½ pints of new milk.
1½ pints of double cream.
11 ozs. of lump sugar.
1 oz. of vanilla sugar.

8 yolks of eggs.
4 whole eggs.
1½ ozs. of ground sweet almonds.
6 ozs. of pure cocoa.

Place one pint of the milk, one pint of the cream, 8 ozs. of the sugar, and the ground almonds in a tin-lined stewpan on the stove to come to the boil, stirring occasionally to dissolve the sugar. Beat up the yolks and the whole eggs in a good-sized basin, and pour the milk and cream, boiling, upon the beaten eggs, stirring vigorously the while. Do not return to the stove. Set the pure cocoa, thinly sliced, in a small stewpan, add the 3 ozs. of sugar, the vanilla sugar, and the remaining half-pint of milk; set on the stove and gradually bring up to boiling point, well stirring at intervals. Whisk well, pass through a fine conical strainer, and add to the custard, beating well together with the whisk. Pass the whole through a fine hair sieve to ensure an even smoothness. When cold freeze as directed, giving particular attention to the spattling, and when nearly frozen beat in the remaining half-pint of cream, half whipped.

This method will give a beautifully smooth, fluffy cream, apparently not quite so rich as No. 1, because, there being some spring left in the eggs and a portion of the cream, it will bulk considerably under the spattle.

TEA CREAM ICE (CUSTARD).

1½ pints of double cream.
1 pint of new milk.
¼ pint of water.
6 whole eggs.
4 yolks.

10 ozs. of lump sugar.
1 dessertspoonful of orange-flower water.
1 oz. of fine tea—Darjeeling, Oolong, or Souchong.

Place the milk, one pint of the cream, and the sugar in a tin-lined stewpan and raise to boiling point, stirring occasionally to dissolve the sugar. Beat the yolks and whole eggs in a basin with the orange-flower water and pour the boiling milk and cream on them, stirring well with the whisk meanwhile.

Place the tea in a small jug or china teapot, made hot with boiling water, and pour in the quarter-pint (or a little over) of boiling water. Cover well down and allow to stand for five minutes if Darjeeling, ten minutes if Oolong or Souchong. Then pour off the liquor carefully and add a quarter of a pint of it to the custard. Mix well together, pass through a fine hair sieve, and when cold freeze as directed, spattling thoroughly. When nearly frozen add the remaining half-pint of cream, half whipped, and beat well in with the spattle. This will give a light, fluffy, but perfectly smooth cream that will bulk under the spattle.

The choice of the tea to be used must depend upon the taste of the confectioner or his customer. Of all the Indian teas the Darjeeling is the most suitable; it gives a thin pale coloured liquor of very delicate flavour, and no astringency. China teas are coming back into favour with folks of refined palate, and either Oolong or Souchong is certain to please them. Oolong also gives a very pale liquor, with a suggestion of Muscat grapes. Souchong has more colour and body, with less delicacy, but is also very fine.

The curious flavour of both Muscat grapes and Oolong tea is tom cat aroma idealised. This was strongly borne in upon the writer when eating Muscat grapes in California. They are tom cat realised and intensified.

Cream Ices.

CINNAMON CREAM ICE.

1 pint of double cream.
1 pint of new milk.
8 ozs. of lump sugar.
6 yolks.

4 whole eggs.
1 oz. of ground sweet almonds.
2 or 3 strips of thinly-cut lemon-rind.
Extract of cinnamon (home-made).

Scald the milk, cream, sugar, ground almonds, and lemon-rind, and pour boiling upon the beaten eggs and yolks. Do not return to the stove, but after well stirring with the whisk pass at once through a fine hair sieve. When cold add a few spoonsful of the extract of cinnamon until the desired flavour is obtained, and freeze as directed, spattling thoroughly. This will give a smooth, fluffy cream that will bulk a little whilst freezing if the spattling be well attended to.

This cream is a great favourite on the Continent, but is seldom made in Great Britain, although it is sufficiently distinctive to be appreciated. The usual method of flavouring is by pounding the sticks of cinnamon with sugar and sifting through a fine sieve. This plan has two features that are objectionable in a greater or lesser degree. The pounded cinnamon distinctly shows in the cream a sort of dingy brown, and the fibrous matter has a woody flavour. Extracted oil of cinnamon has a fine flavour when perfectly fresh, but rapidly deteriorates, and is apt to be used without due regard to its pungency.

It is therefore recommended that 4 ozs. of cinnamon be broken into short lengths and put into a $1\frac{1}{2}$-pint bottle, that one pint of pale brandy be added to it and securely corked. Once a day for a fortnight it should be shaken, and at the end of that time decanted, passed through coarse filtering paper, rebottled with a quarter-pint of simple syrup, and kept in a cool, dry, dark place when not in use. This will give a beautiful flavour, with just the touch of spirit required. Should any form of the flavour be used other than this spirituous one, a dessertspoonful of pale brandy should be added to the custard before freezing.

PISTACHIO CREAM ICE (1) (CUSTARD).

$1\frac{1}{4}$ pints of double cream.
1 pint of new milk.
6 yolks.
4 whole eggs.
9 ozs. of lump sugar.

3 ozs. of fine pistachio kernels.
2 ozs. of Valencia almonds.
1 dessertspoonful of orange-flower water.
1 tablespoonful of noyeau (liqueur).

Little green colour and little water.

Blanch the pistachio kernels and the almonds. Pound them fine in a small marble mortar, adding the orange-flower water to prevent them oiling. Lift out into a basin, and add a few spoonsful of water to thin them down.

Scald the milk, one pint of the cream, the sugar, and the pounded pistachio and almonds in a tin-lined stewpan, stirring occasionally to be certain that the sugar is dissolved. Beat up the eggs and yolks in a basin, and pour the boiling milk and cream upon them, whisking well whilst pouring. Do not return to the fire, but pass at once through a fine hair sieve to remove the fibrous matter of the nuts. When cold add the noyeau and a suspicion of green colour, and freeze as directed, spattling thoroughly. When nearly frozen add the quarter-pint of cream remaining, which must be half whipped, and beat well into the cream with the spattle. This cream should be rich and smooth, but light and fluffy as well, and quite distinctive in flavour.

All about Ices.

PISTACHIO CREAM ICE (2) (CUSTARD).

1 pint of double cream.
1 pint of new milk.
8 ozs. of lump sugar.
8 yolks of eggs.
1 oz. of ground sweet almonds.
1 oz. of pistachio kernels.

1 dessertspoonful of orange-flower water.
1 tablespoonful of noyeau (liqueur).
1 tablespoonful of maraschino (liqueur).
Little green colour.

Pound the pistachio kernels in a small marble mortar after blanching them, adding the orange-flower water to prevent oiling. Scald the cream, milk, sugar, ground almonds, and pounded pistachios, and pour boiling upon the beaten yolks in a basin. Return to the stewpan, and again set on the stove to set the yolks. Stir continually until the custard begins to thicken, when at once remove from the stove, whisk well, and pass through a fine hair sieve to remove the fibrous matter of the nuts and to ensure perfect smoothness. When cold add the noyeau and maraschino, mix well, tint a pale green, pour into a freezer, and freeze as directed, spattling well.

This ice will be very rich and smooth, but rather close-textured, and will answer admirably for moulding in Neapolitan or other moulds. Small pieces of pistachio nuts are sometimes added to these ices for the sake of appearance, but they become so hard that they are troublesome to eat, and in that state appear to have no flavour.

PINE APPLE CREAM ICE (CUSTARD).

1 quart of double cream.
1 quart of new milk.
1 lb. of lump sugar.
1 small Singapore pine.

12 yolks.
6 whole eggs.
2 dessertspoonfuls of pale brandy.
2 dessertspoonfuls of noyeau (liqueur)

Drain the syrup from the pine and put it into a copper sugar-boiler with the sugar. Stir over the fire until the sugar is dissolved. Cut one-third (the softest portion) of the pine into ¼-in. cubes, and boil these in the syrup until soft and quite transparent. Drain the syrup away from them and let them stand to get cold and as free as possible from moisture. Pound the rest of the pine to a pulp in a marble mortar, lift out, and boil with the syrup until the whole nearly reaches the caramel, carefully avoiding discolouration. Reduce with milk until thin enough to blend easily with the cream, etc. Now put the cream (less half a pint), the milk, and the boiled pulp into a tin-lined stewpan and scald. Beat up the eggs and yolks in a basin, and pour the boiling liquid upon them, beating vigorously with the whisk meanwhile. Do not return to the stove, but pass at once through a fine hair sieve, less only the fibrous portion of the pine. When cold pour into a previously prepared freezer and freeze as directed, spattling thoroughly. When nearly frozen add the remaining half-pint of cream, half whipped, with the brandy and noyeau, and beat well together. When this is thoroughly amalgamated add the small cubes of pine, beat well into the cream, spattling until the cream is quite firm.

This ice will be smooth, light, and fluffy, and of beautiful flavour, quite unlike that made from the raw cream. Individual taste must decide between them. They are both good, but the custard base one will possess much more body and tenacity than that made by the other plan.

Cream Ices.

PLAIN ITALIAN CREAM ICE (CUSTARD).

1¼ pints of double cream.
1 pint of new milk.
9 ozs. of lump sugar.
10 yolks of eggs.
1 oz. of ground sweet almonds.
3 thin strips of lemon-rind.
2 bay-leaves.

Put the milk, the cream (less half a pint), the sugar, the almonds, lemon-rind, and bay leaves into a tin-lined stewpan, and bring to the boil. Pour when boiling upon the beaten yolks, whisking well whilst pouring. Return to the stove, and just set the custard without boiling. The moment the custard ceases to follow the movement of the whisk remove from the stove, and at once pass through a fine hair sieve to remove fibrous matter and bay-leaves. When cold, freeze as directed, adding the balance of the cream, half whipped, when nearly frozen, and spattle thoroughly. This cream will be rich, smooth, and moderately solid, and will mould splendidly.

AVELINE PRALINE CREAM ICE (CUSTARD).

1 pint of double cream.
1 pint of new milk.
4 ozs. castor sugar.
1 oz. ground sweet almonds.
8 yolks of eggs.
1 teaspoonful essence of Vanilla.
4 ozs. castor sugar ⎫
4 ozs. avelines or hazel nuts. ⎬ made into praline.
1 teaspoonful of lemon juice. ⎭

Set the avelines on paper in the oven to become slightly roasted. Whilst very hot remove the outer skins by rubbing and fan away from the nuts. Melt the 4 ozs. sugar in a small copper sugar-boiler with the lemon juice, stirring gently to ensure even melting. Shoot in the warm avelines and gently coat with the melted sugar, by which time it will be slightly caramelled. Pour out on to an oiled slab to cool and set. When cold, pound fine in a mortar and pass through a 12-mesh sieve. Should the praline become at all oily, as it may if not carefully pounded, reduce to a paste by adding gradually a very little cream or milk, but keep dry if possible. Put the cream, milk, 4 ozs. of sugar, and ground almonds in a tin-lined stewpan and bring to the boil. Beat the yolks in a basin to break them up, and pour the boiling cream, etc., on them, beating well with the whisk. Turn the custard back into the stewpan and return to the fire, stirring all the time until the mass begins to thicken, but do not let it boil.

Place the praline in the basin and pour the custard over it, well stirring. Stir occasionally as it cools, and when cold pass through a hair sieve to remove the fibrous matter of both almonds and avelines. Add the vanilla, pour into a previously set up freezer, and freeze, with plenty of spattle work. Mould in a straight-sided mould, and freeze for at least an hour before turning out for serving. This ice will be solid, beautifully smooth, and of delicious flavour.

ALMOND PRALINE CREAM ICE (CUSTARD).

1 pint of double cream.
1 pint of new milk.
4 ozs. of castor sugar.
6 yolks of eggs.
4 whole eggs.
1 small laurel leaf.
1 dessertspoonful of noyeau (liqueur).
1 dessertspoonful of pale brandy.
4 ozs. blanched Valencia almonds. ⎫
4 ozs. of castor sugar. ⎬ made into praline
1 teaspoonful of lemon juice. ⎭

Treat this exactly as for the aveline praline, except that the custard must not be

All about Ices.

returned to the fire after pouring upon the yolks and eggs. This cream will therefore bulk more under the spattle whilst freezing, resulting in a lighter and more fluffy ice. Mould, freeze, and serve in exactly the same way.

ORANGE FLOWER CREAM ICE (CUSTARD).

1 pint of double cream.
1 pint of new milk.
6 ozs. of castor sugar.
10 yolks of eggs.
Zest of 2 ripe oranges (rubbed on sugar).
Juice of 2 oranges.
2 tablespoonfuls of orange-flower water.
2 drops of oil neroli added to the orange-flower water.
1 tablespoonful of orange curacoa.

Rub the zest of the oranges on a piece of cut loaf sugar, cut away the saturated portion, and place it in a small basin. Squeeze the orange juice on the zest, add the orange-flower water, the oil of neroli (which is the essential oil of orange-flowers), and the curacoa. Let these steep together until the sugar impregnated with the zest is fully dissolved. Prepare the custard exactly as for the almond praline, avoiding returning to the fire after pouring on to the yolks. Strain at once, and when cold strain the flavouring zest, mix with the custard, and freeze, with plenty of spattling. This cream will be smooth, fluffy, and light, and a beautiful colour. Any shaped mould can be used, but an orange-shaped one is the best. If the orange-shaped mould be used, one or two green marzipan leaves and a stalk may advantageously be set in position when sent to table.

SECTION III.—DESSERT ICES.

ICED PUDDINGS.

Of all the iced puddings, the one best known is the "Nesselrode," apparently named after Count Nesselrode, Foriegn Minister and Chancellor of Russia under the Tzars Alexander and Nicholas.

The composition of this pudding varies considerably, scarcely any two confectioners agreeing thereon. It is always admitted that it must be a rich custard, that it must be flavoured with maraschino, and must contain fruit. Currants, sultanas, and even candied peel are sometimes used. Chestnuts in some form are generally insisted upon, but seldom used even by those who insist. When used in the form of marron glacé (when, by the way, they are not chestnuts at all, but "marrana," a distinct form of the same family), it is questionable whether there is any reason beyond costliness for their use, for their delicacy of flavour is entirely lost by freezing, even were it not overshadowed by the more distinct maraschino, etc.

The formula that most commends itself to the writers, after trying many, is given here. It will, if carefully made and properly frozen and moulded, give results that are certain to please refined tastes.

NESSELRODE PUDDING.

1¼ pint double cream
1 pint new milk.
8 ozs. lump sugar.
2 ozs. icing sugar.
10 yolks eggs.
1 oz. ground sweet almonds.

2 ozs. marrons (glacé or drained) cut into small cubes.
8 ozs. Metz fruits
(cherries, apricots, green almonds, chinois, figs, etc.):
1 wineglassful maraschino.

½ wineglassful fine pale brandy (fin champagne).

Set the milk, one pint of the cream, the lump sugar, and the ground almonds in a tin-lined stewpan on the stove to come to the boil. Beat the yolks of eggs in a basin to well break them, and pour the boiling milk and cream upon them, stirring vigorously the while. When well blended turn the whole back into the stewpan, and return to the fire just to bring the whole to within an ace of boiling point. Stir with the whisk constantly, and the moment the custard begins to thicken remove from the fire, and after well whisking pass through a hair sieve into a basin to cool. It is important that the yolks be not allowed to be fully cooked, or the custard will be lumpy and curdled instead of smooth and velvety.

Cut the marrons into small cubes and put on one side. Cut the fruits into small pieces, put in a basin, and add the maraschino and brandy so that the fruit may be well impregnated. After steeping for half an hour the liqueur may be drawn from the fruit in a small strainer and added to the cold custard, which must be put in a well set up freezer and frozen thoroughly and well spattled.

All about Ices.

Half whip the ¼ pint of cream with 2 ozs. of icing sugar, and beat well into the frozen custard. When quite smooth, add the steeped fruits and cut marrons, and again freeze solid. The pudding will then be ready for moulding. The best mould for this pudding is a basket one with impression of fruit on top. A very usual plan is to attempt to tint the fruits on the mould top with carmine or other colours, but it is seldom satisfactory, and is best left alone. If the top does not fit tightly, pack with strips of paper. Set the mould, top downwards, on some broken ice and quickly fill, pressing into all crevices. Cover the filled mould with a small sheet of paper and press the bottom into place. If not very expert at handling it is well to tie a piece of tape or string from top to bottom to keep the parts well together. Set the mould at once in the middle of a pail of ice and salt, previously half filled, and fill up tightly at once and freeze for two hours before serving. In setting up this pail less salt must be used than for freezing by movement, as rapid melting of the ice is not desired.

This pudding must be sent to table with a sauce composed of clear syrup, 25 deg. to 26 deg. by the saccharometer, tinted pink with liquid carmine, and strongly flavoured with maraschino and pale brandy, served in a sauceboat.

When the pudding is required to be sent to table, and not a minute before, dish it up as follows:—Have ready a silver dish with a paper d'oyley on it. Lift the mould from its bed of ice, dip it into a pail of cold water for a few seconds, wipe the moisture away with a cloth, prise off the top and bottom of the mould with a short thick knife, remove the sheet of paper from the bottom, prise open one side of the mould, and set the pudding on the d'oyley, avoiding touching with the fingers. Send to table at once.

VICTORIA PUDDING.

1 pint double cream.
1 pint new milk.
8 ozs. lump sugar.
12 yolks eggs.
3 ozs. ratafias.
5 ozs. glacé cherries.
2 ozs. fine green angelica.
1 wineglassful kirsch.
½ wineglassful pale brandy.

SAUCE.

½ pint simple syrup.
2 yolks eggs.
1 dessertspoonful kirsch.
1 dessertspoonful pale brandy.

Set the milk, cream, and sugar in a tin-lined stewpan and bring to the boil, being careful that the sugar is thoroughly dissolved. Beat the yolks in a basin to break them down, and pour the boiling milk and cream on them, whisking thoroughly the while Do not return to the fire, as this pudding is intended to be rather lighter in texture than would be possible if the yolks were more nearly cooked.

Set the ratafias in a small basin and pour the kirsch and brandy over them, so that they may be thoroughly soaked. Cut the cherries and angelica into small pieces, and place them in a basin with the syrup intended to be used for the sauce, so that they may become saturated. Keep them in a warm place, when the syrup will the more readily drain away after saturation. The object of so treating the fruit is to prevent its becoming hard and tasteless in the pudding, as it is liable to do unless saturated with either syrup or liqueur.

When the custard is quite cold, turn into a freezer previously set up, and freeze well, with plenty of spattling to give a light, smooth fluffiness. When well frozen, add the well-drained fruit and again spattle until smooth and solid. Then turn in the soaked ratafias and carefully blend, and spattle until smooth and firm enough to mould. A fluted side

Dessert Ices.

mould is a suitable one for this pudding, which must be filled, covered, and embedded in ice and salt as before.

When sent to table it must be accompanied by the sauce as above in a separate vessel. The sauce must be made by bringing the syrup to the boil, pouring it upon the yolks, beaten in a basin with the kirsch and brandy, and whisked until cold. It should be a light creamy froth.

ALEXANDRA PUDDING.

- 1 pint double cream.
- 1 pint new milk.
- 8 ozs. lump sugar.
- 12 yolks eggs.
- 4 ozs. glacé figs.
- 2 ozs. glacé cherries.
- 3 ozs. small savoy biscuits.
- 1½ wineglasses yellow chartreuse.

Sauce.

- ½ pint simple syrup.
- 2 yolks eggs.
- 1 tablespoonful yellow chartreuse.

Set the cream, milk, and sugar in a tin-lined stewpan and bring to the boil, being careful to see that the sugar is entirely dissolved. Beat the yolks in a basin to break them down thoroughly, and pour the boiling cream and milk on them, whisking vigorously the while. Do not return the custard to the stove, but at once set on one side to become cold.

Cut up the figs and cherries into small pieces, and put them in a small basin with two-thirds of the chartreuse. Divide the savoy biscuits into their original single form, pour one-third of the chartreuse into a flat dish and set the flat sides of the biscuits downwards on the chartreuse, so that they may absorb the liqueur and become partially soaked. When the custard is quite cold, freeze, with plenty of spattling to obtain a light, fluffy smoothness, and then add the fruit and chartreuse, and again freeze and spattle until solid.

The best mould for this pudding is a square or oblong one, as the partially soaked biscuits have to be arranged in three layers between the cream. One-fourth fill the mould with the cream, then set one-third of the biscuits, rounded side downwards, side by side on the cream, put in another fourth of the cream and another third of the biscuits diagonally with the first layer, and so on until the mould is filled. Cover the cream with a sheet of paper, put on the bottom of the mould, and if necessary tie the mould with tape before setting in its bed of ice and salt. The sauce must be made exactly as for the Victoria pudding, except for the difference of flavour as given above.

ICED CHRISTMAS PUDDING.

For this pudding it will be necessary to make a pint of lemon-water ice in addition to the formula given below for the inner portion of the pudding.

Inside of Iced Christmas Pudding.

- 1 pint double cream.
- 1 pint new milk.
- 8 ozs. lump sugar.
- 8 yolks eggs.
- 1 oz. ground sweet almonds.
- A few small pieces of thin lemon rind.
- 4 ozs. seedless raisins, cut in halves (or muscatels, halved and stoned).
- 2 ozs. fine sultanas.
- 2 ozs. fine currants.
- 2 ozs. finely shredded citron peel.
- Little caramel colour.
- 1½ wineglasses of orange curacoa.

All about Ices.

SAUCE.

½ pint simple syrup.
2 yolks eggs.
Little caramel colour.
1 dessertspoonful orange curacoa.
1 dessertspoonful pale brandy.

Set the cream, milk, ground almonds, lemon rind, and sugar in a tin-lined stewpan on the stove to come to the boil, being careful that the sugar is entirely dissolved. Add a little caramel colour to tint to a pale coffee-cream. Beat the yolks of eggs in a basin to thoroughly break them up, and when the cream and milk have reached the boiling point pour them on to the eggs, well whisking them the while. When thoroughly blended turn the custard back into the stewpan, and return to the stove just to allow the custard whilst being well stirred to slightly thicken, but not to boil. When this point has been reached pass at once through a fine hair sieve to remove the fibrous remains of the almonds and the pieces of lemon rind.

If seedless raisins are used they will only need to be cut in halves. If the richer muscatels they will need to be stoned as well as halved. Set them with the rest of the fruit in a basin with the curacoa, so that they may become saturated. Whilst the custard is getting cold, prepare and freeze a pint of lemon-water ice (see lemon-water), and have it ready for use when the pudding proper has been frozen.

When the custard is cold pour into a previously well set up freezer and freeze well, giving it plenty of spattle work. Then add the fruits and liqueur, and spattle until smooth and solid.

Set the two halves of a round or bombe mould, the top and bottom (if either should be separate) being fixed in position on a bed of ice, and quickly but thinly line them with the lemon-water, pressing the ice into position with the fingers. Have a basin of cold water at hand in which to dip the fingers. As soon as the lining has been placed in position at once fill in each half with the frozen pudding, and set them together and clamp them into position. At once embed them in ice and salt and freeze for at least two hours. Send to table with a small piece of holly stuck in the top, and the sauce as above in a separate sauceboat.

The sauce is made as for the Victoria pudding, except as to the flavour and colour.

PLOMBIERE ICED PUDDING.

For this pudding it will be necessary to make and freeze one pint of cherry water ice (see cherry water ice), and to incorporate with it when frozen 3 ozs. of bright glacé cherries, cut into small pieces, and set aside in a basin with one dessertspoonful of kirsch. This ice when frozen must be used for lining the mould.

Prepare also three glacé apricots, two to be cut in small cubes and one in thin slices, and separately treated with a dessertspoonful of kirsch, the cubes in a basin, the slices in a plate. The body of the pudding must be made as follows:—

1 pint of double cream.
1 pint of new milk.
8 ozs. of lump sugar.
8 yolks of eggs.
Half of a small young laurel leaf.
A very thin fillet of lemon peel.
A dessert-spoonful of pale brandy.
1 dessertspoonful of orange flower water.

Put the cream, milk, lump sugar, and half laurel leaf and lemon into a tin-lined stewpan, and set on the stove to come to the boil, being careful to thoroughly dissolve the sugar. Beat the yolks of eggs with the orange flower water in a basin to break up well, and as soon as the cream and milk reach the boiling point pour on to the beaten yolks

Dessert Ices.

and well stir with the whisk. Turn all back into the stewpan, and return to the fire to slightly thicken, but not to boil, and at once pass through a hair sieve into a basin to cool Add the brandy, and freeze with plenty of spattling, and when firm add the steeped cubes of apricot and again freeze quite firm.

The mould for this pudding should be a round one, opening into two. If the top and bottom should happen to be separated as they sometimes are, fix them in position first of all. Rest the two half moulds on a bed of broken ice, and quickly line them with the cherry water ice, pressing into position with a half lemon or with the fingers, dipped into cold water to prevent the ice adhering to them. Quickly fill in each half, directly they are lined, with the apricot custard ice. One of the halves should not be filled quite so full as the other, and on the less filled one the slices of steeped apricot must be set close together, one in the centre and the others round it. Close the two halves, press tightly into position, and if necessary bind together with a piece of tape or string, and at once imbed in ice and salt and freeze for two hours before turning out for the table. Serve with a sauce made as for Victoria pudding, but flavoured with kirsch, pale brandy, and orange flower water.

MELON ICED PUDDING.

First make a pint of pale-green pistachio cream ice, and when frozen incorporate with it 2 ozs. of very finely shred angelica saturated with the maraschino which forms part of the flavouring of the pistachio cream. The reason for saturating the fruits in this way before blending with the body of the ice is to prevent them freezing into hard tasteless pieces.

The body of the pudding must be prepared as follows:—

1 pint of double cream.
1 pint of new milk.
8 ozs. of lump sugar.
12 yolks of eggs.

6 ozs. bright glacé cherries
1 wineglassful of mandarine (liqueur).
Zest of one orange.

Cut the cherries into long fillets, and set them in a basin with the mandarine to become saturated.

Put the cream, milk, lump sugar, and the orange zest in a tin-lined stewpan to come to the boil, stirring gently to ensure thorough dissolving of the sugar ; beat the yolks of eggs in a basin to break them up, and when the cream mixture reaches the boiling point pour it on to the yolks, beating thoroughly with the whisk the while. Do not return to the fire, as this cream is intended to be very light when frozen. When cold, freeze with plenty of spattle work, and when quite firm add the saturated cherries, and again freeze and spattle until firm and fluffy.

A fluted melon mould should be used for this pudding ; the two halves set in a bed of small ice, lined with the pistachio cream, and at once filled in with the mandarine flavoured ice, pressed well together, tied if necessary, and quickly imbedded in ice and salt to freeze solid—say two hours. The quantities as above will be sufficient for one very large mould or two ordinary sized ones.

The best sauce for this pudding is simple syrup, tinted orange, and flavoured with the zest and juice of one orange ,and a tablespoonful of mandarine liqueur. It should be strained quite clear, be very cold, and served separately in a sauce boat.

Melon stalk and leaves are sometimes made from marzipan and used for decoration with this pudding, but as in service the pudding is cut and handed round, the decoration is seldom seen, and is therefore wasted labour.

All about Ices.

MARBLED. ICED PUDDING.

This pudding can only be made singly when a number of other ices are being dealt with, as the quantity of each sort required is so small. Of course, when a number are required for a large dinner it is an easy matter to calculate the quantities required.

Any contrasting colours are suitable for the purpose—two, three, or more, properly arranged, giving very pretty effects.

The best shaped moulds for the purposes are either square or oblong, as they more readily lend themselves to both packing and after cutting up.

The combination suggested below is a very pretty one, and will make four large or six smaller square moulds.

Prepare and freeze one quart each coffee cream, vanilla cream, pistachio cream, and strawberry cream. Cut up into thin fillets 4 ozs. of red fruit paste lunettes or brochettes and lightly mix into the pistachio cream, and 4 ozs. of green lunettes in the same shape, which must be carefully blended with the vanilla cream. Having prepared the moulds and set them on an ice bed, fill one at a time, putting in a large spoonful of one colour after another, pressing into position, blending the colours a little of one into the other. Dip the spoon into a basin of cold water between the different colours to insure the cream leaving the spoon easily. When each mould is filled, cover and imbed in ice and salt at once, and freeze for two hours.

When sent to table, the best sauce is as follows :—For each mould :—

¼ pint simple syrup.
¼ lb. red currant jelly.

1 dessertspoonful orange curacoa.
1 dessertspoonful Jamaica rum.

The jelly rendered down with the syrup, strained, and when cold blended with the curacoa and rum, and served separately in a sauceboat.

DIGESTIVE OR BROWN BREAD ICED PUDDING.

This is a pudding that is only favoured by faddists and food cranks, but as there is an appreciable and increasing number of such folks to be catered for, it is as well to make what they require as unobjectionable as possible. Brown bread is used for ice making in many different ways, such as ordinary crumbs, thin slices, toasted slices, and even as pap, all of which we consider nasty and objectionable. After trying various methods to neutralise the objectionable features, we have adopted the plan as below for this pudding, with moderately good results. Whereas in the plain brown bread cream ice we endeavour to keep the crumbs as crisp as possible, in this pudding we actually soak them, but not with the watery moisture they can absorb from the cream, but with some good-bodied malaga or marsala.

1 pint of double cream.
1 pint of new milk.
8 ozs. of lump sugar.
8 yolks of eggs.
1 oz. ground sweet almonds.
2 thin fillets of lemon rind.

3 ozs. of brown breadcrumbs.
1 wineglassful malago or marsala.
1 tablespoonful of pale brandy.
4 ozs. muscatel raisins, stoned and quartered.
2 ozs. finely shed drained orange peel.

Rub through a rather coarse sieve enough crumb of brown bread to weigh 5 ozs., and carefully roast these on paper in a warm oven until nicely dry and browned, by which time they will weigh about 3 ozs. Place these in a basin whilst still warm, and pour over them the wine.

Stone and cut the raisins, cut the peel into fine shreds, and place both in a basin and mix well with the brandy.

Dessert Ices.

Set the cream and milk in a tin-lined stewpan, with the sugar, the ground almonds, and the lemon rind, and set on the stove to come to the boil, taking care that the sugar is thoroughly dissolved. Beat up the yolks of eggs in a basin, and pour the boiling cream and milk upon it, beating well all the time with a whisk. Turn all back into the stewpan, and return to the fire to slightly thicken, but not to boil.

Pass at once through a hair sieve, and set on one side to become cold. Freeze with plenty of spattling, and when solid turn in the brown breadcrumbs, refreeze, and then add the fruit and again freeze with plenty of spattling.

Use a round mould, pack in the frozen pudding, imbed in ice and salt, and freeze for two hours. Serve with a sauce made the same way as for Victoria pudding, but flavoured with brandy only.

MUFFIN ICED PUDDING.

Use either a plain round or a deep mould, half round, with a large bottom cover. Slightly cover the mould with a little clear melted butter, and line it with strips of waxed paper, closely fitting. Cover the paper entirely with a charlotte-like lining of halves of muscatel raisins, split flat and stoned, and set with their cut sides to the waxed paper. They will adhere firmly enough, and having plenty of sugar in them and being partly protected by the paper they will not freeze very hard. Now make your pudding filling as follows :—

  1 pint of double cream.   6 whole eggs.
  1 pint of new milk.   1 dessertspoonful of kirsch.
  6 ozs. of lump sugar.   1 dessertspoonful of noyeau.
  2 ozs. of icing sugar.   1 dessertspoonful of Jamaica rum.

Set the milk, half of the cream, and the lump sugar in a tin-lined stewpan, and place on the stove to come to the boil, being careful to see that the sugar is dissolved before the boiling point is reached.

Whip the eggs in a basin to break well up and lighten them, and pour the boiling milk and cream upon them, beating well with the whisk meanwhile. Do not return to the fire, as this cream must be beaten very light whilst freezing. When cold, freeze with plenty of spattle work into a very light fluffiness. Half whip the rest of the cream with the icing sugar, and beat it into the frozen cream until all is as light and firm as possible. Fill in the prepared mould, cover and imbed in ice and salt, and freeze for two hours.

When ready to send to table dip the mould into water slightly warm for a few seconds, and turn the pudding on to a d'oyley-covered dish. The paper can be removed from the sides in strips, and should readily leave the fruit. Serve with sauce prepared with simple syrup, flavoured with kirsch and rum, and just tinted with caramel and carmine.

This is a most delicious pudding, and is certain to please both by its appearance and its flavour and texture.

DESSERT ICES.

This is a somewhat vague, and occasionally an inaccurate title, inasmuch as all ices become dessert ices when they are served in that particular course. The term, however, is generally understood to include large and small moulded ices (always excepting puddings which are entremets), blended ices, such as Neapolitan, bombas, and eccentric combinations of many kinds and colours. The larger moulds, pints and quarts, are used for every kind of cream and water, and served as dessert ices, generally only one kind to each mould. Many of the smaller moulds are also used with one ice only, appropriately

All about Ices.

chosen to suit them, especially where particular fruits or flowers are represented. Moulds such as those representing asparagus requires two kinds, a green one at the top and a yellow one at the stalk end. In the case of small fruits it is frequently the custom to tint them more or less artistically, laying on the colours with a camel-hair pencil or by sprinkling, according to the fruit represented, after turning out of the moulds, and if well done the effects are good, but there is a growing objection to the practice. Whilst our votes are entirely for the amendment, the final judgment must rest with those who eat the morsels.

If it is desired to use colours, they must be carefully chosen and properly prepared. The liquid ones in ordinary use will answer for sprinkling, as the spray must be fine. A perfectly new fine toothbrush lightly dipped at its end into the colour and scratched with the point of a knife will send a fine spray in a given direction. For painting with a camel-hair brush it is advisable to blend a little solution of gum arabic with the colours to give them body. It is essential, if any toning or shading of colour is to be obtained, that more than one depth of each colour used must be prepared.

Another method, not so general, is to mix a little dry colour with icing sugar and blend them quite dry and free from lumps and tie up in two pieces of fine muslin and shake a little of the coloured sugar through by tapping the sugar doodle gently. A natural-looking bloom can be shaken the same way over coloured plum moulds by using very finely ground rice flour instead of coloured sugar. After filling the small moulds they must be carefully and tightly closed and set in ice and salt for at least an hour to become thoroughly firm. There are different ways of holding the hinged halves of the moulds together. The best, or rather the most secure, is to tie them with a piece of tape or twine, but this takes time, and in inexpert hands the filling is apt to become soft. Some of the moulds are provided with pins, which are entirely satisfactory. The writer is accustomed to provide small square pieces of thin tough paper and to wrap the small moulds that have no pins in them, tightly twisting the ends. Paper is a bad conductor, so moulds so wrapped need longer freezing to ensure good results.

When the small moulds have been in the mixture of ice and salt sufficiently long to be quite firm remove one at a time, dip into warm or tepid water, strip off the paper, re-dip in cold water, hold the mould in a cloth, open it, turn out the ice, colour it if so desired, set on a paper d'oyley, and keep in an ice cave until required to be sent to table.

Small ices of all varieties, either one or more kinds, can be filled after freezing in the ordinary way into small china or paper soufflé cups, and kept until needed in an ice cave. If the cups are filled above the level of the tops an ice cave is an essential for keeping them, but if filled level only they can be packed in carefully-arranged layers, with tinned or paper discs between, in an ordinary freezer, well set up. This latter is the usual way of sending ices ready for serving for balls and other gatherings.

NEAPOLITAN DESSERT ICES.

The Neapolitan form of parti-coloured bricks is a most popular one, and well suited for serving large numbers of people. The moulds are made in different sizes—brick shape, with top and bottom covers. The most useful size is 8 in. long, 3 in. wide, and 3 in. deep, inside measurement, as this will cut twenty-four ices, each 3 in. long by 1 in. wide and deep, which is a good size for serving at most functions.

For filling these moulds either three or four different ices must be made, using in each case rather less sugar than usual, as the ices must be frozen firmly enough to handle. Any combination of colours can be used, and it will be sufficient to suggest one or two. No. 1, vanilla cream, coffee cream, strawberry water, orange water; No. 2, strawberry cream, pistachio cream, tangerine water; No. 3, white coffee cream, chocolate cream,

Dessert Ices.

green tea cream. The above are three most effective combinations, both of colours and flavours, No. 3 being an inspiration that when first made was instantly successful. No. 3 will serve as an object-lesson in filling, cutting, and packing.

Both top and bottom of the mould will need a piece of white paper between itself and the ice to enable the operator to easily separate them. Set the mould, with paper and bottom cover fixed, on a bed of small ice, and having frozen the three creams required, one-third fill with the green cream, using a flat ice spoon dipped in water to lift and spread the cream level. Then fill in the white cream in the same proportion, and last the chocolate cream. Spread quite smooth, lay on the paper and cover, press closely together, and tie a strip of tape tightly round the mould. Set at once in ice and salt and pack well down for two hours. Finish all the moulds in the same way.

When well frozen and ready to pack away for serving have ready prepared the requisite number of paper wraps, cut, say, $3\frac{1}{2}$ in. by $4\frac{1}{2}$ in. from fine white thin surface paper, and also the caves or freezers in which the blocks are to be packed, well set up.

Lift the moulds from their bed, dealing with only one at a time. Cut the tape, dip the mould into a pail of cold water, prise off both covers, strip the paper from one side only, and holding the block of ice, paper side downwards, gently lift the mould away by pressure at each end. Do not touch the ice with the fingers, but use the stripped paper to press with if necessary. A cold marble slab is the best to work on if possible. Now with a sharp thin knife, dipped into lukewarm water, cut a block 1 in. wide quite straight through the block at one end. (The moulds are generally marked to show where to cut.) Turn the cut piece on its flat side, give it a half turn round, and quickly cut into three strips, each 1 in. wide, each piece having one-third of its length a different colour. Li.t each piece on to one of the paper squares, fold the paper up and over the edges, and at once set in its proper place for keeping frozen. An assistant should wrap and pack the pieces as fast as they are cut, so that the operation is as quickly done as possible. Proceed with the rest of the brick, and as soon as that is finished lift another mould, and so on to the end. The blocks are generally served on paper wraps, but can if desired be lifted on to small d'oyleys first.

NEAPOLITAN ICES—TUTTI-FRUTTI.

This is a very simple form of ice blocks, as it consists of only one form of the frozen cream, and can be made, therefore, in small quantities if required. Make as follows:—

$1\frac{1}{4}$ pint of double cream.
1 pint of new milk.
8 yolks of eggs.
2 whole eggs.
8 ozs. of castor sugar.
8 ozs. of glacé fruits, various, bright colours.
Wineglassful of kirsch.

Cut the fruit, cherries, apricot, fig, greengage, pineapple, and angelica into small pieces, and steep in the kirsch for an hour. Set the milk, one pint of cream, the sugar, and a small laurel leaf in a tin-lined stewpan on the stove to come to the boil. Put the yolks and eggs in a large basin, break them up with a whisk, and when the milk and cream reach the boiling point pour on to the beaten eggs, whisking well meanwhile. Strain through a hair sieve, and when cold freeze with plenty of spattling. Half whisk the rest of the cream, blend the steeped fruit with it, add gradually to the frozen cream, well spattling until the whole is frozen stiff and very light. Fill into the prepared moulds as before and freeze solid. When frozen turn out, cut, wrap, and pack in freezer or cave as previously directed.

This cream can also be used for packing in fancy mould and serving as a dessert ice if desired.

All about Ices.

MOSAIC NEAPOLITAN ICE.

For making this ice three colours are necessary—*i.e.*, pink, coffee, or chocolate, and white or yellow. The two following sets are given as examples, both being good:— (1) Strawberry cream, chocolate cream, vanilla cream; (2) strawberry water, coffee cream, vanilla cream.

For each brick mould to be filled six plain pencil-shaped moulds, inside diameter 5-16 in., and six larger moulds, inside diameter ¾ in., both being the same length as the large moulds, will be needed, but can be used successively. Fill the 5-16-in. moulds with pink ice and freeze quite solid. Partly fill the ¾-in. moulds with the dark ice, turn out the frozen pencils, set them along the middle of the ¾-in. moulds, press together, and again freeze solid. Set a ½-in. layer of the yellow cream in the bottom of one of the brick moulds, turn out three of the small-cored chocolate or coffee moulds (whichever set is used), and set them equi-distant on the vanilla cream, so arranging that each one shall be in the middle of the after cuttings. Fill in sufficient of the vanilla cream to cover and to reach two-thirds of the depth, then turn out and set three more of the cored pieces accurately in their places. Fill up the mould, cover and freeze as before directed. When the moulds are turned out and cut up into strips 3 in. by 1 in. by 1 in. the effect should be, and will be if carefully done, very pretty.

As the small moulds will freeze their contents very quickly, a set of six of each size can be handled continuously for filling a number of the large bricks; and although the labour may appear rather troublesome, it is surprising how quickly a number can be finished when once the knack has been acquired

NEAPOLITAN ICES A LA RUSSE.

To make these ices, which resemble in arrangement one of the forms of Russian cake, generally called "Petersburg," supplementary moulds are not needed, although a special size brick mould is necessary, 8 in. long by 1½ in. wide and 1½ in. deep. Careful, speedy, and skilful handling is also essential.

The simple and easy way is to use two kinds of ice only, of contrasting colours, of which one should be pink. Assuming that the two sorts chosen be strawberry cream and pistachio cream, it will be sufficient to describe here the handling of two moulds (the number can, of course, be increased indefinitely), as two moulds only can be dealt with successfully at one time.

Fill half the moulds required entirely with the strawberry cream, and the other half entirely with the pistachio cream, cover with paper, and freeze hard as directed. It is as well to pack the moulds of each kind in a separate tub, so that no mistake be made in opening. Lift out one mould of each sort, dip into cold water, remove the lids, and press out on to a cold slab. Let an assistant rinse the two moulds and set on the paper and bottom covers. Quickly and accurately divide each block into three lengthways. Turn each strip on its side, and again divide into three. Thus divided you will have nine bars from each mould, and the moulds must at once be refilled with them as follows:—

No. 1 mould.—Bottom row: A bar of red at each side and a bar of green between Middle row: A bar of green at each side and a bar of red in between. Top row: A bar of red at each side and a bar of green in between. Cover with paper and press on lid, and repack in ice to become solid.

No. 2 mould.—Bottom row: A bar of green at each side and a bar of red between. Middle row: A bar of red at each side and a bar of green between. Top row: A bar of

Dessert Ices.

green at each side and a bar of red in between. Cover and freeze as before for an hour at least.

When set and turned out cut in 1-in. lengths, wrap, and pack away as previously directed. This arrangement of the bars is necessary, so that each two moulds can be exactly refilled, and also gives a variation of colour scheme. Each small square will then give you nine smaller squares, and the effect, if carefully finished, is very good indeed, but care and skill are essential.

MELON MOULD DESSERT ICE.

Use a melon-shaped mould, and line both halves with plain pistachio cream. Fill the inside of both halves with tangerine water ice, close lightly together, and freeze as directed. If carefully moulded the effect will be very pretty when the moulded ice is cut and served.

SPINACH MOULD CREAM ICE.

For this a special mould in the form of a bunch of spinach leaves is necessary. The top of the mould and about one third downwards should be filled with pistachio cream ice, and the lower portion with vanilla cream ice. In filling, the green portion must be tapered a little way over the portion to be filled with the yellow, so that the colours may blend and tone into one another instead of showing a definite line of meeting.

SMALL TANGERINES ICED.

Procure the requisite number of equal-sized tangerine oranges, squeeze them a little to loosen the skins, remove carefully a small round piece with a round cutter 1 in. in diameter from the stalk base, and deftly remove the insides through the aperture. This can easily be done by dividing the small sections with the handle of a teaspoon. Be careful not to break the skins. Use the removed portions to make a tangerine water ice, and freeze as directed. Fill the ice when frozen into the empty skins, set on the round pieces first cut out, and place in a set up ice cave to become solid before serving. These little morsels can be served either entire or preferably cut nearly through and partly opened out. In this form they are more easily attacked with a spoon. Ungetatable delicacies are sometimes tantalising. In this connection the nigger's mournful lament—
"Eliza Jane's a bright mulatter;
She's a charmin' gal, but you can't get at her."
may be understandable.

ORANGE SECTIONS ICED.

The ordinary Denia, St. Michael, or blood oranges may be prepared in exactly the same way, filled with the orange water ice made from the removed portion, frozen in a cave and cut into quarters when served. Greater care will, however, be necessary in removing the pulp, as it adheres to the skin with greater tenacity than does that of the tangerine variety.

ICED SOUFFLE.

This form of dessert ice is but little known to the average British confectioner, and, curiously enough, one that he appears afraid to attempt. The writer is loth to believe that the ordinary Britisher is afraid of anything, and he hopes and believes that the British confectioner has his full share of the national pluck and dogged pertinacity.

All about Ices.

When it is made perfectly clear that with ordinary perseverance all the forms of iced soufflé can be successfully and profitably made, it is hoped that this favourite delicacy will be much more general, and one more source of profit be utilised instead of neglected.

SOUFFLE DISHES OR MOULDS.

These are generally round, although oval ones are occasionally used. The large ones are (or should be) electro-plated, and consist of an inner and an outer piece. The inner one, which is plain, with upright sides, should slip easily into the outer one, which has a flanged top and side handles, and is only used to serve the soufflé after it is frozen. These dishes can be obtained from any silversmith making plant for our trade. The sizes vary, but the proportions should always be about the same—*i.e.*, the diameter should be twice the depth. Thus 5 in. diameter, $2\frac{1}{2}$ in. deep, or 6 in. diameter and 3 in. deep are very useful sizes, the smaller one for a 1-quart size and the larger for a $1\frac{1}{2}$-quart size. In preparing the inner piece for holding the soufflé, a band of stiff paper should be fastened round the dish so that it stands at least 3 in. above the top edge, rather more than doubling its depth. Into this deepened mould the prepared soufflé is poured. The mould is then set in the ice cave and thoroughly frozen. If any form of decoration on top of the soufflé is desired the top of the cave can be lifted when the soufflé is half frozen and the surface sufficiently solid to carry whatever is arranged or sprinkled upon it.

When thoroughly frozen the paper band must be carefully unrolled, leaving the frozen soufflé standing up above the case, which must then be slipped into the outer one and sent to table. Small cases made in the same form of plate or single ones of thin china are also used, and treated in exactly the same way, or even, as in the case of paper ones, only filled to the tops of the moulds. Small ones are also made from more solid mixtures that can be piled high above the moulds without using paper frames, but these are somewhat different in composition.

ICE CAVES.

Reference was made to these useful and necessary utensils in the opening chapters, but the caves there dealt with were the usual ones for storing and delivering frozen ices. For that purpose the ordinary caves, which have hollow walls and well-shaped tops for carrying the ice or ice and salt, are essential, but for quickly freezing soufflé in the workshop a cheaper and more readily effective form is advocated.

Iron is the best conductor, but is liable to rust and difficult to keep clean. Iron plate tinned is easily kept clean, but is not a rapid conductor, and, being thin, not very durable. Galvanised iron is therefore recommended as being almost as good a conductor as plain iron, easily cleansed, strong, and durable, as well as cheap. Copper is good, and many a small stockpot has been utilised upon occasion when other utensils have run short. Aluminium should answer admirably, but it is dear, and, being soft, easily dented. A useful size is 8 in. in diameter by 9 in. high, made with a wide flanged lid that fits easily and has a handle on top. This will carry all ordinary-sized soufflé, and, having only a small inner chamber, will freeze rapidly. This cave should be set up in a freezing tub, with 4 in. of finely-broken ice at the bottom. Sprinkle a little salt on this, set the cave in position, put on the lid, and pack the sides with ice and salt to within 2 in. of the cave top. Lift off the top, see that the interior is clean and dry, set the soufflé in the inner mould, put on the top, close the lower edges against salt water by filling up the interstices with a little lard, running the finger round to press into position, and then cover entirely with small ice and salt, and freeze until solid. The time required for this operation will

Dessert Ices.

vary according to the size and richness of the soufflé, which can be inspected if necessary by lifting off the ice and then the lid of the cave. Under ordinary conditions three hours is the minimum time required, and it may be much longer.

In the following formulæ all the principal types will be included, and the intelligent confectioner will be able to make endless varieties of flavour and colour if he adheres in the main to the proportions of saccharine strength here given. Two points must therefore be kept in mind—(1) the richer in saccharine strength the mixture used, the greater the difficulty of freezing firmly, and the reverse ; (2) the greater the density of the body to be frozen, the less must be its saccharine strength. All the formulæ here given are properly balanced, and if carefully made to the required density may be depended upon to give first-rate results. First efforts may not be successful, but intelligent observation and perseverance are certain to bring success.

SYRUP FOR SOUFFLE.

Clarified sugar in the form of syrup of a definite saccharine strength is an essential for soufflé making. For nearly all forms 21 deg. by the saccharometer is the proper strength. The usual simple syrup made with 12 lbs. of sugar to the gallon of water (B.P.) is too heavy, varying with the sugar used from 26 deg. to 30 deg. This if at hand can, of course, be used by reducing with the water until it registers at boiling point 21 deg., but it is easier to make a little on purpose. With fine cane sugar 5 lbs. to 3 quarts of water will give the required strength, but whatever sugar be used, it will be well to test the strength when boiling, and either reduce or increase its density as required. The sugar must be put in a copper sugar-boiler with the water and just a pinch of cream of tartar. Beat one white of egg with a little of the water and stir into the hot syrup ; let it boil well up and simmer a little while until the white of egg is thoroughly coagulated, when the syrup should be strained through a fine hair sieve, or double muslin. It can be bottled and kept for use as required.

BROWN BREAD ICED SOUFFLE.

½ pint of syrup (21 deg.).
4 yolks of eggs.
¼ pint of double cream.
4 ozs. of brown breadcrumbs (roasted).
Little vanilla sugar.
2 tablespoonfuls of pale brandy.

Place the crumbs in a small basin and add the brandy just to moisten them. Put the syrup, yolks, and vanilla sugar in a small copper egg bowl and beat over a hot water bath. A little water in a stewpan on the stove is the best method of heating, but the water must not touch the bottom of the egg bowl. Beat until the syrup and yolks are about 120 deg., then lift off and whisk until cold, by which time the mixture should be as light and thick as a sponge batter. Half whip the cream, add the brandy and crumbs, and gently but thoroughly stir into the soufflé. At once pour the whole into the previously prepared mould, sprinkle a few well-dried brown breadcrumbs on the surface, and at once set in the cave as directed.

STRAWBERRY CREAM SOUFFLE.

⅓ pint of syrup (21 deg.).
3 yolks of eggs.
¼ pint of cream (nearly).
2 tablespoonfuls pale brandy.

FOR THE FILLING.

6 oz. strawberries (sliced).
¼ pint double cream.
2 oz. pulverised sugar.
Few drops of liquid carmine.

All about Ices.

Make the soufflé exactly as for brown bread, adding the brandy to the cream before half whipping it. Before filling the soufflé into the prepared mould set a hollow tin tube 1½ in. to 1¾ in. diameter in the centre of the mould, placing a weight or something heavy to hold it in position. Fill in the soufflé round it so that the tube remains exactly in the middle. Carefully adjust in the cave without disturbing the position of the tube, and freeze until solid. When solid lift off the top of the cave, remove the tube carefully by lifting with a spiral motion, and with a spoon at once fill in the cream whipped with the pulverised sugar, tinted a pale pink with the carmine and the sliced strawberries stirred into it. When the centre has been filled cover the top of the soufflé with the balance of the strawberry cream as lightly as possible, and sprinkle sliced strawberries on top. At once cover again and freeze until the cream is solid, when the soufflé can be dished and served as before directed.

VICTORIA SOUFFLE.

4 yolks of eggs.
½ pint syrup (21 deg.).
½ wineglassful maraschino.
½ wineglassful pale brandy.

¼ pint of double cream.
4 ozs. mixed macaroons and ratafias (crushed).
3 ozs. glacé cherries (quartered).

Put three-quarters of the crushed macaroons and ratafias and 2 ozs. of the cherries into a basin (the quarter reserved should be free from powder), and pour the maraschino and brandy over them, allowing them to steep whilst preparing the body of the soufflé. Beat the yolks and syrup into a solid batter as for the preceding soufflé. When quite cold and light half whip the cream, gently stir into it the steeped biscuits and cherries, and blend with the soufflé as lightly as possible. Pour gently into the prepared mould, previously prepared, and strew the dry biscuit nibs and 1 oz. of quartered cherries lightly on top. Set in the cave and freeze solid as directed.

Note.—Should the batter be at all soft after stirring in the cream and steeped biscuits and cherries, it is advisable to defer sprinkling the biscuit nibs and cherries until the soufflé is partially frozen.

CARAMEL SOUFFLE.

4 yolks of eggs.
½ pint of syrup (21 deg.).
⅓ pint of double cream.
Small quantity of new milk.

1 teaspoonful of vanilla sugar.
1 oz. of finely filleted and browned almonds.

First prepare the caramel. Place one-third of the syrup in a very small copper sugar-boiler and boil down over the fire until it reaches the caramel. Take one-third of the cream and add half its bulk of new milk, mixing together. Add a little of this mixture to the caramel and gently stir together. Boil this down until nicely browned, but not burned. Add more of the cream and milk gradually, boiling down each time, but carefully avoid burning, or the delicacy of the flavour will be lost. When the last of the cream and milk are added blend only; do not boil down again, as the mixture must remain sufficiently liquid to blend when cold with the other two-thirds of the cream before or after half whipping with the vanilla sugar.

Prepare the body of the soufflé as previously directed, and when ready gently blend with the half-whipped caramelled cream, and mould as directed. The browned filleted almonds should be sprinkled on top of the soufflé when half frozen, so that their weight does not carry them down from the top.

Dessert Ices.

Fine almonds must be used. Jordans are the best, and the filleting should be carefully and finely done. An additional delicacy of appearance is given if the fillets be crystallised after browning, but this is not essential, and is seldom done. All the same, it is good.

The usual method of making this soufflé is simply to caramel a portion of the syrup and add it to the batter before beating up, but there is no comparison in flavour with the caramel cream as given above. The colour will be a very delicate coffee cream.

PISTACHIO SOUFFLE.

4 yolks of eggs.
½ pint of syrup (21 deg.).
⅓ pint of cream.
3 ozs. pistachio kernels.
½ wineglassful of kirsch.
½ wineglassful of noyeau (liqueur).
Very little green colour.

Blanch the pistachio kernels and finely fillet half an ounce of them. Pound the rest in a small mortar until quite smooth, using a little of the noyeau or kirsch to prevent them oiling. Scrape quite cleanly into a small basin, and stir in the rest of the liqueurs.

Prepare the soufflé batter as previously instructed, and when quite cold and light add a very little green colour just to tint the batter. Half whip the cream, stir in the pistachio paste and liqueurs, and then blend gently but thoroughly with the soufflé batter. Pour carefully into a prepared mould and set in the cave, and when half frozen sprinkle the filleted pistachio kernels on the top, and finish freezing as before instructed.

GREEN COFFEE SOUFFLE.

4 yolks of eggs.
¼ pint of syrup (19 deg.).
½ pint of cream.
2 ozs. of crushed ratafias.
2 ozs. unroasted coffee, either Moc or peaberry.
1 oz. vanilla sugar.

Half roast the coffee berries, slowly and gently, in a small copper sugar-boiler, stirring a little with a wooden spattle, so that they brown evenly, but very slightly. Add the syrup to the hot berries and simmer for two minutes, by which time the syrup will be reduced to about 21 deg. Remove from the fire and cover well down for at least fifteen minutes, by which time the syrup will have absorbed the flavour of the berries without perceptibly deepening in colour. Strain out the berries, put the syrup and yolks into the small egg bowl, and heat and beat up as previously instructed. When cold and light half whip the cream with the vanilla sugar, and gently blend with the soufflé batter and pour into the prepared mould and freeze in the cave. When half frozen the top can be covered with the small pieces of crushed ratafias. Finish the freezing until quite solid before sending to table.

NEAPOLITAN SOUFFLE.

This soufflé can only be made economically when a large number have to be served, as four varieties are necessary. Any four well contrasted colours can be used; even two or three can be made effective, but four are more so. There are two ways of setting the colours, the usual being to have them in layers. This plan is the better for serving, as the soufflé being cut downwards, a portion of each colour would be served together. The objection (if it can be so called) to this plan is that the bottom layers do not show when the dish is handed round, as they are below the rim level. The newer plan, in which the

All about Ices.

varieties are divided horizontally, is more effective in appearance, but not so easy for service.

In the former plan one sort only is prepared at a time, divided into the two, three, or four moulds, and partially frozen, whilst the next one is prepared, and so on until all are filled and finished freezing. By the newer method one large batter sufficient for the four sorts can be prepared, divided into four basins, and the different colours and flavours added with the whipped cream to each. For this purpose a tin cross, composed of two pieces of tin each 5 in. by 6 in., each one cut 3 in. deep on the 5-in. side, and fitted one into the other in the form of a cross and soldered together. In shape this will be like a large Good Friday bun cross, and will fit inside the 5-in. mould. A circular piece of tin 7 in. in diameter should have a 5-in. cross cut with a $\frac{1}{8}$-in. channel in its centre. This will fit over the crossed pieces, which will slide through the cut cross.

Set the crossed pieces inside the papered mould, and fill in the different-coloured soufflé in the quartered spaces right up to the edge of the paper. Slip on the cut cross, and gently draw out the inside frame, leaving the quartered colours intact. The withdrawal of the cross will, of course, lift a little of the thick light batter, but the top frame will minimise this lifting. Each case must, of course, be filled separately, and the cross and frame be washed and used wet each time.

COFFEE SOUFFLE.

4 yolks of eggs.
$\frac{1}{3}$ of a pint syrup (21 deg.).
2 wineglassfuls extract of coffee.
$\frac{1}{3}$ pint of double cream.
1 oz. vanilla sugar.
1 dessertspoonful of Jamaica rum.

Prepare the soufflé in the usual way, adding the extract of coffee to the syrup and yolks of eggs. When cold and light, half whip the cream with the vanilla sugar and the rum, and gently blend with the beaten soufflé. Pour into the prepared mould and freeze as directed, after sprinkling on the top small pieces of broken sugar wafers.

CHOCOLATE SOUFFLE.

5 yolks of eggs.
$\frac{1}{4}$ pint syrup (21 deg.).
$\frac{1}{3}$ pint of double cream.
3 oz. fine pure cocoa.
1 oz. vanilla sugar.
1 dessertspoonful of pale brandy.
$\frac{1}{2}$ oz. finely filleted pistachio kernels.

Prepare the soufflé mixture in the usual way, and when cold and light slowly melt the pure cocoa without making very warm. The cocoa should be finely shredded, and for preference melted in a basin in a hot water bath. Add a little of the cream gradually, gently stirring and blending, until the cocoa is sufficiently softened to be easily mixed with the rest of the cream, which must be half whipped after adding the vanilla sugar and the brandy. When smoothly blended stir gently into the beaten soufflé, and at once pour into the previously prepared case and freeze as directed. The finely filleted pistachio kernels must be sprinkled on top, preferably when the soufflé is partially frozen.

This soufflé needs great care in blending the cream, and in the final admixture, and at its best it is always a little closer in texture than any of the others.

SOUFFLE DES ANGES.

8 yolks of eggs.
$\frac{2}{3}$ pint of syrup (21 deg.).
$\frac{1}{4}$ pint of double cream.
wineglassful of maraschino.
wineglassful of orange-flower water (triple).

3 drops of oil of neroli.

Dessert Ices.

For the Cap.

¼ pint of double cream.
3 ozs. castor sugar.
1 tablespoonful of maraschino.
Wineglassful orange-flower water.
Few drops liquid carmine.

Prepare the soufflé as previously described, adding the orange-flower water and oil of neroli to the yolks and syrup. When cold and beaten very light, half whip the cream with the maraschino, gently blend with the soufflé, and pour into the prepared mould. Freeze as directed, and when half frozen the cap of cream must be roughly piled on top and the freezing finished. The cap of cream must be prepared as follows: Put half a pint of cold water into a large basin, add the castor sugar, the orange-flower water, the maraschino, the carmine, and the cream. Whisk with a willow birch whisk, using a right and left stirring motion only. As the cream rises in a froth skim off the top with a perforated skimmer and set to drain on a fine plain hair sieve. From time to time the drainings can be added to the first basin, and the whisking continued until cream will no longer rise. The frothed cream will bulk largely, and when quite thoroughly drained will give a large pale pink-coloured crown to the soufflé that will be very effective.

ITALIAN SOUFFLE.

5 yolks of eggs.
½ pint of syrup, 19 deg. by the saccharometer.
2 inch stick of cinnamon.
2 small fillets of thin lemon rind.
1 teaspoonful essence of vanilla.
½ pint of double cream.

Set the syrup in a small sugar-boiler with the cinnamon and lemon rind, and simmer gently for two or three minutes, by which time the syrup will be reduced to a density of 21 deg. Cover and allow to steep for at least fifteen minutes, and then strain into the copper egg-bowl, add the yolks, and heat and beat up as before instructed. When quite light and cold, half whip the cream with the essence of vanilla, gently stir into the soufflé, pour into the prepared mould, set in the cave, and freeze as directed.

ICED BOMBES.

These dessert ices take their name from their form. The moulds used are round, generally in two pieces, hinged together. Occasionally the form is varied by an opening at both top and bottom, in which case the top is generally a fancy fruit design, and the bottom a simple cap. When the ornamental top is used it is advised that an ice of a distinct colour from the body of the bomb be used. This must, however, be left to the taste of the operator, who may have to adapt his method of filling to the moulds available for use. Bomb (English), bombe (French), bomba (Italian), as below, are given in orthodox forms only.

CHOCOLATE CREAM BOMBE

Prepare one pint of chocolate cream ice and freeze as directed. This must be used to line the two halves of the mould, pressing into position with a small tablespoon occasionally dipped into cold water. Before lining the mould have ready the filling as below:—

1 pint of double cream.
½ oz. of vanilla sugar.
4 ozs. pulverised sugar.

Set cream and sugars together in a basin and lightly whip, and as soon as the mould

All about Ices.

has been lined with the chocolate cream fill in the two hollow halves and quickly set together, put in connecting pin, and set in ice and salt to become solid.

In all cases when the moulds are being lined they must rest on a bed of small ice, so that the lining may remain as firm as possible, and no time must be lost in lining, filling, and embedding the moulds.

STRAWBERRY AND LEMON BOMBE.

1 pint of strawberry cream ice.   1¼ pint of lemon-water ice.
Small quantity Italian meringue.

The quantities here given are, of course, only approximate, and must depend upon the size of the mould and the skill of the operator. If the moulds are thinly lined the proportion of the filling will, of course, be greater than if the lining be thick and clumsy.

After the lemon-water ice has been well frozen a small quantity of well-beaten Italian meringue (three whites to each quart of ice) should be added and well beaten into the ice just before filling into the strawberry-lined mould.

TANGERINE ORANGE AND STRAWBERRY BOMBE.

The tangerine-water ice should be well frozen and used as the lining for the mould, which must then be filled with the cream as follows:—

1 pint of double cream.   4 ozs. pulverised sugar.
6 ozs. fresh strawberries.   Little liquid carmine.

When the fresh fruit is not in season a bare half-pint of strawberry syrup may be substituted for the fruit and sugar.

Pulp the fruit through a hair sieve, add the sugar, with a few drops of liquid carmine, and add to the cream, carefully but not over-whipped. Line the halves of mould with the tangerine-water ice, and quickly and carefully fill in the strawberry cream, close tightly, and freeze until solid.

PISTACHIO AND COFFEE BOMBE.

Prepare and freeze the pistachio cream ice for the lining, and then make the filling of coffee cream as follows:—

1 pint of double cream.   ½ oz. of vanilla sugar.
3 ozs. of pulverised sugar.   Extract of coffee, *quantum suff*.

Whip the cream with the sugars until light and thick, being careful not to overwhip, and add sufficient extract of coffee to give the desired flavour. Line the halves of the mould with the pistachio cream, quickly fill in the coffee cream, close tightly, and freeze until solid. This is a delicious combination, and always a favourite.

ORANGE AND MARASCHINO BOMBE.

The lining for this bombe is plain orange-water ice, of which one pint should be made and frozen. The filling must be made as follows:—

1 pint of double cream.   1 wineglassful of maraschino.
4 ozs. of pulverised sugar.   Few drops of green colour.

When the orange water is frozen set the cream, sugar, and maraschino in a basin and carefully whip light, erring rather on the side of under than over whipping. Tint a pale green colour—very pale indeed.

Line the mould with the orange-water ice, carefully but quickly fill in the maraschino cream, close tightly, and freeze until solid.

Dessert Ices.

VANILLA AND AVELINE PRALINE BOMBE.

Prepare and freeze one pint of vanilla cream ice for lining the mould, leave it in the freezer to become solid whilst the following filling is prepared:—

    1 pint of double cream.   3 ozs. powdered aveline praline.
    3 ozs. pulverised sugar.   1 tablespoonful of kirsch.

Set the cream, sugar, and kirsch together in a basin and lightly whip, being careful not to overwhip, and gently stir in the praline. Line the mould with the vanilla cream ice, fill in the praline cream, quickly close, and freeze until solid.

PISTACHIO AND ALMOND PRALINE BOMBE.

Prepare and freeze one pint of pistachio cream ice and let it rest in the freezer whilst the following filling is prepared:—

    1 pint of double cream.   3 ozs. of powdered almond praline.
    3 ozs. of pulverised sugar.   1 tablespoonful of noyeau (liqueur).

Treat exactly as for aveline praline bombe above.

PISTACHIO AND CHERRY BOMBE.

Prepare and freeze one pint each of pistachio cream ice and cherry-water ice. Fill one-half of the mould with each, close tightly, and freeze until solid. This is very simple and easy, but an effective contrast of colour and harmony of flavour.

POMPADOUR BOMBE.

For this mould it is necessary to have made two small utensils like those for the Neapolitan soufflé, except that the bottom edges must be rounded to fit the bombe mould. In shape it is like two cheese-knives, in the form of a cross. Any tinsmith can cut and fit the pieces together in a few minutes, and the cost should be a few pence only. The mould when turned out shows four distinct colours in quarters, and is very effective in appearance.

Prepare and freeze a small quantity of tangerine water, lemon water, strawberry cream, and coffee cream, say for two quart moulds, one pint of each ice. Set one of the

Fig. 1.

crosses in each half mould, bot relatively at the same angle, and fill as follows:—Assuming that the crosses are set in the order as below, fill in the four spaces with the different ices as marked on the line drawing (Fig. 1), so that when the half moulds are closed each portion will fit into its proper position. The crosses should be dipped into water before being set in position, and the sections should be filled as quickly as possible. When all are filled the crosses must be withdrawn carefully, the halves closed quickly and tightly, and the mould at once embedded in ice and salt and frozen solid.

All about Ices.

HARLEQUIN BOMBE.

For this mould, which is equally as effective as the Pompadour, only two varieties of ices are required. Prepare one pint each of orange-water ice and green chartreuse cream ice. Freeze them thoroughly, set the crosses in the half moulds, and fill in as shown in the line drawing (Fig. 2), so that when the halves are closed each quarter of the mould will

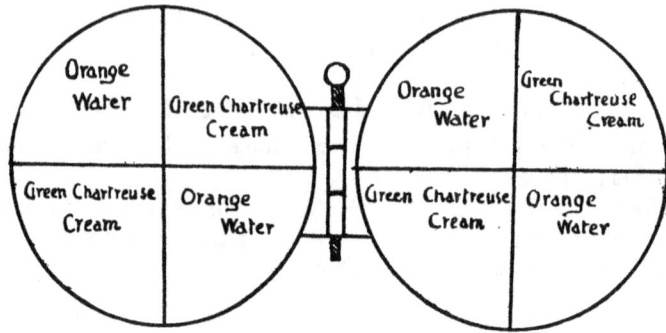

Fig. 2.

be divided into two distinct colours. Fill and close the mould as quickly as possible, imbed in ice and salt, and freeze until solid.

In lifting the crosses, if the pierced cross described for use with Neapolitan soufflé be used the lifting can be more easily done.

The five varieties of bombes that will complete this section are quite distinct from the foregoing, being all of them different in form and with soufflé centres.

COFFEE AND GREEN COFFEE BOMBE.

1 pint of coffee cream ice (custard type).   Green coffee soufflé (4 yolks into). See soufflés.

Prepare and freeze the coffee-cream ice, using the custard type, and allow to stand whilst the soufflé is being beaten up. The moulds used for this type are not of the true bombe form, but are cylindrical, and rather wide in proportion to their depth, being especially suitable for both lining and filling. Although not of the bombe shape, they are always so called, and a well recognised custom must perforce be observed. The prettiest form of the cylindrical mould is the fluted one, but quite plain ones answer all purposes. Should the mould used have an ornamental top, both top and sides should be lined with the coffee cream ice and the soufflé be filled into the centre. Should the mould be plain topped, it is advised that a disc of waxed paper or glassine be cut to fit the flat before lining the sides. This will come away without any rough surface, and can be peeled off after the mould has been turned out. Of course, the bottom of the mould should also be paper covered before putting on the bottom cap. If the plain-topped mould be used, a few pieces of crushed ratafias can be sprinkled on the soufflé centre after stripping off the paper top. Sufficient for a three-pint mould.

VANILLA AND BROWN BREAD BOMBE.

1 pint of vanilla cream ice (custard type).   Brown bread soufflé (4 yolks into).

Treat in all respects the same as for coffee as above, except that if made in the flat-topped mould, after turning out and stripping off the paper disc, the top should be covered with a small pile of dried brown bread crumbs before sending to table. Sufficient for a three-pint mould.

Dessert Ices.

MARASCHINO AND ITALIAN CREAM BOMBE.

1 pint of maraschino cream ice.   1 oz. finely-filleted pistachio kernels.
Italian soufflé (5 yolks into).

Prepare and freeze the maraschino cream ice, and let it rest whilst the soufflé is being prepared. Line the mould (sides only if flat topped, or top as well if fancy topped) with the maraschino ice, and fill in the centre with the Italian soufflé. Cover, imbed, in ice and salt, and freeze solid. When turned out for the table, sprinkle the filleted pistachio on the top of the mould. This quantity is sufficient for a three-pint mould.

CHERRY AND MARASCHINO BOMBE.

1 pint cherry water ice.   Soufflé des Ange (8 yolks into).
1 oz. filleted glacé cherries.

Prepare and freeze the cherry-water ice, and leave whilst the soufflé is being beaten up. Line the mould with the cherry-water ice, and fill the soufflé into the centre. Cover, imbed in ice and salt, and freeze until solid. When turned out sprinkle the filleted cherries on the top before serving. These cherries will, of course, be most effective if the mould be a flat-topped one, as the contrast of colour will be more effective against the yellow soufflé background than on the red cherry-water ice. Sufficient for a large three-pint mould.

VANILLA AND CHOCOLATE BOMBE.

1 pint of vanilla cream ice (custard type).   Chocolate soufflé (5 yolks into).

Prepare and freeze the vanilla cream ice, and allow to rest whilst the chocolate soufflé is made and blended. Line the mould with the vanilla cream, and fill in the centre with the chocolate soufflé. Cover and imbed in ice and salt, and freeze until solid. This quantity will be sufficient for a large quart mould, the chocolate soufflé being closer in texture than any of the others.

In the foregoing pages, methods have been explained for making all types of ices, except the very cheap and low-class ones, with which the writers have no wish to associate themselves. There are, of course, many fancy names given to different ways of dressing, dishing, and serving ices, but the foundation of each and all of them is some variant of one other of the types that have been given. It would be hopeless to attempt to particularise them all, for every chef evolves titles at his own sweet will as opportunity or necessity arises, blending and combining fruit, etc., with ices in one or other of the foregoing types, and it would mean endless and unnecessary repetition. The careful student who has mastered the fixed principles underlying the formulæ given for the various types should be able to make his own combinations and variants; and whatever we may say or desire to the contrary, he will probably continue the practice that so largely obtains of naming or mis-naming his dishes in the usual ridiculous fashion.

SECTION IV.
ALL ABOUT JELLIES & CREAMS.

The old-fashioned method of making calves' feet jelly with calves' feet has largely fallen into abeyance, the use of gelatine being almost universal. There is much to be said in favour of the latter plan, chiefly because of its cheapness and convenience and saving of time. There is also much to be said against it. Of course, the substance required to give solidity to the various syrups and juices is always gelatine, but whilst the gelatine obtained by boiling down calves' feet is perfectly neutral in flavour, and that from cows' feet (a very usual substitute) is practically so, it is the exception to find the dried gelatine of commerce entirely free from a suggestion of glue. Gelatines vary in price from under 1s. per lb. to over 3s. per lb., a difference sufficient to account for a very great variance in quality. When the variety of animal substances from which it is possible to extract gelatine, and their probable maturity, be considered as compared with the tender growth of calves' feet, the difference in taste, or rather absence of taste, will be easily understood. At the same time there are plenty of good brands available that will give first-rate results, but they are not cheap. In making jellies, which are a luxury, it is very false economy to use low-grade gelatine, for its gluey taste cannot be hidden, even by extra flavouring. The outside difference of cost between the very best and the very worst would scarcely exceed 6d. per quart mould. Indeed, it is doubtful if it would come near that, because the higher grades of gelatine generally have a higher setting power. It is not within the province of the writers to recommend any particular maker's goods, but it is advised that a really reliable brand be decided upon and always used, so that the formulæ may always be the same. Exceptional types will sometimes take eight quarts to the pound, whilst some poor ones will only take four. Not only have these low grades more of the gluey taste, but, more having to be used, the taste is accentuated. In the formulæ that will follow good quality will be assumed, and a setting capacity of six quarts to the pound, of ordinary saccharine strength. The saccharine richness of jellies is one of the principal factors in setting capacity. In very hot weather it is well, therefore, to avoid the too generous use of sugar or syrup, unless a corresponding increase in gelatinous strength be arranged for.

The writer recalls an urgent message from an old friend many years ago, who on a hot summer's day could not get his moulds of calves' feet jelly to set, even with the help of ice, and they were needed in an hour for a wedding breakfast. He said, "I have clarified 4 ozs. of French leaf gelatine and added it to the twelve moulds, and have put them in without decoration, for they will not set. What do you advise?" They were tasted, and found to be very syrupy. "How much sugar did you use?" "Six pounds to the six feet, rather small." "Was the stock well set?" "Yes, very well. "How many flavours?" "Two only, six moulds of each." "Pour six moulds into this pan, add a quart of the coldest spring water you have, blend, and put back into the moulds; do the same with the other six, and most likely your jellies will be set in time." They were. The entire trouble was too great saccharine richness

All about Jellies and Creams.

JELLY BAGS.

These can be bought ready made, but can be made more cheaply at home, either of thin white felt or thick white flannel. It is advisable to have two or more different sizes, and if used very frequently these sizes should be duplicated, so that dry bags are always available. Clean dry bags will pass jelly much more quickly than wet or even damp ones. There is no absolute rule as to the exact dimensions, the form, of course, being conical, but with rounded instead of pointed ends. A good idea for obtaining a useful shape is to cut a large sheet of brown paper quite round, divide equally into three or four, take one piece and fold into two, and trim the pointed end round. When the sides and rounded end are joined together you have the shape of the jelly bag. This plan will help you to obtain the correct shape with felt or flannel. The three pieces size cut from the circular pattern is advised as giving a larger mouth to the bag, but either will answer all requirements. The rounded ends to the bags will greatly facilitate cleansing. When these bags are being cleansed they should never be wrung out, but allowed to drip and dry without being twisted out of shape. Each bag must have four strong coarse tape loops sewn equidistant apart on the top edges to suspend the bags when in use. New bags should always be well washed in hot water and carefully dried before using.

Enclosed cupboards with a door at one side, an open top with a spear point at each corner to carry the loops, and a close-fitting lid, and also a bottom shelf to carry the pan for catching the jelly, are sometimes used, but we confess to considering them nuisances. They have one advantage and one only; they certainly conserve the heat, and in that way help to more rapidly pass the contents of the bag. They are, however, awkward to manipulate, and when vessels have to be quickly changed, door, sides, etc., are dreadfully in the way. It is generally convenient to make jelly in a warm kitchen; and two fondant bars, or even two wooden rods, or, better still, a wooden cradle frame with four hooks or knobs to carry the loops, can be set across the backs of kitchen chairs, tables, or any suitable erection, giving free access to both bag and pans.

In establishments where jellies are made on a large scale a square sheet of felt or flannel is sometimes used; eyelets are let into each side, and the square is laced into position, with allowance for a more or less decided droop in the centre. In this way very large quantities are made at once in steam-heated rooms especially fitted.

CALVES' FEET JELLY STOCK.

6 calves' feet.
$12\frac{1}{4}$ quarts of water.
4 lbs. crushed sugar.
18 to 20 lemons, according to size.
20 coriander seeds.

The rind of six lemons.
1 pint of whites of eggs.
2 inches of stick cinnamon.
4 bay leaves.

Well wash the feet, cut them each into four, put into clean stock-pot with eight quarts of water, gradually bring to the boil, and simmer slowly for eight hours. Then strain the stock into a pan, add a further four quarts of water, and put back to simmer for another six hours, after which strain into a second pan and keep in a cold place to set. When cold and set carefully remove the fat from the top of the stocks and gently wash the surface to remove every atom of fatty matter. Put both first and second stock in a large copper stewpan, add the sugar, lemon-juice, lemon-rind (very thinly taken from the lemons without any of the white pithy under-skin), the cinnamon, bay-leaves, and coriander seeds, and set on the stove to melt. As soon as the stock has melted, but before

All about Ices.

it becomes very hot, beat up the whites of eggs with half a pint of cold water, and stir them into the stock. Gradually bring to the boil, stirring all the time, and when the jelly reaches the boil it will rise up quickly, and must be at once drawn back and allowed to subside. Boil up the second time, again draw back, and allow to slowly simmer until the coagulation of the whites is complete and the clear jelly begins to show between the masses of coalgulated albumen. Draw back still further and let rest for a few minutes longer, by which time the separation will show more clearly in larger spaces. Place a large pan under the previously fixed jelly bag, pour in the whole of the jelly, and change the pans under the bag until the jelly runs quite bright, pouring each lot into the bag as quickly but as carefully as possible. This jelly should be very pale in colour and brillantly clear, and will serve as the base stock, from which numberless flavours and colours can be made.

In very hot weather it may be necessary to increase the quantity of calves' feet, or to cut down the quantity of other things proportionately. It will not be sufficient to simply decrease the quantity of water, because that increases the saccharine density of the whole, accentuating the difficulty of setting.

It is suggested that to avoid trouble in setting and to minimise the gelatine flavour, in warm weather the above formula be strictly adhered to, but that the stock be strengthened by the addition of a little fine gelatine, anywhere from 2 ozs. to 4ozs., according to strength and temperature at the time it is put on the fire to clarify.

GELATINE JELLY STOCK.

1 lb. fine leaf or shred gelatine.
3 lbs. lump or crushed sugar.
Juice of 22 to 24 lemons, according to size.
The finely-pared rind of 8 lemons.
12 whites of eggs.
4 bay leaves.
20 coriander seeds.
$6\frac{1}{4}$ quarts of water (including lemon juice).
2 inches of stick cinnamon.

Set the gelatine to soak for an hour in five quarts of water, by which time it will be greatly swollen. Add the sugar, the lemon juice and rind, water to make up to six quarts, cinnamon, bay-leaves, and coriander seeds. Beat the whites with the remaining half-pint of water and add the other ingredients. Set on the stove and finish in all respects like the calves' feet stock.

This jelly base stock is not quite as rich in saccharine as the calves' feet, will be a little firmer, and is suitable for converting into many flavours, as will be hereafter shown

GELATINE AND ISINGLASS.

The gelatine-yielding substances in the animal kingdom cover a very wide range comprising the skins of all animals, bones, horns, hoofs, intestines, and tendons, the coarser of these in their less purified condition forming the various grades of glue. The purification as well as the clarification (in some cases synonymous terms) of these substances in the manufacture of edible gelatine is of necessity very complete, and whilst the various types differ largely in colour, taste, and congealing power, nearly all are harmless. Whatever may be the source from which they are derived, therefore, most of the gelatines of commerce are perfectly wholesome, although many of them are scarcely describable as nice. As all are gelatines the coarsest glue may be set at one end of a long line and the finest edible gelatine at the other, and the maker of confectionery dainties

All about Jellies and Creams.

must decide for himself how far down the line from the top his desire for cheapness will take him. If he be a wise man he will be pretty near the top.

A nice point worth considering here is how far a confectioner using even high-grade gelatine to make "calves feet jelly" is contravening the conditions of the Sale of Food and Drugs Act. It may not be a probable contingency, but it is certainly within the realms of possibility that some such point may be raised by the authorities.

Here is an extract from the specification for a patent taken out in 1844 by a well-known house whose manufactured gelatine is of very high grade and deservedly popular:—

"The shoulders and cheeks of ox hides are preferred, but other parts may be used The hide and skin pieces are cleansed in water, cut in small pieces by a machine, and reduced to pulp in a pulp mill. The pulp is pressed between rollers, mixed with water, and then subjected to heat varying from 150 deg. to 212 deg. F., whereby gelatine is produced. When a very pure quality is required liquid gelatine is mixed with a small quantity of ox blood at a temperature not exceeding 160 deg. to 170 deg., and further heated. The albumen of the blood becomes coalgulated and rises as a scum; the heat is then withdrawn, after which the scum is removed and the purer liquor allowed to settle, and afterwards it is run into coolers to congeal and dry."

Here also is another extract from the patent process of another and equally celebrated British maker:—

"The gelatine is extracted from hide pieces which have been subjected to the bleaching action of sulphurous acid. The strained and purified product is spread in a thin layer on a marble slab till it partly solidifies, when it is cut up and washed to free it from all traces of acid. It is again re-dissolved at the lowest possible temperature, then re-solidified and dried in thin sheets on nets."

Both these makers produce very high-grade gelatine, giving admirable results; and whilst no objection can be taken to their use, it is a trade discrepancy to describe jelly made with them as "calves' feet."

Isinglass is the gelatine derived from the air bladders of certain fish, or, to be strictly accurate, in its raw state it is the cleansed sounds or bladders themselves. The writers have distinct recollection of the leaf or lump form in which isinglass formerly came into confectioners' hands, when it was absolutely necessary to melt and clarify it before it could be used for setting creams and blancmanges. It was hard, brittle, and distinctly fishy in taste.

Russian isinglass is altogether the best, and is prepared from the sounds of sturgeon These are cleaned and steeped in water to remove the fishy taste and smell, and the inner and outer coat separated, the inner coat only being used to produce the very finest quality This is rolled into very thin sheets stretched and dried, and is then shredded by machinery into thin thread-like filaments, opaque, and greyish-white in colour, and more or less easily soluble in water by heat.

The outer coat of the sounds is used to make an inferior quality, which is chiefly used for clarifying wines and other liquids.

Brazilian isinglass comes next in value for confectioners' use. It is produced in exactly the same way from the sounds of a large fish common to the waters of Brazil and Guiana (Silurus Parkerii).

Manila and East Indian isinglass is produced in practically the same way, but its source is doubtful and its quality very varied. The sounds of the common cod, hake, and other fish of the same species are also used to produce gelatinous substances, but are of little use to the confectioner. It is also upon record that the bones of many fish, more particularly the deep sea flat fish are used to produce isinglass, but of this we are unable to speak with certainty. Certainly they contain a high percentage of gelatinous matter.

All about Ices.

Gelatine may therefore be assumed to be what it purports to be and varying in grade, but isinglass, so-called, is often only gelatine in a shredded form. As isinglass of good quality is more expensive than the very best gelatine, the substitution in the shredded form is often made. Its detection is very simple. Steeped in cold water, isinglass retains its curious milky opaqueness. The fine shreds increase in bulk equally in all directions, so that relatively the form and colour are the same with increased bulk. Gelatine becomes more or less transparent according to whether an admixture has been made or not. The expansion also is never quite equal, the filament becoming more ribbon-like. Isinglass is in every way preferable to gelatine for setting creams and blancmanges, as it is less tough in proportion to its power of congealing, and if the shredded form be used, is much more easily prepared. Whilst Russian is the best, good Brazilian is much cheaper, and can always be depended upon to give good results. Other and lower grades should be avoided, as should also the very white samples, which are seldom genuine and generally weak.

TO CLARIFY ISINGLASS.

If the leaf, strip, ribbon, or honeycomb form be used, it must be cut or broken into small pieces and well washed. If the shred form (not too fine) be used it will not need washing. To each ounce used take one pint of cold water and set together in a clean stewpan. Slowly bring to the boil, gently stirring, and then draw back and allow to simmer slowly for twenty minutes, or until the whole of the isinglass is thoroughly dissolved. Saturate a small cube of lump sugar with weak acetic acid, drop it into the dissolved isinglass, and when it is melted stir together and let slowly simmer for a few minutes longer. Then skim carefully any scum that is thrown up, and pass the liquid through a piece of fine dry tammy or silk into a basin. Thus clarified isinglass may be used for fruit or other jellies whose brillance is not a necessity, and instructions for which will be found in the proper place.

DECORATED MOULDS.

The decoration of moulds of jellies and creams offers wide scope for the exercise of artistic taste by the confectioner. The value of the moulds as decorative assets in the table arrangements is out of all proportion to their additional cost. For this purpose many things are available, nearly all fruits, both fresh and preserved, being suitable—fruit peels, angelica, pistachio kernels, gold and silver leaf, and under certain conditions even flowers and flower petals. Of course, it is preferable as a general principal that whatever is used be edible, but the excusable exceptions may be gold and silver leaf, the quantities being infinitesimal, and sometimes flowers.

There are moulds such as macedoines or charlottes, in which the fruit either pervades or lines the shape; they are a very interesting class, and will be separately treated. The general instructions here given must be understood to refer to the moulds that, whilst chiefly filled with clear jelly or some definite type of cream, have the top of the mould decorated before the main filling is put in.

The moulds to be ornamented must be set in a deep flat pan or bain-marie, and a little finely-broken ice placed round them to ensure setting as the sections of the work are built up. Where different colours are being used they can be mixed in very small basins, or even teacups, and filled into their respective places, with a more or less small spoon according to the amount required.

Having used one layer, be certain that it is firmly set before adding to it, or the layer of one colour or the fruit set in it will be apt to lift out of position. Never use warm jelly

All about Jellies and Creams.

for decorating unless it be for the first layer used. Jelly that is only just liquid is much easier to work with and much more expeditious in results

In moulds of cream, which are opaque, a natural background is provided for the decorative tops, but where the mould is a clear jelly it is often advisable to provide a background to bring the decorated portion into prominence. One of the most effective methods of producing this background is simply to whip a small quantity of the filling jelly until quite firm and opaque, and run a layer of this on to the decorated top, tapping it well into every portion of the mould pattern that it covers. Great care will be necessary in filling the mould afterwards, or the whip, being lighter than the rest, will rise. When the whip is firm a spoonful of almost set jelly must be run over and allowed to set before another is added. This must be several times repeated until the covering has a good firm hold, when the filling up may be completed, but never with warm jelly. One considerable advantage of this whipped background is that the jelly increases so in bulk by whipping that less fills the mould. On a large number of moulds the saving will be considerable.

Whilst some few of the moulds, especially the fruit creams and fruit jellies, naturally suggest what their decoration shall consist of, there are numberless others to which many styles are equally suitable, and which the skilful operator will naturally vary as opportunity occurs. If a few simple examples are given here, just to suggest others, and particular styles be given where they especially apply, it should be sufficient to form the nucleus of a wide variety. For this set it is elected to use chiefly oval moulds that have six or eight raised castellated sections as a top pattern.

No. 1.—Clear jelly in each section. Set a black grape in each section and gradually cover. In the centre space clear jelly and five or six very finely filleted blanched pistachio kernels. Gradually cover. Background of white whipped jelly or use to fill with a white cream.

No. 2.—Clear jelly in each section, alternate black and Muscat grapes. In the centre space clear jelly, a pinch of very finely chopped pistachio kernels, and when set five or six overlapping thin slices of banana well coated with almost set jelly. This will not need a background, but will be very suitable for a pale pink or green cream.

No. 3.—Clear jelly in each section. A medium-sized strawberry in each section, pink jelly in the centre space, with five or six overlapping slices of strawberry set in a row. If used for a clear jelly should have a white whipped jelly background, but is also suitable for a mould of strawberry cream.

No. 4.—Pale pink jelly in the sections, and in each a winter strawberry, the fruit of the abutilon tree. Between each section a few fine fillets of pistachio kernels, and in the centre space five or six overlapping slices of the fruit set in clear jelly. This fruit is round, red-skinned, with bright yellow seeds showing, and the inside flesh apricot colour. It is a delicious fruit, and although little known here, is a great favourite in both France and Italy. There must be many places where it is grown and wasted in England, if one only knew where. On the rocky terrace gardens of Torquay there are a number of trees in full bearing. In the late autumn the fruit can be bought at Covent Garden Market.

No. 5.—Put in a breakfast-cup nearly filled with clear jelly two pages from a book of gold leaf. Break up well by beating with a small pointed cook's knife; place a little of this jelly when nearly cold in each section, and in each place a peeled mirabel well drained from syrup. When set and well covered fill in the centre space with some of the same jelly, into which six finely filleted pistachios have been mixed when the jelly was almost set. Use this mould either for a pale yellow or blush-rose cream, or if for jelly set in a background of either white or pale pink whipped jelly.

All about Ices.

No. 6.—Clear jelly in half the sections, pink in the other half. In each place a bright red cherry. When set cut the same number of thin slices from a peeled banana, remove the centres with a small cutter, dip each piece into jelly (half of each colour), and set on the cherries like hat-brims. The portion of the tiny hats standing above the small sections, as well as the centre space, will be filled in with clear jelly, a star of angelica diamonds being arranged in the centre space. Suitable for a white or pink cream or for a clear jelly; in the latter case a white whipped jelly background is an improvement.

No. 7.—Clear jelly in the sections. In half of them also a well-drained peeled mirabel, and in the other half a green Muscat grape. When well set fill in the centre with clear jelly and arrange one or two bunches of large bright, fresh, red currants. This is most effective against a white, yellow, or pale pink background, either of cream or whipped jelly.

No. 8.—Pale red jelly in each section, and in each a ripe mulberry. Between each section an angelica diamond in clear jelly, and in the centre space finely filleted pistachio kernels in clear jelly. This requires a white background, either of cream or whipped jelly.

No. 9.—Prepare a breakfast-cup nearly full of clear jelly with three sheets of gold leaf. Break up very fine. A quarter fill each section, and drop into each a few fillets of pistachio kernels. When set fill up, and cover the bottom of the mould very thinly with the jelly. Peel a small tangerine orange, remove the white pithy portion and divide into sections. Set these pointed edges downward in the layer of jelly between the sections filled with pistachio, and all radiating outwards from the centre to the sides. Be very careful in setting them in position so that all are true. Gradually add the gold leaf jelly until all are covered and set. A yellow background either in cream or whipped jelly will bring this into prominence.

LEMON JELLY.

Either of the forms of foundation jelly—*i.e.*, that made with calves' feet or with gelatine—will serve for lemon jelly, without any addition for flavouring. It is, however, advised that if made specially for lemon jelly a few threads of saffron be added to give a pale yellow tint.

ORANGE JELLY.

There is an old tradition amongst confectioners that orange jelly cannot be made bright. It is, of course, all nonsense to say that it cannot, because if oranges be substituted for some of the lemons, and thinly-sliced outer skin of oranges be used instead of the slips of lemon peel, and treated exactly as given for either calves' foot or gelatine stock, the resulting jelly will be deeper in colour, but as bright as if made with all lemons.

It will have a strongly-marked orange flavour, but it will not be the fresh fruit flavour. It will therefore be quite accurate to say that the fresh fruit flavour cannot be retained if the jelly be bright, as no amount of passing through a jelly-bag will remove the slight milkiness of the fresh fruit, unless it has been subjected to heat and some clarifying agent used. For the sake of this freshness of flavour, therefore, it is usual to sacrifice the clarity of the jelly. The usual plan is as follows:—

2 ozs. fine leaf gelatine.
6 oranges.
2 lemons.
½ pint simple syrup.
½ pint of water.

All about Jellies and Creams.

Rub three of the oranges with lumps of sugar until they are quite saturated on all sides, using not more than six cubes in all. Cut and squeeze the oranges and lemons into a basin upon the saturated cubes. Add the syrup, stir well, and allow to stand until the cubes are dissolved. Pass through a fine silk sieve or a thin flannel bag. Dissolve the gelatine by heating in the water and skim carefully. Add the strained juice and syrup, and when nearly cold pour into a mould, previously decorated appropriately.

ORANGE CURACOA JELLY.

Use either of the stock jellies given, and to each nominal quart mould add a small wineglassful of orange curacoa. The liqueur will give the necessary colour. When nearly cold fill up a mould that has been appropriately decorated previously.

ORANGE-FLOWER JELLY.

This jelly must be made especially because of its blended fruit flavour and also because, bulk having to be made up in the later stages, it must have greater stability.

- 4 ozs. fine leaf gelatine.
- 3 oranges.
- 3 lemons.
- 12 ozs. sugar.
- 1 liqueur glass fin champagne.
- $1\frac{1}{4}$ quarts of water.
- 4 whites of eggs.
- $\frac{1}{4}$ pint orange-flower water (triple).
- $\frac{1}{4}$ pint champagne.

Soak the gelatine in the water for half an hour, add the sugar, the finely-sliced rind of two oranges, the strained juice of the oranges and lemons, and the whites of eggs well beaten in with the whole. Boil, simmer, and pass in exactly the same way as previously described for jelly stock, until quite bright. It will be a brilliant but pale orange-yellow. When nearly cold add the orange-flower water, the fin champagne, and well blend, without stirring sufficiently to make top froth. Have nicely decorated moulds ready, and when quite cold and just on the point of setting gently add the bubbling champagne, carefully blend, and with great care fill up the moulds. Fine sparkling saumer or sillery may be substituted for the champagne if desired. Perhaps it will be as well to add that fin champagne is very old liqueur brandy.

TANGARINE ORANGE JELLY.

This jelly is very seldom made, as it is somewhat troublesome. It can be made by boiling in the ordinary way, and is very good indeed in that form. It is, however, much more delicate it the fresh flavour be conserved, and for very fine results the following plan is recommended as the best:—

- 2 ozs. fine leaf gelatine.
- 10 tangerine oranges.
- 3 lemons.
- 1 wineglassful of kirsch.
- $\frac{1}{2}$ pint simple syrup.
- $\frac{2}{3}$ pint of water.
- 1 tablespoonful orange-flower water (triple).

Remove the rind from the oranges and clean away the strings of white pithy matter round and between the sections. Cut the oranges into small pieces, remove the pips, and pound to a pulp in a marble mortar. Remove into a basin, pound the rind of three of the oranges in the mortar, and add to the pulp in a basin. Add the strained juice of the lemons and the syrup with one-third of the water, and let stand for half an hour. Then strain through a fine silk sieve or a thin flannel bag. Melt the gelatine with the rest of the water in a small copper sugar-boiler. Skim carefully, and add to the strained juice and syrup. When nearly cold add the orange-flower water and the kirsch. Fill into a previously decorated mould.

It is usual to add a drop or two of liquid carmine to this jelly, but we confess to preferring the natural colour.

MARASCHINO JELLY.

Either of the original stock jellies may be used for this, adding a wineglass of maraschino to each quart mould. This jelly is generally tinted a very pale pink, but there is no reason why it should be, as maraschino is quite colourless.

CASSIS JELLY.

This is a very unusual but a beautiful and full-flavoured jelly, cassis being a rich, deep red syrupy cordial-like liqueur, made from black currants.

The usual stock jelly will answer admirably, using a large wineglassful of the cassis and a dessertspoonful of pale brandy to each quart. The cassis and the brandy should be previously well mixed together, as there is less difficulty in mixing the syrupy cassis when it has been thinned down with the spirit. A few drops of liquid carmine will help to give a brilliantly deep colour to this exquisite jelly.

JELLY VICTOR.

Either of the stock jellies given will be suitable for this; the flavouring equal quantities (half wineglassful to the quart mould) of maraschino and curacoa (not orange curacoa). It is generally deepened in colour with a very little caramelled sugar. The decoration should be ripe morella cherries in the same jelly, with a background of filleted pistachio nuts. A white background of whipped jelly brings the red and green into greater prominence, but is not usual.

JELLY VICTORIA.

Either of the stock jellies will be suitable for this mould. The flavouring should be equal quantities of pale brandy and maraschino, a wineglassful in all to each quart. Take a teacup nearly full of the jelly and in it break up very finely one sheet of gold leaf. When nearly set turn it into a soup-plate, and when quite set cut out pieces with a teaspoon and set them in the pinnacles of the mould, using a few drops of just liquid jelly to ensure filling all portions of the shape. In the middle portion of the mould set a radial star of long and short fillets of bright glacé cherries, covering well with clear jelly. Blanch, wash, and finely shred ½ oz. of Sicilian pistachio nuts, and when the rest of the jelly is nearly set turn in the pistachio fillets, blend, and fill up the mould. Care must be taken not to fill in the jelly as long as the nuts sink; they must be equally distributed all through the finished jelly.

JELLY POMPADOUR.

Either of the stock jellies will answer admirably for this mould. The flavouring should be for each quart mould a wineglassful of yellow chartreuse and a dessertspoonful of triple orange-flower water.

Use a mould with rather high castellated points. In each point set a section of tangerine orange from which every atom of white pith has been removed. These sections of orange should be as nearly perpendicular as possible, with the bevelled edges to the

All about Jellies and Creams.

outside. Set them in some of the flavoured jelly. When quite set and nearly covered, a background may be made as follows:—In two small basins set half a teacupful of the flavoured jelly. Add a few drops of liquid carmine to one. Whip them until quite firm and opaque, then turn them into soup-plates and allow them to get quite firm on ice. With a teaspoon dipped into warm water cut out alternately small oval pieces, and arrange in a mosaic pattern on a bed of almost set clear jelly in the mould. When all are filled in and set, gradually cover with almost set jelly, and allow to become quite set before adding the rest, which must be almost set, or the lighter whipped jelly will rise to the surface.

GELEE A LA DURER.

The ordinary stock jelly will be suitable for this, but it must be almost colourless. Flavour with two-thirds maraschino and one-third kirsch, a wineglassful to the quart mould. For each mould use 1 oz. each of preserved ginger (free from syrup and dry), glacé pineapple, glacé apricot, and glacé cherries, all cut into fine cubes. Set the fruit in a soup-plate with sufficient jelly to cover it, and all to stand until slightly set. Break up gently with a spoon and carefully stir into the rest of the jelly when it is on the point of setting, and very carefully fill up the mould. Each small piece of fruit, being coated with jelly, will the more easily retain its place in the mould than if it were simply stirred into the jelly as a whole.

This jelly is a melange of fruits, and in no way resembles a macedoine, in which whole or cut fruits are arranged.

VANILLA JELLY.

For this jelly take either of the ordinary stock jellies, and add to each quart mould one dessertspoonful of vanilla extract and one dessertspoonful of pale brandy. The colour should be deepened with a little caramelled sugar. Almost any form of decoration may be used.

COFFEE JELLY.

This is sometimes made by adding an extract of coffee to one of the jelly stocks, but it is never satisfactory. It is a jelly that is seldom asked for, but, properly made, it is very good indeed. Try this plan:—

- 4 ozs. fine sheet gelatine.
- 12 ozs. crushed sugar.
- 3 lemons.
- 3 ozs. Mocha coffee berries (freshly roasted).
- $3\frac{1}{2}$ pints water (including the juice of lemon).
- 5 whites of eggs.
- 1-in. piece vanilla bean.
- Few threads of saffron.
- 10 coriander seeds.

Soak the gelatine in three pints of the water for half an hour; add the sugar, the strained juice of the lemons (made up to half a pint with water and beaten up with the whites of eggs), the piece of vanilla, the whole coffee berries, the saffron, and coriander seeds. Bring up to the boil, stirring all the time; boil well up and allow to subside; again boil well through to coagulate the whites of eggs; draw back and allow to simmer very slowly, until the clear jelly begins to show through the albumen; draw back from the fire, cover and in a few minutes, when the separation shows more clearly, pass through a dry jelly bag until it runs quite bright.

This jelly is best moulded quite plain, but should be served either with nougat, caramel, praline, or plain cream.

All about Ices.

GREEN COFFEE JELLY.

This jelly should be made in exactly the same way as the preceding one, substituting for the roasted coffee 4 ozs. of berries roasted only to a pale golden colour, so that they do not darken the colour of the jelly. Add to each quart mould one tablespoonful of pale fine brandy.

TEA JELLY.

For this jelly either of the stock jellies will be suitable. For each quart mould add nearly ¼ pint of infusion of tea as below and one dessertspoonful of pale brandy.

TEA INFUSION.

1 oz. Darjeeling orange pekoe   ¾ pint boiling water.

Steep for five minutes only, then pour off quite clearly. Should any sediment or small broken leaves come away, pass through a silk sieve or piece of fine muslin. Plain, slightly sweetened whipped cream should be served with this jelly

BELGRAVE JELLY.

This jelly takes its name from the mould in which it is made more than from the type of jelly used. It must, however, be pale in colour and very bright. The mould has six castellated points, and is round, or nearly so, as the points are continued in pillar, form the full depth of the mould. A cover stretches from side to side, having six round perforations corresponding to the pillar forms. In these perforations are suspended six hollow spirals, with a small air tube in each. When the mould, either decorated on top or not, is filled within 1¼ in. from the top the lid is set in place and the spirals adjusted, and surrounded by ice to set very firmly. When quite set, a little warm water is run into one of the spirals, which can then be twisted out, leaving the space empty. This is then filled in with some white, yellow, or pale pink cream and the other spirals taken out and filled in one at a time until all are done. When set and turned out well the white or pale pink spirals in the clear jelly are very effective.

We confess, however, to having had considerable trouble with this mould, and also— and this was very comforting—seen many others have trouble in the same way. Unless the jelly is very firmly set when the spirals are withdrawn, especially if more than one is withdrawn before refilling, the jelly is apt to collapse. That difficulty surmounted, it is almost impossible to force either cream that will set or simple whipped cream down to the bottom of the spiral forms ; and when only partly filled they look bad, if the entire shape does not collapse after turning out. After many failures it occurred to the writer one day to try filling the spiral shapes with blanc mange. This, being much thinner than any of the creams, ran readily into the entire shapes, and a perfect mould was the result. Great care is, however, necessary, and the filling must be run in slowly, so that it never fills the entire passage, except from the bottom, or the imprisoned air will prevent proper and complete filling.

RUM PUNCH JELLY.

Either of the stock jellies given can be used for this jelly. For each quart mould use a wineglassful of old Jamaica rum and half a wineglassful of brown brandy. Add the zest of an orange, or the thinly-pared rind will serve ; let it steep for an hour in the blended

All about Jellies and Creams.

spirits, strain through a silk sieve, or better still, filter through a piece of filtering paper in a glass filtering funnel, and add to the jelly before moulding. It is usual to add a little caramelled sugar to darken this jelly. Most styles of decoration will be suitable.

MACEDOINE OF JELLY.

Either of the stock jellies will be suitable for this mould, but it is advisable to have it very pale and very brilliant. There is no recognised rule as to what fruits shall be used. The object is so to arrange the fruit that when turned out the group shall be graceful and harmonious. The arrangement must be left entirely to the taste and skill of the operator, who must, of course, always bear in mind the fact that the point of view will be reversed when the mould is turned out on its dish. Cherries, strawberries, red, white, and black currants, and grapes readily lend themselves to effective treatment, and many small plums, like mirabels and small gages, as well as apricots and nectarines, especially if a few firm leaves be added, can be effectively arranged. Larger fruits must be cut in suitable form. A centre background of the larger yellow and green fruits, with a curtain of bunches of alternate red and white currants gracefully drooping round them, is particularly striking; but no doubt many combinations will suggest themselves to the thoughtful workman after a little practice.

Of course, the mould must be gradually built up, with a layer of clear jelly well set before beginning the arrangement of fruits, and only small quantities can be added at a time, each layer being well set before the next one is added. Many arrangements of individual fruits can be made in jelly, all of which can be effective if care be taken, but these, of course, would not be macedoines, which means mixture or blends, but would be named in accordance with the fruit used, or jointly with the fruit and any specially flavoured jelly.

Plain-sides moulds, either oval or round, should always be used for macedoines, so that the view of the fruit arrangement be not in any way obstructed. Macedoines are sometimes made by using two moulds, both the same shape, but one smaller than the other. The small mould is set inside the other upon a thin layer of jelly, and slightly weighed to keep it in position. The larger mould, or rather, the space between the two, is gradually filled in with clear jelly and allowed to set quite firm. Warm water is carefully poured into the inner mould, which is then lifted out, and the arrangement of fruit and jelly is gradually completed in the centre space. This plan has its advantages, less fruit being required, and consequently a little less labour. It is, however, not so effective as the former plan, and unless the jelly is unusually brilliant the view of the fruit is partially obscured.

One final word on macedoines. If fresh fruits are used, lemon or orange flavoured jellies are the most suitable. If preserved fruits, the jelly should always be a liqueur-flavoured one, such as maraschino or yellow chartreuse.

GELEE A LA RUSSE.

In three small basins whip quite firm rather less than half-pints of clear jelly; that made from the gelatine stock will be suitable. Flavour the first one with maraschino, leaving the colour quite white. When whipped pour into a soup-plate and set on ice to become firm. Flavour the second with mandarine (liqueur), and colour pink with liquid carmine. Set to cool on ice as for the first. Flavour the third one with curacoa, and tint to coffee-colour either with extract of coffee or caramelled sugar. Pour into a soup-plate when whipped, and set on ice as for the other two.

All about Ices.

To fill the mould use a teacup nearly filled with clear jelly almost cold enough to set, but not set. With a knife dipped into warm water divide the jelly in the soup-plate into cubes, only a portion at a time, or it will quickly adhere again. With a teaspoon lift out the cubes, dip each one into the semi-liquid jelly in the teacup, and arrange in rows alternately in the mould. The coated cubes will fit irregularly into one another So on until the mould is filled. The mould must be set in ice to insure rapid setting Carefully filled, this is a most effective mould when turned out.

PANACHEE JELLY.

This is in character much the same as a la Russe, but only two colours are used, white and pink, and the pieces are large and set in position with a tablespoon. It is very easy and effective, but not so decorative as the gelee a la Russe. The more usual plan is to fill the mould with alternate layers of the two colours of whipped jelly, and if carefully done in very thin layers it is very effective. If this plan be adopted it will be necessary to warm and re-whip the jellies for each layer, as it will not run properly into shape.

RUM JELLY.

This jelly can be made from either of the jelly stocks given, flavoured with old Jamaica rum, one wineglassful being used to each quart mould. It is generally tinted with a little caramelled sugar. Almost any kind of decoration is suitable.

NOYEAU JELLY.

Use the ordinary jelly stock either of calves' feet or gelatine, flavoured with noyeau (liqueur), one small wineglassful to each quart mould. This jelly is generally tinted a pale pink, but there is no tangible reason why it should be coloured at all, noyeau being quite colourless.

CHAMPAGNE JELLY.

Champagne jelly is a great favourite with many ladies, and here and there are to be found male admirers. To be at all satisfactory it must retain, as far as possible, its sparkling character. Should it be flat it has ceased to have any reason for existence. The usual way is to stir a glass of champagne into some ordinary jelly stock, allow the effervescence to exhaust itself, and then to wonder why it does not please the customer. If care be used the following plan may be depended upon to give entire satisfaction:—

- 4 ozs. fine leaf gelatine.
- 12 ozs. of loaf sugar.
- 4 lemons.
- 2¼ pints of water (including lemon juice).
- ¼ inch stick cinnamon.
- 1 bayleaf.
- 5 or 6 whites of eggs.
- 1 pint bottle of dry champagne.
- 3 or 4 threads of saffron.
- 1 tablespoonful pale brandy.

Put the gelatine to soak in two pints of the water until well swollen. Add the sugar, the thinly-sliced rind of one lemon, the lemon juice, made up to a quarter of a pint and beaten up with the egg white, the saffron, the bayleaf, and the small piece of cinnamon. Set on the fire to boil, stirring all the time. Boil up twice, being sure that the second time the boiling thoroughly coagulates the whites. Simmer slowly for ten or fifteen minutes, withdraw from fire, cover up, and allow to stand a few minutes for the separation of the clear jelly from the albumen. When this shows clearly pass at once through a clean dry jelly bag, and continue repassing until the jelly runs brilliantly clear

All about Jellies and Creams.

This jelly will set rather firmly if allowed to do so, because allowance has been made for the addition of the champagne. It is best not to allow it to become set on the ice, although it may be cooled there. When it is quite cold and on the point of setting, but not before—and care must be taken that it is exactly in this condition—add the brandy, and then the small bottle of champagne may be lifted from the ice, where it has been cooling, opened, and poured in, gently stirring to blend, but not to expel the carbonic gas, leaving the jelly flat and unprofitable.

With the jelly at setting point and the wine icy cold, the completed jelly, set on ice, should be solid in half an hour. When sent to table the jelly should be not only of delicious flavour, but sparkling in appearance and sparkling on the palate.

LEMON SPONGE JELLY.

Either of the jelly stocks given will be suitable for making this mould. Use an ornamental castellated mould, and decorate it with clear jelly and bright fruits. When this is set take half a pint of clear lemon jelly, add the strained juice of one lemon to it, and whip it in a basin until white and almost solid. At once pour it into prepared mould and well tap, so that every portion of the pattern is filled. The mould should remain in ice as long as possible, and be served quite cold. Care should be taken not to overweight the top with the decoration, as the body of the mould has very little stability.

ORANGE SPONGE.

Can be made in exactly the same way, substituting some strongly-flavoured orange jelly for the lemon as above.

ROSE JELLY.

Flavour some very brilliant and almost colourless jelly, made by either of the stock plans given, with a wineglassful of rosewater, two drops of attar of roses, and a tablespoon of pale brandy to each quart. Decorate your mould with a little of the flavoured jelly and roses in one or other of the following ways:—

(1) Small red moss rosebuds in each point, with three small fully-opened white roses in a line along the middle.

(2) Clear jelly with gold leaf in the points, and two Marechal Neil or Niphetos roses, with small leaves, parallel at an angle along the middle, the blossoms pointing to the ends in each case.

(3) Clear jelly to thinly line the top of mould, and a small spray of white or yellow roses, buds, and leaves.

When covered and set, tint the flavoured jelly to a very pale pink with liquid carmine, and when nearly set carefully fill up the mould.

COLOURING JELLIES PINK.

In all cases where tinting has to be done liquid carmine has been recommended, because it is practically tasteless and blends more easily with jellies of moderate acidity. With jellies of unusual acidity like very sharp lemon, carmine, being in an alkaline solution, is very apt to precipitate. For tinting these and any other jellies analine pinks may be used, but must always be added whilst the jelly is warm, or, irrespective of the percentage

All about Ices.

of acidity, the colour will immediately separate into fine particles, which nothing but reheating will dissolve. Once properly blended, there will be neither separation nor precipitation. These colours must, however, be used with great discretion. They are very powerful, and sometimes of particularly nasty flavour.

ICELAND MOSS JELLY.

This is essentially a medicinal preparation, having, it is claimed, great value in pulmonary and phlegmatic troubles generally. It is intensely bitter in flavour, and for the sake of making it more palatable the moss is generally well washed before using. This washing certainly reduces the bitterness, but with the bitterness goes also most of its tonic value. If, therefore, it is worth while to take the nasty stuff at all it should be taken *au naturel* and not washed out.

- 4 ozs. dry Iceland moss.
- 2 ozs. fine leaf gelatine.
- 8 ozs. lump sugar.
- 4 lemons (rind of one).
- 1 wineglassful of pale brandy.
- 3 whites of eggs.
- $3\frac{1}{4}$ pints of water (including lemon juice).
- 1 wineglassful of sherry.

Put the moss, rinsed once in cold water to remove any dust, into a stewpan with the gelatine and two pints of water, and let it steep for at least half an hour. Then add the sugar, the rind of one lemon, and the juice made up to $1\frac{1}{4}$ pints with water, and the whites beaten with the juice and water. Set on the fire and bring to the boil, and then let it slowly simmer for half an hour. Throw in a few threads of saffron, bring up to the full boil again, draw back, and allow to stand until the separation of the albumen shows clearly. Pour through a jelly-bag, and continue to return as it runs through until the jelly is quite bright.

This jelly is much more efficacious in chest troubles if it is slowly sipped whilst quite warm, and, if so taken, the brandy and sherry should be added just before drinking. Neither of these is recommended here medicinally; they are flavourings simply, and can be omitted if need be.

FRUIT JELLIES.

In the making of these, if the freshness of the fruit flavour be desired, then something of clarity and brilliance must be sacrificed. The clarification by boiling and coagulating whites of eggs with the jelly will totally alter the flavour of most fruits.

If time and the quantity of fruit used be of no moment, then unquestionably the plan of setting fruit and sugar in layers and allowing the clear fruit syrup to run away is the best. Of course, the careful workman can use up any fruit and sugar remaining after the juice has drained away by boiling with any similarly coloured fruit and making into jam. He can do this, but, alas! it is so very seldom that he does. In practice, therefore, we find for the ordinary confectioner it is easier to mash his fruit, pass it through a ten-mesh brass sieve, and run it through a thin flannel jelly-bag until moderately bright, adding simple syrup to sweeten and sufficient clear spring water, to reach the proper strength, and setting with melted gelatine or isinglass. The gelatine is the easier to use, as it can the more readily be melted moderately clear.

All about Jellies and Creams.

TO MELT THE GELATINE.

Allow for each quart mould from 2½ ozs. to 3 ozs. of fine leaf gelatine, according to its strength. Set it in a large basin and cover it with water, and let it steep for an hour. At the end of the time it will be fully expanded and will have taken up rather more than its own weight in water. Drain away the water and put the wet swollen gelatine in a clean copper sugar boiler, stand this in another pan of water, set on the stove, and gradually melt it, using a clean spattle, but stirring it as little as possible. When quite clear and melted cover down tightly to avoid a skin forming on top, and keep warm to use as directed.

SIMPLE SYRUP

should be made by using 3 lbs. of lump sugar to each quart of water, slowly melting and bringing to the boil, carefully skimming off any scum that may come to the top. If the sugar is very dirty it may be necessary to pass through a fine tammy cloth, and if more than usually unclean a white of egg may be beaten up with the syrup, allowed to coagulate, and then be passed through a bag or fine silk sieve. As a rule, however, the addition of two or three drops of dilute acetic acid to one piece of sugar will be sufficient to throw the scum to the top, where it can be skimmed off. The syrup when quite clear should be stored in glass fruit bottles to keep quite free from flying dust and dirt.

STRAWBERRY JELLY.

1 lb. fine fresh fruit (juice of).
½ pint of simple syrup.
Clarified gelatine (3 ozs.).
Spring water to fill mould.
Few drops of liquid carmine.
1 teaspoonful of proof rum.

When the fruit juice has passed quite clear there should be rather better than a half-pint of it. To this add the simple syrup, then gently but thoroughly stir in the warm melted gelatine, add the required water, and still in the basin, carefully add liquid carmine until the proper tint has been obtained. Add the rum, and when nearly cold, pour into the prepared decorated mould and set in ice. Serve as cold as possible.

RED CURRANT JELLY.

Juice of 1¼ lb. red currants (weighed on the stalks).
½ pint of simple syrup.
Clarified gelatine (equivalent to 3 ozs).
Spring water to fill quart mould.
1 teaspoonful of kirsch.

Carefully pick and crush the currants and put into a clean copper sugar-boiler with half a pint of spring water, and simmer for a few minutes. At once pass through a small thin bag until bright, add the syrup, gelatine, and enough spring water to fill the mould, and when nearly cold the kirsch. If the fruit be fully ripe the juice should be deep enough in colour without the addition of carmine. When cold and nearly set pour into a previously decorated mould and set on ice. Serve as cold as possible.

RASPBERRY JELLY.

1 lb. of fine ripe raspberries (juice of).
¼ lb. of fine red currants (juice of).
½ pint of simple syrup.
Clarified gelatine (equivalent to 3 ozs.)
Spring water to fill quart mould.
1 teaspoonful of pale brandy.

The juice in this case should be taken off cold by crushing and passing as before described. The small quantity of red currants is added to give the necessary acidity. When the juice has run clear treat as above. Do not add colour. Add the brandy when nearly cold to avoid the alcohol being volatilised.

All about Ices.

RASPBERRY AND RED CURRANT JELLY.

½ lb. of fine ripe raspberries.
¾ lb. of fine ripe red currants. (weighed on stalks).
Spring water to fill quart mould

½ pint of simple syrup.
Clarified gelatine (equivalent to 3 ozs.).
1 teaspoonful of kirsch.

Take off the juice cold and treat exactly as for raspberry jelly. Do not add colour, and add the kirsch when nearly cold. Serve as cold as possible.

CHERRY JELLY.

1½ lb. cherries (Flemish or Duke type).
4 ozs. loaf sugar.
⅜ of a pint of simple syrup.

Clarified gelatine (equivalent to 3 ozs.).
Spring water to fill up a quart mould.
1 teaspoonful of kirsch.

Pound the cherries in a clean mortar, stones and all; lift into a clean copper sugar-boiler and simmer slowly for five minutes with a quarter-pint of the water. Add the loaf sugar and simmer until quite clear. Pass through a thin flannel bag until bright. Add the syrup, the melted gelatine, and sufficient cold spring water to fill up a quart mould. When nearly cold add the kirsch and pour into a previously decorated mould. Set on ice, and serve as cold as possible.

The type of cherries given above are the bright red semi-transparent ones. The small pale ones are sometimes called Kentish or Flemish, and are very acid. The rather darker-coloured ones, known as May Dukes or Dukes (in error for Medoc), are best of all, being richer and fuller in flavour, but not quite so acid. Pounding the stones with the fruit will accentuate the flavour, with an added one of ratafia.

MORELLA CHERRY JELLY.

This type of cherry is also semi-transparent, is distinctly acid, very rich and full in flavour, and of a very deep colour. It must be treated in exactly the same way as for cherry jelly, substituting pale brandy for the kirsch.

1½ lb. Morella cherries.
4 ozs. of loaf sugar.
⅜ of a pint of simple syrup.

Clarified gelatine (equivalent to 3 ozs.).
Spring water to fill up a quart mould.

1 dessertspoonful of pale brandy.

In the season when cherries cannot be obtained cherry jelly can be made from the fruit especially bottled for ice-making, instructions for which will be given in the proper place. Morella cherry jelly can also be made from either of the jelly stocks given by adding cherry brandy in the proportion of a wineglassful to each quart mould, but it must then be classed as a liqueur, not as a fruit jelly.

WHITE CURRANT JELLY.

Make exactly as for red currant jelly, substituting white for red currants. The flavour will be exactly the same, but the natural colour will be a little greyish. It is therefore advised that a drop or two of infusion of saffron be added to give a very pale yellow tint.

All about Jellies and Creams.

GRAPE JELLY.

- 1 lb. Muscat grapes.
- 1 lb. sweet water grapes.
- 2 lemons (juice only).
- ½ pint of simple syrup.
- Clarified gelatine (equivalent of 2½ ozs.).
- Wineglassful of infusion elder-flowers.
- Spring water to fill up a quart mould.
- Little infusion of saffron.
- 1 dessertspoonful of pale brandy.

Crush and squeeze the grapes through a coarse hair sieve, with the juice of the lemons and half a pint of cold spring water. Add the infusion of elder flowers (dried flowers will do, simmered for a few minutes in water). Pass through a thin bag until clear, add the saffron, the clarified gelatine, and sufficient cold spring water to fill up the quart mould. Tint with a few drops of infusion of saffron, or if preferred one or two drops of liquid carmine or aniline green, and when nearly cold the brandy. Pour into a previously decorated mould, set on ice, and serve very cold.

PINEAPPLE JELLY.

- 1 pineapple (canned Singapore or fresh).
- ½ pint of simple syrup.
- 2 lemons (juice only).
- Clarified gelatine (equivalent to 3 ozs.).
- Spring water to fill up a quart mould.
- 1 tablespoonful of kirsch.

Cut the pine into slices (if fresh removing the outer rind) and pound to a pulp in a clean mortar. Lift out into a clean vessel, add the lemon juice and a quarter-pint of water, and bring to the boil and simmer for a few minutes. Pass through a thin flannel bag and let the juice run clear. Add the syrup, the clarified melted gelatine, and sufficient cold spring water to fill the quart mould. Tint a little deeper colour with a few drops of caramelled sugar, and when nearly cold add the kirsch and pour into a previously prepared mould. Set on ice, and serve as cold as possible.

PEACH JELLY.

- 5 large ripe peaches.
- 2 lemons (juice only).
- ½ pint of simple syrup.
- Spring water to fill the quart mould.
- Clarified gelatine (equivalent to 2½ ozs.).
- 2 or 3 drops of liquid carmine.
- 1 dessertspoonful of pale brandy.

Halve the peaches and remove the stones. Pass the peaches through a coarse hair sieve, crack the stones, crush the kernels, and add them with the lemon juice and half a pint of spring water to the peach pulp, let stand half an hour, and then pass through a thin flannel bag until clear. Add the syrup, the melted gelatine, and sufficient cold spring water to fill up the quart mould. Tint with liquid carmine to a suggestion of pink colour only, and when nearly cold add the brandy and fill into a previously prepared mould. Set on ice, and serve very cold.

APRICOT JELLY.

- 1½ lb. ripe apricots.
- ½ pint of simple syrup.
- Clarified gelatine (equivalent to 2½ ozs.).
- Cold spring water, sufficient to fill up quart mould.
- 1 dessertspoonful of kirsch.
- 1 teaspoonful of pale brandy.

Halve the apricots (reserve the stones) and pound to pulp in a clean marble mortar. Lift into a copper sugar boiler, pound the stones and add to the pulp. Add half a pint of

All about Ices.

spring water, simmer for ten minutes, and pass through a thin flannel bag until the juice runs clear. Add the syrup, the clarified melted gelatine, and sufficient cold spring water to fill up a quart mould. When nearly cold add the kirsch and brandy and fill up a previously prepared mould. Set on ice, and send to table as cold as possible.

If fresh apricots are not available, apricot pulp can be used instead, but a teaspoonful of noyeau (liqueur) should be substituted for the brandy, as the flavour of the kernels will be lacking.

CRANBERRY JELLY.

1½ lb. large ripe Michigan cranberries.
½ pint of simple syrup.
Clarified gelatine (equivalent to 3 ozs.).
Cold spring water to fill up a quart mould.
1 dessertspoonful of pale brandy.

Set the cranberries in a copper sugar-boiler with half a pint of water. Set the sugar-boiler in another vessel of water and break down the fruit with heat. When thoroughly pulped pass through a thin flannel bag until the juice runs clear. Add the syrup, the clarified gelatine, and what cold spring water is needed to fill up the mould. When nearly cold add the brandy, pour into a previously prepared mould, set on ice, and serve very cold.

There will be sufficient colour in the fruit to give the required tint. This jelly has a curious acid astringency that is very pleasant, but it is somewhat an acquired taste.

BARBERRY JELLY.

8 ozs. fine ripe barberries.
½ pint of simple syrup.
2 lemons (juice only).
1 dessertspoonful of pale brandy.
Clarified gelatine (equivalent to 2½ ozs.).
Spring water to fill up quart mould.

Boil the barberries in half a pint of spring water until quite soft and pulpy. Cover them up and let stand for half an hour, then pass through a thin flannel bag until clear; add the syrup, the clarified gelatine, and enough cold spring water to fill up a quart mould, and tint a pale pink with carmine. When nearly cold add the brandy and pour into a mould and set on ice. Serve very cold.

ASPIC JELLY.

Aspic or savoury jelly is largely in demand for use with cold dishes, but except where used for coating or masking cold entrées and removes it is very seldom eaten, or perhaps it would be more correct to say that very little is eaten in proportion to the amount used. It may therefore be useful to, upon occasion, use a more economical one for decoration only, and two types are therefore given below.

ASPIC JELLY.—No. 1.

1 large knuckle veal (8 to 10 lbs.).
4 calves' feet (split in halves lengthways).
1 carcase chicken (from which the breasts have been removed).
4 gallons water.
6 small carrots.
1 large head celery.
3 large onions.
1 small bunch parsley.
1 small bunch thyme.
3 sprays marjoram.
3 bay leaves.
8 cloves.
2 ozs. salt.
30 peppercorns.

All about Jellies and Creams.

Place the knuckle of veal, the calves' feet, and the chicken's carcase, with the water, in a stockpot, and slowly bring to the boil. Skim well, and simmer slowly for three hours ; again skim well, and add the vegetables and seasoning, coarsely cut, except the herbs, which are best tied in a bunch. Simmer again for at least two hours longer and then strain into shallow pans, and set in a cold larder until next day. If desired, one gallon of water may be added to the stock and again simmered for two hours to get a weak second stock. If this is done, however, an extra ½ oz. of salt and a few more peppercorns will be needed, and when making into jelly next day, should the second stock not be very well set 4 ozs. of leaf gelatine must be added. This plan is not, however, advised, as the added second stock will greatly reduce the richness of the jelly. When cold and set the layer of fat must be carefully removed from the stock and the top carefully washed with warm water to ensure freedom from any particle of grease. Place the stock in a large stewpan and slowly melt over the fire. Beat up twelve whites of eggs, with a pint of water, ½ pint of white wine vinegar, and ⅛ pint of Tarragon vinegar. Add this to the melted stock, beat well together, and bring to the boil, whisking all the time. Boil up twice, so that the coagulation of the whites may be complete. Stand back on the stove and let slowly simmer for half an hour, until the separation of the coagulated whites is clearly shown. Then pass through a jelly-bag until quite bright. This jelly will be almost colourless. If required to be a pale yellow, a few drops of infusion of saffron may be added. If darker a very little caramelled sugar, and if pink a few drops of liquid carmine will give the required tint. Keep in a very cold larder.

ASPIC JELLY.—No. 2.

2 quarts good white stock.
2 quarts water.
12 ozs. fine leaf gelatine.
3 small onions.
2 small shalots.
Small bunch parsley.
Small bunch thyme.
A spray of marjoram.
2 bay leaves.
8 cloves.
6 peppercorns.
Salt if necessary (depends upon the stock).
¼ pint white wine vinegar.
1 tablespoonful Tarragon vinegar.
6 whites of eggs.

Treat this as if you were dealing with the stock in No. 1, except that the gelatine must be set to soak in the water at least an hour before it is put on the fire to melt, and boil with the other ingredients.

Very common so-called aspic jelly is often made without using the white stock at all, but doubling the water and leaving all the other ingredients as given. If used for decoration solely, the cheap form is as suitable as the best, but we have a lot of sympathy ready for any hapless guest who may attempt to eat the fraudulent imitation.

SECTION V.—CREAMS.

CREAMS.

Moulded creams are almost endless in variety, and may roughly be divided into two classes—viz., those that depend for their main body upon whipped cream and those having as a foundation boiled custard. The former are far the more numerous, and have again many divisions. One set or class, the fruit creams, consist of sweetened fruit pulps or syrups blended with the creams. Another set, also a large one, is variously flavoured with liqueurs, vanilla, nuts, etc., and there are many combinations and overlappings. All of them have this in common, that they are set or solidified with some gelatinous substance, generally either isinglass or gelatine, melted in readiness.

If a large number of moulds be required for a banquet or other function, it is an economical plan to melt the isinglass or gelatine in bulk, and measure the required quantity into the prepared creams. These arrangements, however, the operator must make as the need arises, the following formulæ giving the necessary ingredients and quantities to produce the varieties specified.

WHIPPING CREAM FOR MOULDS.

This is best done in a shallow basin, and with a willow whisk if possible. The confectioner's workshop of old always had one or two of these bunches of small white willow hanging handy for use, but they are seldom seen to-day, and the more or less suitable wire whisk is now almost universal. One other great advantage of other days was freshly skimmed cream, free from preservative of any kind, and although it cost rather more per quart than "separated" cream, toned up with boracic acid, it was much more economical to use, as it bulked so largely when whipped. "Preserved" cream thickens fairly well, but bulks in a very limited degree, and nearly a pint is now required to fill a quart mould equally with a half-pint of unpreserved skimmed cream. This is one of the penalties we pay for progress, and the almost universal invasion of chemistry into the commercial world.

Great care must be used in whipping cream not to overwhip it (a very common fault), or the particles of butter-fat will begin to separate themselves from the watery buttermilk, and the mass will be useless except for butter-making. It is a good rule to underwhip, never carrying the operation beyond the glossy stage or the consistency of a well-beaten sponge batter. Cream that is whipped stiff enough to lose its glossy surface shows the danger signal, and butter is almost certain to supervene.

In cream-making, where the sugar has not to be used for blending with pulp or for syrup-making or sweetening, it is advisable to add it to the cream before whipping, as it is a safeguard against disintegration, and also saves unnecessary after-stirring.

All about Ices.

Pound the almonds in a marble mortar as fine as possible, adding the orange-flower water to prevent oiling. Lift out into a basin, and add one pint of cold water. Let them stand for a few minutes, then strain through a tammy cloth into a basin, two persons twisting the ends of the cloth. Return the nut paste to the mortar, repound, and add nearly another pint of cold water, and again squeeze through the cloth. Add the syrup to the milk of almonds, and also the melted isinglass, stir well together, strain through a fine hair sieve, and when nearly set pour into a mould and put on ice. Ground almonds may be used instead of pounding whole ones if desired, but they never give the same fresh flavour nor the same amount. The best quality almond paste (No. 1), two-thirds almonds and one-third sugar, now on the market, will give very good results, especially if a little extra syrup be added to the strained almond milk.

BLANCMANGE (WHITE, No. 2).

1¼ lb. of No. 1 almond paste.
¼ pint of simple syrup.
1¾ pint of cold water.
1 oz. of isinglass.
1 dessertspoonful of pale brandy.

Mix together the paste and water until quite smooth and strain through a fine hair sieve, add the syrup, the melted isinglass, and the brandy, strain again to guard against any small stringy pieces of isinglass being left, stir occasionally until nearly set, and then pour into a decorated mould.

Blancmange is sometimes, nearly generally, occasionally always, made with milk, gelatine, sugar, and essence of almonds, and to this is even added a little cream to enrich the mass, but the result is unspeakably nasty, almost as nasty as that other so-called blancmange composed of cornflour, milk, sugar, and essence of almonds. The beastly imitations are probably responsible for the present lowly repute of what is really a most dainty dish of great nutritive value

Creams.

heat. Add the isinglass previously steeped in cold water, and make into custard with the yolks as described in Italian cream. Stir occasionally as it cools, and when nearly cold stir in the soaked crumbs, and pour into a decorated mould, and set on ice.

MINT CREAM (PALE GREEN).

1 pint of double cream.
4 ozs. of pulverised sugar.
½ ozs. of isinglass.
3 ozs. (liquid) of crème de menthe.
1 teaspoonful of noyeau (liqueur).

Whip the cream with the sugar and the crème de menthe, and to finish, follow the instructions for curacoa cream.

CARAMEL CREAM (COFFEE COLOUR).

1 pint of double cream.
4 ozs. of pulverised sugar.
1 teaspoonful of vanilla sugar.
½ oz. of isinglass.
1 tablespoonful of pale brandy.
Crème caramel à discretion.

Make a little cream caramel by boiling down a few ounces of sugar and water with a drop or two of lemon juice until it reaches the caramel point of discoloration. Add a little at a time half the weight of the sugar in double cream, and boil down after each time of adding, until the whole of the cream is caramelled to the rich deep caramel colour. Then add gradually sufficient water to reduce to a thick syrup of a rich deep treacle colour Strain, and put on one side for use. Whip the cream, sugar, and vanilla sugar, melt the isinglass, add the brandy to it, colour and flavour the whipped cream with the cream caramel, and then pour in the brandy and isinglass, blend together, and pour into a decorated mould, and put on ice to set.

CREAM DES ANGES (YELLOW)

This is more like a gelatinised soufflé than an ordinary cream, but it is of quite distinctive character, and worthy of popularity. It is entirely new, if that is in its favour.

½ pint of simple syrup.
6 yolks of eggs.
¼ pint of double cream.
1 oz. of isinglass.
3 ozs. (liquid) of maraschino (liqueur).
1 oz. (liquid) of orange-flower water (triple).
1 teaspoonful of vanilla sugar.

Steep the isinglass in cold water for half an hour, drain away the water and place in a small copper egg-bowl with the yolks, the syrup, the maraschino, and the orange-flower water, and whisk together to mix. Place the pan in a hotwater bath so that the steam only reaches the bottom of the pan, and whisk constantly until the batter is 140 deg. F. Lift off and beat until very stiff and almost cold. Have the cream half-whipped with the vanilla sugar, and stir into the sponge, and blend thoroughly, and at once pour into two small decorated moulds, and set on ice to become cold and firm. The moulds will need tapping to ensure all parts being filled. Serve very cold.

BLANCMANGE (WHITE, No. 1).

14 ozs. of blanched sweet almonds.
2 ozs. of blanched bitter almonds.
½ pint of simple syrup.
1 oz. of isinglass.
Nearly a quart of cold water.
1 tablespoonful of orange-flower water.

All about Ices.

PRUNEAU CREAM. (WHITE).

1 pint of double cream.
4 ozs. of pulverised sugar.
Instructions as for curacoa cream.
3 ozs. (liqueur) of pruneau.
1 oz. (liqueur) of kirsch.
½ oz. of isinglass

KIRSCH CREAM. (PALE PINK).

1 pint of double cream.
3 ozs. of pulverised sugar.
4 ozs. (liqueur) of kirsch.
½ oz. of isinglass.
A few drops of liquid carmine.
Instructions as for curacoa cream.

NOYEAU CREAM. (PALE PINK).

1 pint of double cream.
4 ozs. of pulverised sugar.
2 ozs. (liqueur) of noyeau.
Instructions as for curacoa cream.
1 oz. (liqueur) of pale brandy.
½ oz. of isinglass.
A few drops of liquid carmine.

ALMOND PRALINE CREAM. (BROWN).

1 pint of double cream.
3 ozs. of pulverised sugar.
3 ozs. of powdered almond praline (see praline).
½ oz. of isinglass.
1 dessertspoonful of kirsch.

Melt the isinglass, and when cooled add the kirsch. Whip the cream and sugar, stir in the powdered almond praline, and then pour in the slightly warm melted isinglass. Blend quickly and thoroughly, and almost at setting point pour into a decorated mould and set on ice to cool.

AVELINE PRALINE CREAM. (MOTTLED BROWN).

1 pint of double cream.
3 ozs. of pulverised sugar.
3 ozs. of powdered aveline praline (see aveline praline).
1 dessertspoonful of pale brandy.
½ oz. of isinglass.

Instructions exactly as for almond praline cream.

PISTACHIO CREAM. (PALE GREEN).

1 pint of double cream.
¼ pint of simple syrup.
3 ozs. of blanched pistachio nuts.
½ oz. of isinglass.
1 dessertspoonful of noyeau.
1 dessertspoonful of kirsch.
1 dessertspoonful of maraschino.
A few drops of apple green.

Pound the blanched pistachio nuts in a small marble mortar, adding the kirsch a little at a time to prevent oiling. Lift out into a basin, and add the simple syrup gradually, working together until quite smooth, and then pass through a fine hair sieve to remove any fibrous matter. Melt the isinglass, and add the noyeau and maraschino as it cools. Whip the cream, pour in the pistachio syrup, tint a pale green, blend, and then stir in the melted isinglass, only just warm, and blend quickly, and at nearly setting point pour into a decorated mould and set on ice.

Creams.

GREEN CHARTREUSE CREAM. (PALE GREEN).

1 pint of double cream.
4 ozs. of pulverised sugar.
3 ozs. (liqueur) of green chartreuse.
½ oz. of isinglass.
A few drops of apple greening.

Treat as for curacoa, tinting pale green before adding the isinglass.

YELLOW CHARTREUSE CREAM. (PALE YELLOW).

1 pint of double cream.
5 ozs. of pulverised sugar.
4 ozs. (liqueur) of yellow chartreuse.
½ oz. of isinglass.
A few drops of infusion of saffron.

Make in the same way as curacoa, tinting the whipped cream before mixing in the isinglass.

MANDARINE CREAM. (YELLOW).

1 pint of double cream.
3 ozs. of pulverised sugar.
3 ozs. (liqueur) of mandarine.
½ oz. of isinglass.
Zest of one tangerine orange.
A few drops of infusion of saffron.

The instructions given for curacoa to be followed here, except that the zest of the tangerine orange must be added to the cream and sugar before whipping, and the cream tinted before adding the isinglass.

CASSIS CREAM. (PALE PURPLE).

1 pint of double cream.
4 ozs. of pulverised sugar.
6 ozs. (liqueur) of cassis.
⅔ oz. of isinglass.
1 dessertspoonful of pale brandy.
A few drops of liquid carmine.

Instructions as for curacoa, the cream to be tinted pink with carmine before adding the cassis and isinglass. To counteract as far as possible the purple tint of the cassis, which is a liqueur made from black currants, the liquid carmine should be treated with a reagent to brighten it. If the original dry carmine has been dissolved in water to which a little liquid ammonia has been added, pour a small quantity into a teacup and add a few drops of fresh lemon juice, and use this for tinting the cream.

BENEDICTINE CREAM. (WHITE).

1 pint of double cream.
5 ozs. of pulverised sugar.
3 ozs. (liqueur) of benedictine.
1 oz. (liqueur) of pale brandy.
½ oz. of isinglass.

Instructions as for curacoa, adding both brandy and benedictine to the melted isinglass.

KUMMEL CREAM. (PALE YELLOW).

1 pint of double cream.
4 ozs. of pulverised sugar.
3 ozs. (liqueur) of kummel
1 oz. (liqueur) of pale brandy.
½ oz. of isinglass.
A few drops of infusion of saffron.

Instructions as for curacoa cream, tinting the cream with saffron before adding the melted isinglass.

All about Ices.

partly whipped cream and thoroughly mix. At first the cocoa will stiffen, but will gradually give way as the cream is added a little at a time. When quite soft and workable turn into the rest of the cream, and mix into a smooth batter; add the previously melted isinglass, cooled a little, mix well, and almost at the setting point pour into a decorated mould and at once cool on ice.

This method of mixing in the cocoa is the correct way, and in expert hands no difficulties arise. With the inexpert there is often trouble in the form of either streaky cream or the separation of the butter particles of the cream. An alternative method is therefore suggested. Instead of the 5 ozs. of pulverised sugar, take a $\frac{1}{4}$ pint of simple syrup. Steep the isinglass in cold water for half an hour, pour away the water, lift the isinglass into the syrup, and slowly melt in a basin held in a pan of hot water. When quite melted and hot, shred the cocoa into thin flakes, and turn it into the syrup, stirring gently until melted. When this has cooled a little, stir a little at a time of the half-whipped cream into it until smooth, and then turn into the rest of the cream as before, quickly mix, and pour into the mould. In the latter plan the vanilla sugar must be added to the cream before whipping.

CHOCOLATE CREAM.—No. 2.

$\frac{3}{4}$ pint of double cream.
$\frac{1}{2}$ pint (bare) of new milk.
5 ozs. of castor sugar.
1 teaspoonful of vanilla sugar.
4 yolks of eggs.
3 ozs. of pure block cocoa.
$\frac{2}{3}$ oz. of isinglass (thread).

Steep the isinglass in cold water for half an hour. Place the milk, cream, sugar, vanilla sugar, and shredded cocoa in a tin-lined stewpan to heat, stirring gently. When hot drain the water from the isinglass, and add to the hot liquid, stirring until melted. Whisk the yolks in a basin to break them up well, and pour the hot cream on them, whisking vigorously the while. Return to the stewpan, and bring up to boiling point, stirring all the time, but do not let the cream boil. At once pass through a fine hair sieve into a basin, and stir occasionally until cold and almost set, when pour the cream into a previously decorated mould and put on ice to set.

CURACOA CREAM. (WHITE).

1 pint of double cream.
5 ozs. of pulverised sugar.
A small wineglassful of orange curacoa.
$\frac{1}{2}$ oz. of isinglass.

Melt the isinglass as before instructed, and when cooled add the curacoa to it, stirring and mixing thoroughly. Whip the cream and sugar together, and stir in the curacoa and isinglass carefully and quickly, and when almost at setting point pour into a decorated mould and set on ice.

The whole of the liqueur creams are made as above, differing only in the flavour and colour.

MARASCHINO CREAM. (PALE PINK).

1 pint of double cream.
3 ozs. (liqueur) of maraschino (Zara).
4 ozs. of pulverised sugar.
$\frac{1}{2}$ oz. of isinglass.
A few drops of liquid carmine.

Treat exactly as for curacoa cream, adding the carmine before the isinglass.

Creams.

VANILLA CREAM.—No. 2.

½ pint of new milk.
½ pint of double cream.
4 yolks of eggs.
4 ozs. of castor sugar.

2 inches of a vanilla bean.
A small piece of lemon rind.
1 teaspoonful of ground almonds.
⅔ oz. of isinglass.

And afterwards, ¼ pint of double cream.

Steep the isinglass in cold water for half an hour. Place the milk, ½ pint of cream, sugar, vanilla, lemon rind, ground almonds, and the swollen isinglass in a tinned stewpan, and bring to the boil, stirring meanwhile to melt the isinglass. Strain through a fine hair sieve into a basin in which the yolks have been beaten, whisking well together. Return to the stewpan and put on fire again, and just bring to boiling point, but do not boil, or its smoothness will be spoiled. Lift from the fire, and stir occasionally until nearly cold to prevent a skin forming on top. Whip the ¼ pint of cream, and thoroughly mix into the custard, which should be almost cold. Stir well to avoid streaks, and when about to set pour into a previously decorated mould on ice. Cool as quickly as possible. This cream is a little closer than No. 1, but very rich and of beautiful texture if carefully made.

COFFEE CREAM.—No. 1

1 pint of double cream.
4 ozs. of castor sugar.

1 teacupful of extract of coffee.
1 teaspoonful of vanilla sugar.

½ oz. of isinglass.

Steep the isinglass in water for half an hour, then lift from the water into a small copper sugar-boiler, add the extract of coffee, the sugar, and vanilla sugar, and melt into a thick syrup, and whilst cooling whip the cream carefully. Pour the almost cold isinglass and coffee syrup into the cream, well mix, and when on the point of setting pour into a previously decorated mould. Serve very cold.

COFFEE CREAM.—No. 2.

½ pint of new milk.
½ pint of double cream.
5 ozs. of castor sugar.
4 yolks of eggs.
½ inch piece of a vanilla bean.

3 ozs. of coffee berries.
⅔ oz. of isinglass.
And afterwards, ¼ pint of double cream.
Little caramelled sugar.

Roast the coffee to a deep rich colour, and put it whilst hot into the milk and cream, which with the steeped isinglass must then be made into a custard, strained and finished with the whipped cream exactly as for vanilla cream No. 2. As the whole coffee berries will give a fine flavour, but very little colour, a deeper tint can be obtained by adding a little caramelled sugar.

CHOCOLATE CREAM.—No. 1.

1 pint of double cream.
3 ozs. of pure block cocoa.

5 ozs. of pulverised sugar.
1 teaspoonful of vanilla sugar.

⅔ oz. of isinglass.

Only partly whip the cream, with the sugar and vanilla sugar. Melt the cocoa in a basin held in a stewpan of hot water, and when quite liquid, but not hot, add a little of the

All about Ices.

Take the rind off two of the oranges, and pound very fine in a small marble mortar. Lift out into a small basin, and add the brandy and orange-flower water, and pass through a fine hair sieve. Cut the oranges in halves, remove the pips, and either pound and pass through the sieve on to the zest or squeeze the juice through without pounding. Add the sugar and colour to the cream, and whip carefully. Blend the liquor with the warm melted isinglass, and when nearly cold add to the whipped cream. Blend, and when almost set pour into a previously decorated mould. Serve very cold.

An alternative plan is to make a syrup of the sugar, juice, and orange-flower water, and simmer the rind in that for a few minutes, afterwards blending with the isinglass and adding to the whipped cream when almost cold. This is very much easier, but the finished cream will lack the freshness so desirable, and have an added cooked peel flavour that is objectionable to a delicate palate.

LEMON CREAM.

1 pint of double cream.
6 ozs. of castor sugar.
Zest of two lemons.
A small teaspoonful of the lemon juice (if desired).
½ oz. of isinglass.
1 teaspoonful of pale brandy.

The cream must be very fresh and sweet, or it will be liable to be curdled by the lemon juice. If there is the least question of its condition it will be better to leave out the juice. If by any chance the cream be made one day to be used the next the juice must not be used even with perfectly sweet cream. Make and finish exactly as for orange cream, but without colour.

MILLE FLEUR CREAM.

1 pint of double cream.
¼ pint of simple syrup.
1 drop of attar of roses.
4 drops of essence of violets
1 dessertspoonful of orange-flower water (triple).
3 petals of white chrysanthemum.
1 dessertspoonful of green chartreuse.
½ oz. of isinglass (Russian or Brazilian thread).

Place the isinglass in a breakfast cup and cover with cold water and steep for half an hour. Pour away the water, and add the swollen isinglass to the syrup in a small copper sugar-boiler, and gently melt by heat. Add the chrysanthemum petals, cover, and leave until nearly cold, and then remove the petals, add the orange-flower water, attar of roses, essence of violets, and the chartreuse. Whip the cream carefully, stir in the flavoured isinglass syrup, and mix carefully, and when almost set pour into a previously decorated mould, in which a few small flower sprays are set in clear jelly. Serve very cold.

VANILLA CREAM.—No. 1.

1 pint of double cream.
5 ozs. of castor sugar (fine).
1½ oz. of vanilla sugar.
½ oz. of isinglass.
1 dessertspoonful of pale brandy.

Melt the isinglass and allow to cool, stirring occasionally to prevent a skin forming on top, then add the brandy. Whip the cream, sugar, and vanilla sugar together carefully, pour in the cooled isinglass, blend all together, and when nearly set pour into a previously decorated mould. Serve very cold.

Creams.

- ½ lb. of fresh ripe mulberries.
- 3 ozs. of red currant jelly.
- 5 ozs. of small crushed sugar.
- ⅔ oz. of isinglass.
- 1 pint of double cream.
- 1 dessertspoonful of pale brandy.
- 1 teaspoonful of kirsch.
- A few drops of liquid carmine, if necessary.

Simmer the fruit with very little water in a copper sugar-boiler until well pulped, add the sugar, and simmer slowly until dissolved, then add the red currant jelly, and reduce to a thick pulp and pass through a fine hair sieve into a basin. When nearly cold stir in the brandy and kirsch, and mix well, adding the carmine if necessary. Whip the cream, add the melted isinglass to the cooled pulp, and stir the whole into the whipped cream, and put into a mould previously decorated with clear jelly, fresh mulberries, and Muscat grapes. Serve very cold.

MILLE FRUIT CREAM.

- 1 pint of double cream.
- 5 ozs. of pulverised sugar.
- 6 ozs. of mixed glacé fruit, cut in small pieces.
- 1 dessertspoonful of kirsch.
- 1 dessertspoonful of orange-flower water (triple).
- Zest and juice of one orange.
- Few drops of infusion of saffron.

Cut up the glacé fruit, cherries, apricots, green and red brochettes, etc., and place in a basin with the kirsch, orange-flower water, and orange juice, having taken the zest off on a piece of loaf sugar. Scrape off the saturated sugar and add it with the sugar to the cream, which must then be carefully whipped. Tint a pale yellow with a few drops of infusion of saffron, strain the liquor away from the fruit into the melted isinglass, stir the fruit into the cream, being careful that it does not adhere in groups, and then pour in the isinglass and liquor together, and blend the whole, pouring into a previously decorated mould just as it is setting. Care must be used that the cream is poured into the mould at exactly the right consistency. If too soft, the fruit will precipitate; if too much set the cream will not shape itself properly to the mould. Serve very cold.

ORANGE CREAM.

- 1 pint of double cream.
- 5 ozs. of castor sugar.
- Zest and juice of three oranges.
- ½ oz. of isinglass.
- 1 dessertspoonful of orange curacoa.
- A few drops of infusion of saffron.
- A drop of liquid carmine.

Take the zest off the oranges on a rough piece of sugar loaf, squeeze and strain the juice. Scrape the saturated sugar from the piece of loaf, and add it with the juice and sugar to the cream, and tint this with the saffron and carmine. Melt the isinglass, and when nearly cold add the curacoa and mix together. Whip the cream carefully, and pour in the isinglass and curacoa nearly cold. Blend together, and pour into a previously decorated mould, and set on ice to become firm and cold.

TANGERINE ORANGE CREAM.

- 1 pint of double cream.
- 5 ozs. of castor sugar.
- Zest of two tangerine oranges.
- Juice of five tangerine oranges.
- 1 dessertspoonful of brandy.
- 1 dessertspoonful of orange-flower water (triple).
- ½ oz. of isinglass.
- Few drops of infusion of saffron.

SECTION VI.
JAMS AND CONSERVES.

Jams and conserves generally, of fine flavour, good colour, and proper consistency are of such importance in the daily work of every confectioner that it is a matter for suprise so few of them take the trouble to make for themselves. There is, however, a growing minority producing the whole or part of their requirements, and in the hope that the number may be largely increased the subject is here dealt with.

There was a time when this branch of the retail trade was in the confectioners' hands, but, like so many others, it has now passed into the grocers', and it is too late to recover it. It is not, however, too late to revert to the ancient custom of making fine preserves for trade use, and by so doing enhance the quality of one's products. It is a curious fact that to-day nearly all confectioners confine themselves to using three jams only, *i.e.*, raspberry, greengage, and apricot, the latter one having come into general use comparatively recently. It is difficult to understand this restriction, which, by the way, is often only in intention, for the three do not invariably consist only of the fruits which give them their name. Entirely outside of the desire to cheapen the cost of the higher-priced jams by admixture with cheaper fruit, there is an understandable and defendable reason for such admixture, which will be made quite clear as we proceed, but if such admixture is made, it should be made by the confectioner, and the advantage be his.

There are two distinct types of factory-made jam entirely outside of varieties. One, the best, that made at the beginning of the season when fresh fruit is boiled at once into the finished jam, and the other, that made from stored pulps as occasion may require.

There are two reasons for storing pulps by the manufacturer. Two great commercial reasons, that is, besides several minor reasons, of greater or lesser importance. The first major reason is the commercially insurmountable difficulty of dealing finally with the great bulk of fruit when it is obtainable. The second is the large capital outlay for sugar which would be necessary to convert all the fruit into jam at once, and the locking up of capital, which would be all the heavier, because the tremendous demand would send up the market price of sugar at such a time. This, of course, would mean that the sale price of jams during the year would be raised on account both of the higher cost price and the interest on locked up capital, whilst, all other circumstances being equal, the market value of sugar would have resumed its normal position.

It may be argued that if all confectioners made their jam for the year at the fruit season the same results would accrue, but in the first place the whole of the trade never will, and in the second their entire consumption would only be a small moiety of the yearly consumption. It is not here suggested that the trade should make all their jam at that season, but it is insisted upon that jam so made is superior to that made from pulped fruits, and that if pulped fruits are used the confectioner should have whatever advantage may accrue, and be perfectly assured of their constitution.

All about Ices.

Most fruits suitable for jam making contain in a greater or lesser degree a mucilaginous substance called pectose in the unripe fruit and pectin in the ripened fruit. These substances, although changing chemically as the fruit ripens, have almost the same physical effect in jam making. They give the jelly-like consistency to the finished jam. The pectose has the greater setting capacity, but is not so tenacious as the pectin. The best illustration of this is shown in jams made from green unripe gooseberries and fully ripened gooseberries.

Those fruits containing the larger percentage of this substance are, irrespective of flavour and individual taste, the most suitable for jams and jellies. In the front rank are red, white, and black currants, raspberries, green and red gooseberries, apples, cherry apples, green figs, apricots, mirabels, damsons, Gisbon plums, oranges, and greengages. In the second rank, cherry plums, unripe and ripe Victoria plums, damson plums, Washington gages, bullace plums, prune plums, bush plums, sloes, Michigan, Scotch, and Dutch cranberries, and quince. At the bottom of the list come strawberries, cherries, blackberries, mulberries, rhubarb, pears, peaches, pineapples, etc. This list is not complete, but is approximately accurate. It may be accepted as a rule that the finer the condition of the fruit the greater the mucilaginous development, and per contra. All the sorts of the currants are suitable, so are all the raspberries. Nearly all varieties of gooseberries can be used, but Warringtons and Crown Bobs are the best. Nearly all types of cooking apples are suitable, the main differences being in colour and flavour, russet types being the least satisfactory, and Wellingtons, Suffields, Keswicks, Blenheim Orange, etc., the best. Cherry apples make magnificent jelly, giving a lovely orange-red colour naturally. Green figs make splendid jam, too seldom seen. Apricots, the fresh fruit, make magnificent jam, but are seldom obtainable at a reasonable price. Mirabels, the real fresh fruit is hardly ever on sale in this country, and then is dear, but an oval bastard variety can often be bought at cheap rates. Damsons are always in large supply, and cheap enough to use freely. Gisbon plums are almost the cheapest plums offered, and make really fine yellow jam. Oranges at the proper season (January and February) are generally cheap. There are many types of greengages, the Reine Claude being the best. They should always be hard and unripe. Of the fruits in the second rank it is not necessary to deal at length, although they all, or nearly all, serve useful purposes. Of those in the last list strawberries are the most important, being amongst the first favourites. These have practically no mucilage in their juice, and must therefore be provided with what they lack, if satisfactory results are to be obtained. The only cherries worth considering at all for jam or jelly making are Morellos, Medoc (May Dukes), and the black varieties, and these contain a very small percentage. Forced rhubarb has a small percentage, very small, naturally grown practically none. Peaches have practically none, blackberries a very little, and mulberries rather more.

This mucilaginous substance, so important in the making of really fine jams and jellies, is very rapidly broken down by even slight fermentation, and in most pulps has greatly deteriorated after storage, even when there are no signs of fermentation at all. The loss is usually very marked in raspberry pulp, less so with all the currants, and least of all with gooseberries and apples. For this reason these pulps are largely used to tone up the depreciated raspberry pulp, the resulting jam being then sold by reputable makers as raspberry and gooseberry, raspberry and currant, etc., etc., Of course, the description would be quite accurate, no matter what the percentage may be, and most confectioners are too lazy or indifferent to attempt to find out.

A very useful agent for remedying the shortage of mucilage is agar agar, or Japanese gelatine, if used with discretion. It has great setting capacity of the pectose character.

Jams and Conserves.

This can be qualified with glucose, and pectin character obtained, but both are liable to give trouble unless used with knowledge. Glucose in particular makes for toughness, and is best absent from confectioners' jams. Agar agar has a great affinity for moisture, and although this characteristic is not apparent in its dry state, it is very apt to attract the moisture from a humid atmosphere when combined with jam or jelly, and invite the growth of mould. This subject will be fully treated in its proper place.

The plant necessary for jam making on a small scale need not be very elaborate, but will, of course, depend upon the quantity desired to be made in any given time. If steam be available a very small tilting pan with a pouring lip will be most useful, this same pan answering for many other purposes, including fondant making. It is, however, not a necessity, and no confectioner need hesitate to make jam because he has not such a pan. A gas stove will answer, but is not advisable, either on the score of economy or efficiency. Unless there be a cooking stove with rings opening over a coal or coke fire, the best boiling stove is a small round iron tubular frame, with a firebrick lining and an open ring top. This can be bought for about £2, fitted with an iron chimney running into any flue, burns coke, and gives splendid results at a very small cost. In addition to this, one or two round-bottomed copper egg bowls, three fine, medium, and coarse mesh brass wire sieves, and a couple of large spattles are at first all that are needed for the actual jam boiling. If jellies are wanted to be made, large felt or flannel jelly bags will be wanted, and, of course, jars for storing the jam when made. The usual size are those holding 7 lbs., which cost about 4s. per dozen at Doulton's or Swift's potteries. The best size and shape, are, however, 14-lb. jars, the same diameter as the 7-lb. ones, but higher, and with sloping instead of sharply-rounded necks.

This brings us to the question of boiling, which, if the best results are to be obtained, should always be in small quantities. The development of factory work and large steam pans have, of course, made for economy of production, but the confectioner who is certain to have no special means of cooling quickly will be well advised in never exceeding 28 lbs. of fruit and sugar at one boiling.

Sugar.—The best possible sugar is, of course, fine refined cane, but this is generally outside practical politics, so we must content ourselves with suitable beet. But, please, let that be suitable, and do not be persuaded to buy something unsuitable, because it costs 1s. per cwt. less. Tate's No. 1 or No. 2 crushed, Say's crushed, Lebaudy's crushed, or any similar grade of French small crushed, or a good make of small Dutch crushed will all give good results. They are hard and more or less coarse in their crystallisation. Much of the Dutch is in very large pieces. Avoid this, for it will only dissolve with difficulty. Choose the small, bright, hard sugar, and use as directed.

FRESH RASPBERRY JAM.

The raspberries should be bought free from stalks and as dry as possible. The smaller the packages in which they are packed the better will be their condition, all other circumstances being equal. For large purchasers the cheaper form will, of course, be the tubs, in which the bulk of the fruit comes to market, but these are never dry, the pressure expressing the juice, and samples are occasionally thirsty, if one may judge by the added water. Reputable growers do not, of course, descend to this trick to increase weight, but it is sometimes done in dry and scarce seasons. In whatever packages the fruit be bought, arrangements should be made to boil the entire parcel as quickly as possible after arrival, and under no circumstances should any portion be allowed to remain unboiled until the following day. First pass the whole of the fruit through a brass sieve, five mesh to the

All about Ices.

inch, into either a large copper pan or an enamelled one, and weigh the pulp into the pan for boiling. Boiling must always be done in untinned copper, and all pans must be not only clean, but bright. If the weight of the boiling pans be previously known, the pulp may be lifted into the boiler with a small enamelled hand-bowl, and pulp and pan weighed together. For each boiling in a 16-inch pan use 14 lbs. of pulp and 14 lbs. of small crushed sugar, put on the fire at once, and stir, to break up the sugar and to prevent burning, the whole time of boiling. The boiling must be as rapid as possible. It is not possible to give the exact time, for the percentage of water to be expelled is a varying quantity. The use of the sugar thermometer is sometimes advised, but it is of little actual use, because the setting point of the jam is governed more by the quantity and quality of the pectin in the fruit than by the actual sugar temperature. The best test is the condition of the webbing of the jam when lifted on the spattle. A little practice will show quite clearly when the webbing is thick enough, and breaks in leaving the uplifted spattle. Overboiling will mean deterioration of colour as well as of flavour. The moment the right point is reached remove the pan from the fire, scrape down the sides with a piece of stiff card, and fill into the clean dry jars, and cool as quickly as possible. Next day cover the tops with rounds of waxed paper, and tie down with vegetable parchment, and store in a cold, dark, dry store room. Care must be taken that the skin formed on top, must not be broken; there is no more fruitful cause of fermentation and mould than the breaking of this sealing skin. No colouring matter is necessary with this jam.

It is customary to use a somewhat higher percentage of sugar than that given here; it makes for greater keeping qualities, but it is somewhat tougher in texture, and is more apt to blow in the oven if baked in goods, and we confess to preferring the proportions here given.

FRESH RASPBERRY AND RED CURRANT JAM.

This is a beautiful jam when carefully made, but red currants are a nuisance if many are to be used. If picked from the stalks, they are easily passed through a fine mesh sieve, but they take a long time picking. The usual way is to wash the fruit (unless very fine and bright), drain it and place stalks and fruit together in the sieve, pressing out as much juice as possible. This is much quicker, but more wasteful, and the stalks, even if they do little harm, do not improve the flavour of the expressed juice. The fruit is sometimes so very cheap, and the juice is so heavy with pectin that the result is often worth the labour.

Use for this jam two-thirds of the raspberry pulp and one-third of the red currant, and for each boiling in the 16-inch pan use to 14 lbs. of pulp 15 lbs. of crushed sugar, and treat exactly as for raspberry alone.

White currants may, if desired, be used in place of red with precisely similar results, except that the jam will not be so deep in colour. Use no colouring matter whatever.

FRESH RED CURRANT JAM.

Treat the fruit exactly in the same way, weigh the pulp, taking 13 lbs. to 15 lbs. of fine crushed sugar, and boil exactly as before. Use no colour.

FRESH BLACK CURRANT JAM.

This fruit must be picked from the stalks, which have a very strong aroma and taste. For table use the so-called whole fruit is generally preferred, but for confectioners' use the

Jams and Conserves.

properly passed fruit is preferable. Pick the fruit, therefore, rinse it in cold water if at all gritty, pass it through a fine mesh sieve, weigh 13 lbs. of the pulp, add one quart of water, bring to the boil, and boil a few minutes to soften the skins, add 15 lbs. of small crushed sugar, dissolve and boil quickly to the webbing point. This is best filled into smaller jars, for it is seldom used so freely as raspberry. No colouring will be needed.

This jam can be made with one-third red or white currant pulp, which will lighten its deep colour a little, and will scarcely affect its flavour, but if sold it must, of course, be properly described.

Most of the black currant jam made, especially the whole fruit type, has very hard skins. The object in view in adding water and boiling before adding the sugar is to obviate this feature as far as may be.

STRAWBERRY JAM.

This jam is not very useful to the confectioner in his daily work, but it is occasionally called for, and is a great favourite as a tea table conserve. Owing to the absence of pectin in its make up, it is practically impossible to make with strawberries and sugar alone, jam of the jelly-like consistency desired. Jam can be, and is, made, without any addition in the form of mucilage, but it is never quite satisfactory. It is generally much too thin or if boiled to a fuller consistence it is tough. It is, therefore, not only permissible but desirable to add mucilage in some one or other form. The most suitable form is the juice of red or white currants because its acidity gives splendid flavour. Next in order comes apple juice, red gooseberry juice, green gooseberry juice, and, last of all, agar agar (Japanese gelatine). Red currants are usually obtainable near the end of the strawberry season-- not always when at the lowest price. The earliest suitable apples are Keswicks, but they are seldom obtainable in time. Red gooseberries also are generally too late (the previous season's are sometimes used), but, as a rule, there are plenty of green gooseberries to be had, and good white canned apples can be used. Agar agar is, like the poor, always with us.

"Scarletts," the small wild variety, are on all counts the best fruit to use whether for whole fruit, or for that which is pulped. If these are not available, choose Paxton's, medium sized, firm, red, fruit, or some such type, avoiding the very watery sorts. Fully ripe fruit is preferable for pulping, and barely ripe for whole fruit. Hand picking from the hulls is essential in both cases. With the whole fruit, there is a tendency to float, especially with large fruit, and constant stirring whilst filling into jars is very necessary. To obviate this trouble, the jam is sometimes turned on to a cooling slab before filling out, the jars being afterwards set in a hot water bath to reheat them, and ensure a firm film-like skin on the surface. This, however, is a very tedious and messy process, and it is best to avoid it if possible.

If glucose be used, as it sometimes is, to counterbalance the pectose-like setting of agar agar, it is well to remember that it rapidly discolours at a high temperature, and to add it near the end of the boiling. Another point to remember is that all other conditions being equal, the smaller the boiling the better will be both colour and consistency.

Each of the following formulæ have been used by the writers successfully, and they are given in their order of merit.

WHOLE FRUIT STRAWBERRY JAM.—No. 1.

14 lbs. strawberries (free from hulls).
8 pints of red or white currrant juice.
16 lbs. of small fine crushed sugar.
A few drops of liquid carmine (if desired).

All about Ices.

To make the currant juice, place any quantity of picked currants, free from stalks, in the boiling pan, and cover them with water. Bring to the boil, and stirring vigorously, boil until thoroughly broken down. Then pour into a thin flannel jelly bag and let the juice run through into a pan. It is not necessary that it run bright like jelly, so pass as quickly as possible. Measure out the proper quantity, put it in the boiling pan with the sugar, and boil until it begins to web on the spattle, stirring continuously. Then add the picked strawberries, stir in carefully, bring to the boil again, and with only occasional stirring simmer slowly until the strawberries look almost transparent. By this time the water should be out of the fruit and the sugar have taken its place. Then boil rapidly up to the firm webbing point adding the liquid carmine when nearly ready and gently stirring to avoid burning on the pan. Pack in small jars as directed.

Picking the currants from the stalks by hand is laborious work, and they can, if desired, be passed through a fine mesh brass sieve instead and the water added afterwards. The addition of water is to give bulk to the juice (it runs more freely through the bag) and to provide moisture to dissolve the sugar where the otherwise smaller quantity of thicker juice would not do so satisfactorily.

WHOLE FRUIT STRAWBERRY JAM.—No. 2.

14 lbs. strawberries (free from hulls).
8 pints of apple juice.
17 lbs. of small fine crushed sugar.
A few drops of liquid carmine.

Cut the apples in halves or quarters (do not peel or core them), put in the boiling pan, adding sufficient water to float them. When thoroughly pulped, stirring only slightly, pass through the jelly bag, and finish as for No. 1.

WHOLE FRUIT STRAWBERRY JAM.—No. 3.

14 lbs. of strawberries (free from hulls).
9 pints of red gooseberry juice.
18 lbs. of small fine crushed sugar.
Very little liquid carmine.

Use ripe but firm gooseberries—Warringtons or Crown Bobs—well cover with water d boil until well pulped, stirring continually. Pass and finish as for No. 1.

WHOLE FRUIT STRAWBERRY JAM.—No. 4.

14 lbs. strawberries (free from hulls).
9 pints of green gooseberry juice.
16 lbs. of fine crushed sugar.
3 lbs. of liquid glucose.
Liquid carmine at discretion to tint.

Use hard green gooseberries, use rather more water than for the red ones, as the pectose is harder to dissolve than the pectin, gently simmer them without stirring, until quite soft, afterwards boiling quickly and stirring constantly until well pulped. Finish as for No. 1, adding the glucose and carmine when the boiling is almost completed.

WHOLE FRUIT STRAWBERRY JAM.—No. 5.

14 lbs. strawberries (free from hulls).
12 lbs. of fine crushed sugar.
3 lbs. of liquid glucose.
2 ozs. of agar agar—or more.
3 quarts of water.
A little liquid carmine.

Separate strands of the agar agar, place in the pan, add the water and let it stand until well swollen and transparent. Add the sugar, place on the fire, well dissolve the sugar, bring to the boil, stirring well to break down the agar agar, and boil up to 240 deg

Jams and Conserves.

by the sugar thermometer (the hard ball), add the glucose, boil up again, and at once turn in the picked strawberries. Boil up to cover the fruit, occasionally stir gently, and slowly simmer until the fruit collapses, and becomes thoroughly permeated with sugar. Then boil quickly up to the webbing point. Great care will be necessary to prevent the fruit floating.

Agar agar varies considerably in strength, therefore in using any particular parcel it will be necessary to try one or two small batches to decide accurately as to the proportions to be used.

STRAWBERRY JAM (PULPED FRUIT).

Any of the foregoing formulæ can be used for this, provided the picked fruit be passed through a fine mesh sieve, the juice added to it, and both boiled for ten minutes to reduce it before adding the sugar—this will save after boiling and materially aid in conserving both colour and consistency.

In using No. 5 formula for pulped fruit, omit the water, but steep the agar agar in the pulp, and as nearly as possible dissolve it before adding the sugar. This cannot be done entirely because it is only partially soluble at 212 deg., and the pulp alone cannot be raised above that temperature. Add the glucose and carmine near the end of the boiling.

LIQUID CARMINE FOR COLOURING.

2 ozs. of powder carmine No. 30 or 36.   1 quart of distilled water.
1 oz. of strong liquid ammonia.

Place the powder in a white glass Winchester quart bottle, pour on the water and shake well once or twice. This will give a red opaque liquid, the carmine being held in suspension only in the water. Half an hour later again well shake and add the liquid ammonia. Shake once more, cork, and in half an hour or less the liquid will be a dull transparent crimson, and fit for use for all liquid bodies. To reprecipitate this colour into a brilliant paste for fondants and royal icing see instructions in "Colours" elsewhere.

FRESH GREENGAGE JAM.

Choose unripe fruit, hard and green, pick off the stalks and pulp them. If the same size pan be used, 18 lbs. of gages and three pints of water should be used at a time, the stirring being continuous and vigorous. When quite soft and broken, turn into enamelled pans to become cool. When sufficiently cool to handle, rub through a four-mesh sieve to remove the stones and thoroughly break up the fruit. Weigh 14 lbs. of pulp and 14 lbs. of fine crushed sugar, and finish boiling in exactly the same way as for raspberry. Fill jars and cool as quickly as possible to conserve the colour. If the fruit be at all ripe the colour will be a yellowish brown instead of a pale light green.

FRESH APRICOT JAM.

Split the fruit with a sharp bright knife, and be careful that the knife is kept clean. Remove the stones, and pulp the halves of fruit exactly in the same way as for greengages, using one quart of water to each 12 lbs. of fruit. Pour into enamelled pans to cool, pass through an eight-mesh sieve to remove the fibrous matter, weigh into the boiler 14 lbs. of pulp and 14 lbs. of fine crushed sugar, and boil as quickly as possible to the proper webbing point. Pour into jars and cool as quickly as possible. This is a very delicious jam, and

All about Ices.

is beautifully solid, but the fruit can so seldom be bought at a reasonable price, as compared with the French, Spanish, Californian, and Australian pulp that it is practically outside confectionery economics in this country.

Apricot conserve for coating purposes is much more heavily sugared than the above, but this will be treated exhaustively when pulps other than fresh fruit are under consideration.

FRESH MIRABEL JAM.

This is the best of yellow jam that can be made, of beautiful flavour and almost transparent. The fruit in shape and size is like an oval damson, and almost straw yellow in colour. The skin is as thin as tissue paper, and the stone very small. If the jam be made with the stones in, the flavour is a little more delicate, and the fruit is so easily pulped that passing is not necessary. For confectioners' use, however, stoneless jam is necessary, and the stones cling, so the mirabels must be pulped the same way as greengages, using 1 lb. of water to each 12 lbs. of fruit. When cool, pass through a four-mesh sieve, weigh pulp and sugar in equal proportions, and boil to the webbing point, and cool quickly. The result will be jam almost transparent, pale yellow in colour, and of delicious flavour.

FRESH GREEN GOOSEBERRY JAM.

Use either Warringtons or Crown Bobs, hard and green. For the very finest jam the stalks and snuffs must be removed before pulping, or many of them will pass through the meshes of the sieve and spoil the appearance of the finished jam. To each 10 lbs. of fruit add a quart of water, and stir continually to prevent burning. As soon as the fruit is broken down, turn out into enamelled pans, and when sufficiently cool pass with pressure through a five-mesh sieve, and boil in the proportions of 13 lbs. of pulp to 15 lbs. of fine crushed sugar. This high proportion of sugar to the watered pulp is necessary, as the proportion of pectose in the unripe fruit is very large, and without extra sugar the jam would be short and granular in texture instead of jelly-like. Boil quickly to the webbing point, and at once pour into dry clean jars. In this jam, which should be a pale green colour, not very clear, the seeds will show distinctly green.

A more delicate green gooseberry jam is sometimes made from the large berries that are green when fully ripe, but as these are dessert fruit, they are much more expensive If these are used, they must be treated in all respects as the unripe fruit, but using equal weights of pulp and sugar. In this jam the pips will be almost black, and the body of the jam will have a yellowish colour. The flavour is quite distinctive and pleasantly acid.

FRESH CHERRY PLUM JAM.

This fruit is fairly common in England as well as in most Continental countries, and comes early in the season. It is a variety of the mirabel, is round, rather larger than the true mirabel, has the same yellow flesh and small stone, and much of the mirabel flavour. Its thin skin is a bright red in colour, and when boiled the jam is deep orange in colour. The fruit can often be bought at very moderate prices, and as it is useful for bottling as well as a tart fruit when fresh, should never be neglected by the confectioner.

Pick off the stalks and pulp with one quart of water to every 14 lbs. of fruit. Pour into enamelled pans, and when cool enough pass through a four or five mesh sieve, and boil pulp and sugar in equal proportions up to the webbing point. If it is desired to

Jams and Conserves.

keep back the skins and make a more jelly-like conserve, use an eight-mesh sieve, and use 13 lbs. of the pulp to 15 lbs. of sugar. A few drops of liquid carmine or infusion of rose pink will give a very brilliant red conserve that will serve many useful purposes. It is, however, suggested to the confectioner that the colouring of all types of conserves for glacéing be done at the time of using, as the colouring will be more brilliant when freshly tinted.

FRESH RED GOOSEBERRY JAM.

This is one of the most economical of the red jams, and answers admirably for cheap work. Its chief value, however, is for blending purposes and to supply the mucilaginous pectin missing in many of the pulps. (See "Pulps.") It is also well worth atttention as a fresh fruit jam, and almost every season is so low in price that some should always be made.

Red Warringtons or Crown Bobs are the two most suitable sorts, both being of the hairy varieties. Choose them when fully coloured, but not too ripe. If bought in this condition, a sufficiently large parcel to cover three days' operations may be bought at once, of course at a lower price. Wash them in cold water to ensure cleanliness, and be certain that all leaves, etc., are picked out. Pulp them with one quart of water to each 12 lbs. of fruit, turn into enamelled pans, and when sufficiently cool pass through a five-mesh sieve to ensure thorough breaking up of the skins. Boil equal weights of pulp and fine crushed sugar up to the webbing point, and store in clean dry jars.

FRESH ORLEANS PLUM JAM.

This is an early plum, not very large, bright red in colour, of beautiful flavour, but with very little pectin in its make-up. With care a very fine jam for immediate consumption can be made with it, but its use is not advised for a storage jam.

Pick off the stalks and pulp with one quart of water to 20 lbs. of fruit. Pour into enamelled pans, and as soon as cool pulp through a five-mesh sieve, and boil 13 lbs. of pulp with 15 lbs. of fine crushed sugar as quickly as possible to the webbing point. The smaller the jars used for this the better will be the jam, both in colour and texture.

FRESH VICTORIA PLUM JAM.

This plum has more pectin than the Orleans, and consequently will produce jam of better texture. It is generally to be obtained at a moderate price, and is a very useful jam for cheaper goods. When ripe the stones are free, and if the fruit be split lengthways the stones are easily removed, and if the fruit be carefully pulped before adding the sugar passing can be dispersed with. The pulping must, however, be very thorough, or pieces of fruit will be in the finished jam.

Use one quart of water for each 12 lbs. of fruit, weighed after the stones are removed, and boil with an equal quantity of sugar up to the webbing point. The jam will be pale in colour, because the pulp is yellow, so, if a deeper tint is needed, a little liquid carmine or rose pink must be added.

FRESH GREEN VICTORIA PLUM JAM.

This fruit if used whilst hard and green, stalked, and pulped exactly as for unripe greengages, passed and boiled in exactly the same way, will give jam of almost as good colour, but not such good flavour. It is, however, a much cheaper jam, as the green plums can generally be bought when the trees are being thinned at less than half the price of English gages. Care must be taken that the fruit be very hard and unripe, or the results will be entirely unsatisfactory. Heating will then develop a dingy red on the skins, and the finished jam will resemble a mixture of sepia and umber.

FRESH WASHINGTON GAGE JAM.

The Washington gage is a large, round, dusky-looking plum of good flavour when ripe, but unfit for jam-making unless used hard and unripe, and before the russet tinge has arrived. If taken in the proper condition it will produce jam as good a colour and almost as good in flavour as the true gage, and it is always much cheaper. Treat exactly as for greengages, being careful to pulp thoroughly, as the stone clings very tenaciously.

FRESH GISBON PLUM JAM.

These plums are sometimes called egg plums on account of their shape. They are when unripe a pale green, and treated exactly as greengages, using one quart of water to each 10 lbs. of fruit, and boiled, pulp and sugar in equal proportions, will give very good green jam.

It is, however, from the ripe fruit, that the best jam is to be made. The fruit has little juice, is a pale yellow with a suspicion of green, is of poor flavour when raw (in this resembling cherry plums), has free stones, breaks down easily, and makes really fine flavoured pale yellow jam.

Pick off the stalks, pulp the fruit, using one quart of water to each 10 lbs. of fruit. Pass when cool, and boil 14 lbs. of the watered pulp with 14 lbs. of sugar up to the webbing point, and at once pour into clean dry jars for storing.

If stored pulps are to be made, Gisbon plums should certainly be one of the kinds chosen; they are heavily charged with pectin, and are valuable for toning up the more or less watered apricot pulps of commerce.

FRESH DAMSON JAM.

This fruit has of late years been sadly neglected by confectioners, in spite of the fact that it is a great favourite with the public. It has considerable stomachic value, it is pleasantly astringent and distinct in flavour, and it is nearly always very cheap. In spite of its many claims, the average confectioner makes only an occasional damson and apple tart, and a few penny covered tarts, in neither of which he ever uses sufficient sugar to make them palatable, and for the rest—nothing! Well, what can be expected? "Ex nihilo nihil fit." For them, damson jam, damson jelly, damson cheese, damson cordial, etc., etc., do not exist. God graciously sends us the fruit, and the alleged confectioner ignores it. Perhaps if our ministers gave a weekly sermon appendix on wasted opportunities, with special reference to the duties of the coming week, some slumbering consciousness might be awakened, but maybe few would be there to hear.

Some of the possibilities of this fine fruit will be shown in a later chapter; here we are concerned with jam-making only.

Pick the stalks from the fruit, wash them in cold water if at all gritty, and pulp carefully, using one quart of water to every 12 lbs. of fruit. Pour into pans as before, and as soon as cool enough pass through a five-mesh sieve to remove the stones and any hard skins. Boil 13 lbs. of fruit with 15 lbs. of fine crushed sugar quickly up to the webbing point, and store at once in clean dry jars.

Jams and Conserves.

The resulting jam should be a deep rich wine colour, of great tenacity and body, and of fine flavour.

Most of the commercial damson jam is boiled with the stones, in which case passing is unnecessary if the pulping be thoroughly done. In either case vigorous stirring must be constant, the high acidity of the fruit rendering it very liable to burn on the bottom or sides of the pan.

JAMS FROM PULPED FRUIT.

When large quantities of jam have to be made and it is desired to avoid using the sugar until the actual jam is required for use, and the fruit has been preserved in pulped form (see Pulps), it is often necessary to blend the pulps so that those containing the higher percentage of undeteriorated mucilaginous matter may help to tone up those that have deteriorated. Apple, currant, and gooseberry pulps are the most useful for this purpose, and following will this be found proportions for admixture that will improve the texture and consistency of the various jams without greatly altering their flavour. Of course, if sold as jams they must be properly described as blended.

After the pulps have been passed, mixed, and weighed, and the proper proportion of sugar added, they must be boiled into jams in exactly the same way as pulped fresh fruits, in most cases requiring rather more boiling, because of the lower percentage of pectose or pectin.

When there is any considerable proportion of apple pulp used with raspberry pulp, or when gooseberry pulp is largely used, gingelly seeds are sometimes added, as these greatly resemble the seed of the raspberry in shape and colour, if of good quality. This seed is the product of Indian sesame (Sesamus orientale), and contains a large percentage of gingelly oil, and is a valuable demulcent. It is in no sense detrimental to health, although it is, of course, an adulterant, masquerading as something else that, by the way, has no food value.

RASPBERRY JAM (BLENDED) (1).

10 lbs. of passed raspberry pulp.
5 lbs. of passed red gooseberry pulp.
15 lbs. of crushed sugar.
A little liquid carmine.

RASPBERRY JAM (BLENDED) (2).

7 lbs. of passed raspberry pulp.
7 lbs. of passed red gooseberry pulp.
14 lbs. of crushed sugar.
$1\frac{1}{2}$ oz. of gingelly seeds.
A little liquid carmine.

RASPBERRY JAM (BLENDED) (3).

10 lbs. of passed raspberry pulp.
5 lbs. of passed apple pulp or juice.
14 lbs. of crushed sugar.
2 lbs. of liquid glucose.
2 ozs. of gingelly seeds.
Liquid carmine to colour.

RASPBERRY JAM PURE (4).

15 lbs. of passed raspberry pulp.
15 lbs. of crushed sugar.
$1\frac{1}{2}$ oz. of agar-agar (thoroughly soften in the pulp before adding the sugar).
Little liquid carmine.

All about Ices.

Glucose, when used, must be boiled as little as possible, as it discolours rapidly, therefore add shortly before the jam is finished.

Carmine also, to retain its brightness, needs very little boiling, and must be added at a late stage. Gingelly seeds, which often need washing, can be added at the start, to ensure thorough permeation by the sugar, otherwise they will float.

The glucose given in No. 3, the one in which apple pulp is used, is intended to counteract the shortness given by apple pulp.

RASPBERRY AND RED CURRANT.

9 lbs. of passed raspberry pulp. 15 lbs. of crushed sugar.
6 lbs. of passed red currant pulp. A little liquid carmine.

This mixture will make an admirable jam, almost equal to that from fresh fruit, but will need a little longer boiling, as well as a little colour.

APRICOT JAM FROM PULP (1).

1 5-kilo can of apricot pulp 10 lbs. of crushed sugar.

Pass the pulp through a six-mesh sieve into the pan, add the sugar, and boil until the webbing point is reached. This jam will be suitable for all ordinary purposes, such as spreading on sandwiches and Swiss roll, tartlets, etc., but not for masking.

APRICOT JAM (BLENDED) (2).

1 5-kilo can of apricot pulp. 5 lbs. of pale apple pulp.
15 lbs. of crushed sugar.

Pass and treat exactly as for No. 1, but the addition of the apple pulp will give a little firmer body to the jam, which will not run so freely if baked in tartlets or notched tarts.

APRICOT JAM (3).

1 5-kilo can of apricot pulp. 11 lbs. of crushed sugar.
1½ oz. of agar agar.

Pass the pulp on to the agar-agar (loosely separated), and allow it to soften and expand before adding the sugar. Then boil to the webbing point.

APRICOT CONSERVE FOR MASKING (4).

1 5-kilo can of apricot pulp. 20 lbs. of small-crushed sugar.

Pass through an eight-mesh sieve, add the sugar and boil quickly, and much higher than usual, so that when used hot it will set firmly. This conserve is best in colour when used directly it is boiled, and as continually heating darkens it, a very usual plan is to boil it with half the quantity of sugar at first, and reboil small quantities as required, adding fine sugar to each small lot.

In choosing apricot pulp care is necessary to select suitable kinds. As a rule the most suitable is the French, as the best kinds are pale in colour. This is always in 5-kilo cans, packed ten in a case. The pulp is gross for net, that is, the cans weigh 5 kilos, cans and all.

Spanish pulp is almost always deeper in colour than the French, but of good quality and flavour. The packages are the same size and weight.

Jams and Conserves.

Italian pulp is much the same colour as the Spanish, although some of it is as pale as the French. It is in 5-kilo cans, as well as larger ones.

Californian pulp is packed in 7-lb. or gallon cans, each case containing twelve cans. This pulp at its best is of finer flavour than the French, varies a good deal in colour, and is generally more watery than any of the other packs. San José is one of the highest grades, but many good packs are available.

Australia and New Zealand are now sending splendid apricot as well as other good pulps here. These are packed in high square-sided tins of different weights, from 10 lbs. to 14 lbs. each, and are well worth sampling.

RED GOOSEBERRY JAM FROM PULP.

14 lbs. of passed red gooseberry pulp.   14 lbs. of crushed sugar.
A little liquid carmine.

Pass through a five-mesh sieve, add the sugar, and boil to the webbing point, adding the carmine when nearly finished. This gives a jam of good consistency and fine acid flavour, and is suitable for all cheaper goods.

GREEN GOOSEBERRY PULP.

This pulp has always a more or less defined pinkish colour, and will not therefore make green jam. It can be used to blend with red gooseberry, but the seeds retain a partial green colour which does not matter in jam that is admittedly gooseberry, but objectionable as a blend with raspberry.

GREENGAGE JAM FROM PULP (1).

14 lbs. of passed greengage pulp.   14 lbs. of fine-crushed sugar.
Very little apple green.

GREENGAGE JAM (BLENDED) (2).

10 lbs. of passed greengage pulp.   15 lbs. of fine-crushed sugar.
5 lbs. of white apple pulp.   Little apple green.

GREENGAGE JAM (BLENDED) (3).

10 lbs. of passed greengage pulp.   16 lbs. of crushed sugar.
6 pints of apple juice.   Little apple greening.

Cut some white-fleshed cooking apples into quarters, put in a copper jam boiler, cover with water, and boil until soft and pulped. Turn into a large flannel jelly bag, and let the juice run until the pulp is quite dry. Measure out six pints into the above mixture, and boil until the webbing point is reached, when a very little apple greening should be added to give a pale tint. This will make jam of good flavour and colour and first-rate consistency.

The pulp remaining in the bag can be passed through a fine mesh sieve and used for making Banbury or Eccles meat.

GREEN VICTORIA PLUM PULP.

This can be used the same way as greengage pulp, and will give almost the same results, except that the flavour will not be so good.

All about Ices.

VICTORIA PLUM JAM (1).

14 lbs. of passed Victoria plum pulp. 2 ozs. of agar-agar.
14 lbs. of crushed sugar. Little liquid carmine.

VICTORIA PLUM JAM (BLENDED) (2).

10 lbs. of passed Victoria plum pulp. 15 lbs. of crushed sugar.
4 lbs. of passed apple pulp. Little liquid carmine.

As this fruit is red-skinned and yellow-fleshed the pulp is rather indeterminate in colour, but readily takes the added colour, and although there is very little mucilage left in it, the addition of the agar-agar in the one case and the apple pulp in the other will result in jam of good flavour and texture. The agar-agar must be well swollen before the sugar is added, or there will be great trouble to dissolve it afterwards.

RED CURRANT JAM (PURE).

14 lbs. of passed red currant pulp. 15 lbs. of sugar.
Little liquid carmine.

Pass through a six-mesh sieve, add the sugar, and boil to the webbing point, adding the colour just before the boiling is finished.

White currant pulp can be used with red in any proportion, provided the proper tint is obtained afterwards, as there is little difference beyond colour in the two fruits.

This jam is not so well liked as it deserves to be, the acid being too pronounced for most tastes. The pulp, however, is so useful for blending with raspberry and black currant, as well as for making into jelly, that its lack of popularity as a jam need not be regretted.

BLACK CURRANT JAM (PURE) (1).

14 lbs. of passed black currant pulp 15 lbs. of crushed sugar.

BLACK CURRANT JAM (BLENDED) (2).

10 lbs. of passed black currant pulp. 5 lbs. of passed red currant pulp.
16 lbs. of crushed sugar.

Pass the pulp through a six-mesh sieve, blend together, add the sugar, and boil to the webbing point. No colour should be needed. The No. 2 jam with the blend of red currants will be not quite so full in flavour, but, still, very good indeed, and the colour will be brighter. Great care will be needed in preparing the black currant pulp, but full instructions will be given in dealing with the preservation of pulps.

MIRABEL JAM (PURE).

14 lbs. of passed mirabel pulp. 15 lbs. of crushed sugar.

Treat as for pure apricot from pulp, and the result will be a pale yellow semi-transparent jam of beautiful flavour.

GISBON PLUM JAM (PURE).

14 lbs. passed Gisbon plum pulp. 15 lbs. of crushed sugar.

Jams and Conserves.

GISBON PLUM JAM (BLENDED) (2).

10 lbs. passed Gisbon plum pulp.   5 pints of apple juice.
15 lbs. of crushed sugar.

Treat No. 1 as for apricot pulp jam, and the result will be a pale yellow jam of good flavour and body.

No. 2.—The apple juice for this must be made in the same way as for greengage jam No. 2. This blend will give a slightly paler coloured jam of greater body and good flavour.

DAMSON JAM (PURE) (1).

14 lbs. of passed damson pulp.   15 lbs. of crushed sugar.

DAMSON JAM (BLENDED) (2).

10 lbs. of passed damson pulp.   16 lbs. of crushed sugar.
5 lbs. of passed red or white currant pulp.

DAMSON JAM (BLENDED) (3).

10 lbs. of passed damson pulp.   5 pints of apple juice.
16 lbs. of crushed sugar.

Pass the damson pulp through a fine mesh sieve, and treat all of these formulæ exactly as for the other plums, being very careful in stirring to prevent burning. No. 1 will give a rich, deep-coloured, full-flavoured jam, very astringent. No. 2 will be lighter in colour, very delicate, and, like No. 3, less astringent. No. 3 will be paler, not so rich in flavour, but of first-rate body, and be more generally liked than No. 1.

JELLIES.

The chief of these in use is, of course, red currant, but there are many others, especially in the United States, where very little jam, except the imported article is used. Jellies consist mainly of the juice of fruit and sugar, boiled to the webbing point, and if made from fresh fruit seldom require any mucilaginous assistance. In the cheaper grades agar-agar or Japanese gelatine, the product of a particular type of seaweed, is often the groundwork upon which many varieties are founded. We have no desire to see these makeshifts popular here, but hope to be able to show in various forms how agar-agar may be used in a perfectly legitimate way by the confectioner.

RED CURRANT JELLY (FRESH FRUIT (1).

The best way to make high grade jelly is to choose large ripe fruit, wash it in a wicker sieve on the stalks, pick from the stalks into an enamelled pan, pass by pressure through a coarse wicker or a five-mesh brass sieve, add the necessary amount of water (as below), heat up to 200 deg. F., and pour into a thin flannel jelly bag for all the juice to run through. Once passing will be sufficient; it need not be quite clear, but get through all the juice possible, leaving the pulp almost dry. Measure the juice, and for every pint add 1 lb. of fine crushed sugar. Boil quickly to the webbing point in a copper pan. No colour will be required; the jelly will be quite bright, of beautiful colour and flavour, and should be at once filled into small pots or glass jars, and when set covered down in the usual manner.

All about Ices.

RED CURRANT JELLY (PULPED FRUIT) (2).

Assuming that the pulp has been passed through a five-mesh sieve before storing, turn out a jar into a copper preserving pan, heat up to 200 deg., turn into a thin flannel jelly bag, and let the juice run through until the pulp is practically dry. Measure the juice, add to each pint 1 lb. 2 ozs. of fine crushed sugar and $\frac{1}{8}$ oz. of agar-agar. Let the latter steep in the juice for half an hour, then add the sugar, and boil to the webbing point.

RED CURRANT JELLY FROM BOTTLED FRUIT (3).

Fruit that has been bottled in water is often used for tart making, the fruit turned out on to a sieve to drain away the water, which is wholly or in part thrown away. It should never be wasted, for much of the flavour as well as the mucilage is in the water. Strain it either through a jelly bag, a fine hair sieve, or a tammy cloth, add to each pint $\frac{1}{4}$ oz. of agar-agar and 1 lb. of sugar after the gelatine has steeped and swollen, and quickly boil to the slight webbing point, adding, if needed, a few drops of liquid carmine. This need not be boiled too highly, as the gelatine will set the jelly. Jelly made in this is particularly useful half melted, or, rather thoroughly melted and allowed to partly cool, for covering after baking small or large open tarts made from the drained fruit, as well as for many other purposes.

If desired, jelly can be made with both fruit and water, in which case the fruit should be passed through a five-mesh sieve, heated with the water, strained, and in the after measuring only two-thirds of the agar-agar used.

White currant jelly from fresh fruit, from pulp, and from bottled fruit should be made in the same way as for red.

BLACK CURRANT JELLY.

This should always be made from fresh fruit very ripe, should be washed, picked, and passed through a five-mesh sieve, and well pulped by boiling for five minutes in half its weight of water. Then turn into a thin flannel bag, and well drain away the juice. Measure this, and to each pint add 1 lb. of fine crushed sugar, and boil to the webbing point. Pour at once into small pots or glass jars, and when cold cover with small round of vegetable parchment dipped into brandy and drained nearly dry, and cover down in the usual way.

The usual covering for all these jars and pots is thin vegetable parchment, cut in squares, dipped into water, and allowed to nearly dry, stretched and tied, and again stretched, and when dry trimmed with scissors.

Black and red currant juice or black and white currant juice can be blended in the proportions of two to one, and will make beautiful jelly not quite so full in flavour or so deep in colour as the black alone

RED GOOSEBERRY JELLY (FRESH FRUIT) (1).

Use firm almost ripe Warringtons or Crown Bobs. Wash well, and boil with sufficient water to cover them, stirring constantly until the fruit is thoroughly pulped. This will take from ten to fifteen minutes if the fruit be in exactly the right condition, but if it does not break down easily, add a little more water, and continue boiling until well pulped. Turn into the thin flannel jelly bag, and run the juice away. If the pulp

Jams and Conserves.

remaining in the bag be still fruity, do not waste it, but use for cheap filling Banbury meat instead of apples.

Measure the juice, and for each pint add a pound of fine crushed sugar, and quickly boil to the webbing point. This will make a fine coloured and flavoured jelly of good consistency, and sharply acid.

RED GOOSEBERRY JELLY FROM PULP (2).

Turn out a jar of red gooseberry pulp, pass through a five-mesh sieve, add one quart of water to each 10 lbs. of pulp, bring up to the boil, turn into the bag, and drain away the juice. To each pint add 1 lb. of fine crushed sugar, and quickly boil to the webbing point, adding a few drops of liquid carmine to brighten the colour, if necessary.

GREEN GOOSEBERRY FROM BOTTLED FRUIT.

Green gooseberries in water (bottled) are generally used for open tarts, and they must be covered after baking, and apricot conserve is much too deeply yellow to give a good appearance, it is always a good plan to strain away the water from the fruit (the water is heavily charged with mucilage), and boil it with sugar in the proportion of 1 lb. of sugar to each pint of juice into a colourless jelly that when spread over the cooked fruit will add to both appearance and flavour at a very small cost.

When fresh fruit is used for open tarts the jelly for covering can be made by first half boiling the fruit in water before using (which will largely prevent the usual shrivelling in the oven), and, after straining the water away, add a few of the parboiled fruits, and boil them down to a pulp in the water, strain through a hair sieve, add sugar in the same proportion as before, and boil quickly to the webbing point.

TART FRUIT GENERALLY IN WATER.

All fruits that are bottled in water for tart making during the winter and spring can be advantageously covered with jelly made from the water, care being taken that any having a lack of mucilage are toned up with a little agar-agar. Of these, cherries and most kinds of plums are the chief. These jellies can always be suitably tinted to enhance the appearance of the fruit. They should be used in semi-set condition, and always be run over the fruit with a dessertspoon.

RASPBERRY JELLY (FRESH FRUIT) (1).

This is a splendid jelly, and far too seldom used. In lusciousness it leaves raspberry jam a long way behind.

Pass the fresh fruit through a five-mesh sieve, heat the pulp to 200 deg. F., and at once pour into a thin flannel jelly bag, and allow the juice to drain away, leaving the pulp almost dry. (The pulp can be added to a batch of raspberry jam the same day to avoid waste.) Measure the juice, and to each pint add 1 lb. of fine crushed sugar, and boil quickly to the webbing point. A more delicate jelly, a little more troublesome to make, can be produced as follows:—Pass the fruit as before through a five-mesh sieve, stand a wooden cradle over an enamelled pan, stand a coarse hair sieve on this, pour the passed pulp into the sieve, cover the whole with a clean cloth, and stand the whole in a cool place until next day, when the juice will have run clear from the pulp. (Throw the pulp away.

All about Ices.

for it is almost certain to be slightly fermented.) Measure the juice, add 1 lb. of fine crushed sugar to each pint, and quickly boil to the webbing point. The flavour of this jelly will be distinctly more fresh than that made from the heated pulp.

RASPBERRY JELLY FROM PULP (2).

Turn out a jar of pulp into the sugar boiler, add one-fifth of its weight in water, heat up to 200 deg. F., turn into the jelly bag, and run the juice away. The pulp remaining may be added to a boiling of raspberry jam, the same day to avoid waste. Measure the juice, and to each pint add one-sixth of an ounce of agar-agar, and when steeped and swollen add 1 lb. of sugar to each pint, and quickly boil to the webbing point, stirring continuously to ensure the dissolving of the gelatine, which might otherwise leave strings undissolved. If necessary, add a few drops of liquid carmine to brighten.

STRAWBERRY JELLY (FRESH FRUIT).

This jelly, like that from black currants, should always be made from fresh fruit. There are many types of this fruit that can be used, and many that are not at all suitable. It may be taken as a general rule that the red-fleshed fruits are the most and the white-fleshed the least suitable. Of the red, the small wild Scarlett is the best of all, next to these Paxtons, Doctor Hoggs, etc., all of them of good body and colour. Of the white-fleshed the Royal Sovereign is for delicacy of flavour an easy first, but like most of the white-fleshed varieties, it is very watery, and cooking entirely destroys its delicate flavour.

Whichever fruit you choose, let it be ripe and in fine condition. Pick off the hulls, pass the fruit through a coarse hair or wicker sieve by rubbing, add an equal weight of fine unblued castor sugar, and mix thoroughly with a spattle   Let it stand for three hours undisturbed, by which time the juice will begin to separate from the pulp. Turn it carefully into a thin flannel jelly bag, so pouring in that the bulk of the juice goes in first and the pulp last. This plan will avoid the pulp partially blocking the pores of the bag, leaving them free for the exodus of the juice. Do this in the evening, and next morning, when the whole of the juice is through, measure it into a copper preserving pan, add to each pint one-sixth of an ounce of agar-agar, and quickly boil to the webbing point; not too high, as the gelatine will give body. It is a good plan to estimate that for every 6 lbs. of sugar used you will obtain six pints of juice, and then to place the estimated quantity of agar-agar in the pan, and allow the juice to filter through the bag on top of the gelatine, which will give it ample time to steep and expand.

If in making this jelly one-fourth part of red currant juice be used to three parts of strawberry juice, adjusting the sugar accordingly, one-third of the agar-agar may be omitted, and the resulting jelly will have greater body and an added pleasant acidity.

CRANBERRY JELLY (FRESH FRUIT).

This is a most useful jelly, being strongly acid and astringent, and, used in small quantities, gives an added zest to game sauces, &c. There are three distinct varieties of cranberries, the largest being the Michigan or Cape Cod kind. The medium-sized ones are the Scottish, and the small ones the German and Dutch variety, which come over here in water in casks, and masquerade as red currants in the penny pie shops. The Michigan ones are well known, are universally used in America as a sauce with roast turkey, and are gaining favour here. These make first-rate jelly. The Scottish variety

Jams and Conserves.

have only lately appeared in London in any quantity, are softer, fuller in flavour than the Michigan, and make splendid jelly. The Dutch may be safely left to the pie shops

Whichever of the two first be used, they should be placed in a preserving pan with sufficient water to cover them when pressed down. Bring up to the boil slowly, stirring continuously with a spattle until entirely pulped. Do not be afraid of being shot when the popping commences. The fruit is hollow, cellular inside, and the air expansion causes the explosions.

When fully pulped, turn into the jelly bag and let the juice run free from the pulp. Measure the juice, and for each pint add, if Michigan, one-sixth of an ounce, if Scottish one-eighth of an ounce, of agar-agar, and when steeped and swollen 1 lb. 2 ozs. of fine crushed sugar, and quickly boil to the webbing point. The result will be a fine, bright, acid, astringent jelly of first-class flavour. The Scottish cranberries will give a rather deeper-coloured jelly than the Michigan.

APPLE JELLY (FRESH FRUIT) (1).

Choose white-fleshed cooking apples for this purpose, either Wellingtons, Suffields, Keswicks, unripe Blenheim Orange, Greenings, or any similar sorts. Wipe them, cut in quarters, being careful that no bruises or bad spots remain, put in the preserving pan and cover with water, and quickly boil to smash. Turn into the jelly bag, and let the whole of the juice drain away. (The pulp remaining may be passed through an eight-mesh sieve, and be used for Eccles or Banbury meat.)

Measure the juice, and to each pint add 1 lb. of fine crushed sugar, after reducing the juice by boiling for ten minutes, and boil to the webbing point. This jelly will be quite firm and of a very pale straw colour if the apples have been carefully chosen. If desired, a portion may be coloured with liquid carmine. Both colours are very useful for decorative work, and are also useful for running into shapes in starch powder, and afterwards crystallising. They are both decorative and of fine flavour.

APPLE JELLY (CHERRY APPLES) (2).

The small cherry apples, once so common in apple orchards, make splendid jelly of a deep orange colour if treated exactly the same way, but with rather more water for boiling, as they have little moisture.

The bright red apple jelly is a useful article for decorative work, and, given a few starch trays and small plaster moulds, can be easily and economically prepared. The best shapes are round for cherries, pear shapes, crescents, etc., etc. When the impressions are made in the starch, which must be dry, well sifted, and struck off quite smoothly, melt the jelly thoroughly and with a fondant funnel and stop stick run into the impressions. Let the trays stand in the drying room for a few hours, sift away all the starch from the fruit shapes, and when about to use for decoration wash away the starch from the surface in warm water, and your bright jelly shapes can be used as desired.

MARMALADE.

In this country the term marmalade has become associated exclusively with the conserve made from oranges or lemons, and apparently suggests nothing else. In the Latin countries, however, it is the generic title of conserves of all kinds. This evolution

All about Ices.

is almost as curious as our exclusive use for one type, because both the Italian title "marmelata" and the Spanish "marmelada" mean in trade parlance "quince" or "honey apple." Both these are only trade terms, and apparently evolved from "melimelon," or "melimelion," and the prefix "mar" (bitter) fairly well fits itself to the product of bitter oranges. It is a curious feature of trade association that in many parts of the Continent marmalade as we understand it is almost universally known not as marmalade, but as "keiller."

PREPARATION OF PEEL AND PULP.

Place the oranges, whether bitter or sweet, in a clean tub, and pour boiling water over them, sufficient to well cover. Let them stand in this for 15 or 20 minutes. Then change into cold water. With a sharp knife cut the peel of each orange into four equal parts and strip the peel away. Throw both peel and pulp into cold water, but in separate vessels. Then with either a sharp knife or slicing machine slice the peel into very thin shreds. Place the sliced peel in a copper pan with plenty of water, and boil gently until the peel is soft and mellow. Drain this on wicker or hair sieves. Place the pulp, preferably torn to pieces, in a copper pan with a little water, sufficient to start the pulping, and boil quickly, stirring continually until the whole is thoroughly pulped. Then pass through an eight-mesh brass sieve to break up evenly and to remove the pithy matter and pips. If only comparatively small quantities be made at a time, the easiest after method is to add the shredded drained peel to the passed pulp, weigh the whole, add an equal weight of fine crushed sugar, and as quickly as possible boil to the webbing point. Where larger quantities are being handled, however, certain proportions of peel and pulp are weighed out of the bulk for each boiling. The following are examples:—

No. 1.—SEVILLE ORANGE MARMALADE.

10 lbs. of passed pulp (Seville oranges).

5 lbs. of shredded peel (Seville oranges).

15 lbs. of fine crushed sugar.

No. 2.—SEVILLE ORANGE MARMALADE.

9 lbs. of passed pulp (Seville oranges).
5 lbs. of shredded peel (Seville oranges).

$11\frac{1}{2}$ lbs. fine crushed sugar.
5 lbs. of glucose, added when almost finished boiling.

No. 3.—SEVILLE ORANGE MARMALADE.

10 lbs. of passed pulp (Seville oranges).
3 lbs. of shredded peel (Seville oranges).

1 quart of passed apple juice.
15 lbs. of fine crushed sugar.

Sweet oranges can be used either alone or in any proportion with the bitter ones, the process being exactly the same.

If it is desired to make the marmalade perfectly bright the juice should be strained clear from the pulp after boiling, and then boiled in the proportions below.

CLEAR ORANGE MARMALADE.

10 lbs. of passed orange juice (Seville).
3 lbs. of passed apple juice.

4 lbs. of shredded peel (Seville).
17 lbs. of fine crushed sugar.

Jams and Conserves.

A very seldom made but delicious marmalade is that from Tangerine oranges. At certain seasons they can be bought very cheaply, and are then well worth using. It will not be necessary to parboil these in boiling water, for there is no great bitterness to remove, and quite sufficient of the flavouring oil will be lost during the boiling of the shredded peels. The peels, however, are rather brittle, and can be handled more easily for 15 minutes' steeping in warm, not hot, water.

TANGERINE ORANGE MARMALADE.

10 lbs. of Tangerine oranges (representing only 8 lbs. of rind and pulp).
3 pints of passed apple juice.
12 lbs. of fine crushed sugar.

ORANGE PUREE.

This is useful for confectioners' purposes, and can be utilised where marmalade with the shredded peel would be objectionable. It is best made with sweet oranges, which should be treated exactly as described for ordinary Seville orange marmalade, except that the peel after shredding, boiling, and draining must be pounded smooth in a mortar and rubbed througd a ten-mesh brass sieve. Then boil as follows:—

10 lbs. of passed pulp.
5 lbs. of passed peel.
3 pints of passed apple juice.
18 lbs. of fine crushed sugar.

Boiled in the usual way to the webbing point.

LEMON MARMALADE.

This is made in exactly the same way as orange marmalade, except that it is necessary to use a higher proportion of sugar. The addition of a small proportion of passed apple juice is a distinct advantage to its consistency. The following will give good results:—

10 lbs. of passed lemon pulp.
5 lbs. of finely shredded lemon rind.
3 pints of passed apple juice.
20 lbs. of fine crushed sugar.

Boil in the usual way to the webbing point.

FRUIT PASTES.

These pastes are seldom used in England except by the sweet-making houses for various fruit shapes, and even then are mostly different in composition. In France, Spain, Portugal, and Italy, as well as Finland, they are largely made in various fancy shapes, with many in imitation of sections of fruit, and in the first three countries (where jams, as we use them, are seldom of home manufacture) they are made in thick sheets, cut out in blocks, and retailed by weight. The chief forms that have a sale here are entire small fruits, like raspberries and strawberries, and sections of larger ones, such as orange and lemon sections, slices of apples, &c., from Finland, and brochettes, lunettes, and twisted knots, which come chiefly from France and Italy.

The foundation of all these pastes is the pulp of the quince and the apple, blended for certain purposes with the pulps and rinds of other fruits. The chief of these are oranges, lemons, apricots, peaches, and pears.

In each case it is essential to use fresh fruit, which must be carefully selected.

Quince must be fully grown, quite hard, with the skin just turning yellow and unbruised, but is seldom obtainable here in quantities, so must give place to apples.

All about Ices.

Apples.—Must be white-fleshed, Wellingtons, Suffields, Keswicks, Blenheim Orange, or any of the white-fleshed Pippins, Codlins, or Greenings, Warner's King, etc., all of which must be fully grown, but hard and unripe.

Pears.—There are very few sorts grown in this country that are suitable for fruit-paste making, and less that are fit for preserving whole. Of the early pears, the Hazel, when hard and green, is quite suitable, and is always fairly low in price. Of the later ones, the Flemish Bon Chrétien, Black Worcester, Verulam, and Catillac, are all good, but large in size and rather high in price. The Chaumontel, which is really a fine dessert pear when fully ripe, gives, when used in the hard, unripe state, the whitest and best-flavoured pulp; but it is seldom sufficiently low in price to admit of its use.

Peaches.—Any of the white-fleshed free-stone varieties are suitable, but are seldom obtainable here at prices low enough to permit of their use.

Apricots.—The early French or Italian fruits are in the London markets about the same time as the early apples, are generally moderate in price, and are preferable to the cheaper canned pulps, because the pulp is firmer and added water has not to be evaporated.

Oranges and Lemons.—For blending purposes these are only employed in small proportions, and are nearly always available.

Pulping.—Quinces, apples, and pears are all pulped in the same way. Place them in a copper or enamelled pan with sufficient water to cover them. Slowly bring the water up to 200 deg. Fah. Do not let it boil, but keep as near this heat as possible, until the fruit can be easily pierced with a thin pointed stick. Lift out carefully into cold water. The peel must then be carefully and quickly removed and the fruit sliced down to the core, which must be discarded. (The cores can afterwards be boiled in water, drawn through a bag, and jelly made with the resulting juice.) A silver knife must be used for peeling and slicing, the pieces dropped on a coarse hair sieve, and an assistant must rub through into pulp as fast as the fruit is sliced.

Apricots and Peaches must first be lightly pricked all over (*see* Preserving), blanched in hot water for a much shorter time, turned into cold water, split in halves, the stones removed, and the pulp passed in the same way as before.

Oranges and Lemons must be treated exactly as for marmalades (rind only), and, after, boiling, the rinds must be pounded and passed, and used as described below.

BOILING THE PULP INTO PASTES.

There are two ways of arriving at the same result, one being to boil the sugar to the hard ball and add to the prepared pulps, the other to use fine unblued pulverised sugar and add it dry. Both will give good results if the instructions are carefully attended to.

All pastes must be cooked in a copper preserving pan stood over another pan containing water that is kept boiling. This is essential, so that a good colour may be assured. The higher temperature of an open fire in contact with the pan would quickly result in discoloration.

QUINCE PASTE.

2 lbs. of quince pulp.

$2\frac{1}{4}$ lbs. fine crushed sugar boiled with water to the hard ball, or use instead $2\frac{1}{4}$ lbs. fine unblued pulverised sugar.

Jams and Conserves.

QUINCE AND APPLE PASTE.

2 lbs. of quince pulp
2 lbs. of apple pulp.

4¼ lbs. of fine crushed sugar boiled with water to the hard ball, or use instead 4¼ lbs. of fine unblued pulverised sugar.

APPLE PASTE.

2 lbs. of apple pulp.

2 lbs. of fine crushed sugar boiled to the hard ball, or use instead 2 lbs. of fine unblued pulverised sugar.

PEAR PASTE.

2 lbs. of pear pulp.
1 lb. of quince or apple pulp.
1 teaspoonful of kirsch.

3¼ lbs. of fine crushed sugar boiled to the hard ball, or use instead 3¼ lbs. of unblued pulverised sugar.
1 drop of Jargonelle essence.

PEACH PASTE.

1 lb. of peach pulp.
3 lbs. of quince or apple pulp.
2 ozs. of blanched bitter almonds pounded to a smooth paste.

4¼ lbs. of fine crushed sugar, or use instead 4¼ lbs. of fine uncoloured pulverised sugar

1 dessertspoonful of noyeau (liqueur).

APRICOT PASTE (1).

2 lbs. of apricot pulp.
2 lbs of apple pulp.
1 dessertspoonful of kirsch.

4¼ lbs. of fine crushed sugar, or use instead 4¼ lbs. of fine unblued pulverised sugar
1 oz. of blanched bitter almonds pounded to a smooth paste.

APRICOT PASTE (2).

2 lbs. of apricot pulp.
5 lbs. of fine crushed sugar, or use instead 5 lbs. of unblued pulverised sugar.

1 lb. of apple pulp.

1 dessertspoonful of noyeau (liqueur).

No. 2 apricot paste is admirably adapted for moulding in starch in any fancy shapes for decorative work, or for running out in small medallions on waxed paper, drying in the warm room, and afterwards cutting into fancy shapes, or setting between dry petits fours, etc. All of the above pastes are boiled—or, rather, evaporated—over the water bath until the proper consistency is obtained, the stirring being continuous. A small piece dropped on a cold plate will quickly show if it be sufficiently evaporated.

All about Ices.

If the pastes be intended for cutting out in fancy shapes, the colours must be decided upon and added just before the paste is ready to turn out. Have ready some shallow wooden trays, line them on bottom and edges with waxed paper, pour in the paste, and spread 3-16in. thick for brochettes and knots and ⅛ in. thick for lunettes, with a gauge-stick, and set in the warm room for 24 hours or more, until sufficiently dry to handle easily, when they can be turned on to a clean slab lightly dusted with sugar, the paper stripped off, and cut into the required shapes.

Brochettes are cut out with a plain round cutter, ⅞ in. in diameter, and threaded on straws ready for crystallising. Five-inch straws will each carry eleven or twelve. If the straws be very fine, two should be used for each set. Only one colour should be on each straw or straws. The usual colours for these are white, orange, bright red, and bright green. The coating with crystals will tone down the deeper tints, so this must be allowed for in colouring.

Knots.—Cut the ¾-in. thick sheets into strips ¼ in. wide and 7 ins. long, and carefully twist into true-lovers' knots with slightly extending ends, and set on the crystallising wires.

Lunettes.—Cut the ⅛-in. sheets into strips 6 ins long and ½ in. wide, turn each end inward until the rolled ends meet, then set them on their edges on the crystallising wires. Should these show a tendency to uncurl, prepare a number of small, stiff paper rings the necessary size, press them flat, open them, and slip over the lunettes to hold them in shape until they are set and firm. The crystallising must not be done until the cut edges are quite dry. The remaining pastes for this purpose are orange and lemon, but they are very seldom used.

ORANGE PASTE.

2 lbs. of apple pulp.
¼ lb. of orange-rind pulp.
1 dessertspoonful of orange-flower water (triple).

2½ lbs. of fine crushed sugar boiled to the hard ball, or use instead 2½ lbs. fine unblued pulverised sugar.
A few drops of infusion of saffron and very little liquid carmine.

LEMON PASTE.

2 lbs. of quince pulp.
1 lb. of apple pulp.
½ lb. of lemon-rind pulp.

3½ lbs. of fine crushed sugar boiled to the hard ball, or use instead 3½ lbs. of fine unblued pulverised sugar.

Both of these to be evaporated over the water bath, exactly as for the other pastes.

CRYSTALLISING THE PASTES.

When dry, set the various forms on the wires in the crystallising tins (see Crystallising), boil some clarified syrup to 32 deg. by the saccharometer, allow it to cool, and when it shows 65 degrees of heat by the thermometer, pour it over and entirely cover the trays of pastes. Set in a warm place for 24 hours, and then examine the fruit. If the deposit of crystals is sufficient, drain away the syrup and allow the fruit to dry in the warm room, when the crystals will be much more in evidence.

The size of the crystals will depend not only upon the strength of the syrup, but also upon its heat. The colder the syrup the finer the crystals, and *vice-versa*.

Jams and Conserves.

BLACK CURRANT PASTE (1).

This paste is useful for lozenges, drops, &c., and is a valuable stomachic and demulcent. It can be made either from fresh fruit or pulped stored fruit, the fresh being the richer in flavour. Pulp the fruit free from seeds, and use in either of the following proportions:

2 lbs. of black currant pulp.   2¼ lbs. of fine crushed sugar boiled to the little ball, or use instead 2½ lbs. of fine unblued pulverised sugar.

BLACK CURRANT PASTE (2).

2 lbs. of black currant pulp free from seeds.   1 lb. of red currant pulp free from seeds.

3½ lbs. of fine crushed sugar boiled to the little ball, or use instead 3½ lbs. of unblued pulverised sugar.

BLACK CURRANT PASTE (3).

2 lbs. of black currant pulp free from seeds.   2¾ lbs. of fine crushed sugar boiled to the little ball, or use instead 2¾ lbs. of unblued pulverised sugar.
½ lb. of passed apple or passed quince pulp.

Evaporate each of these in exactly the same way as for quince paste, and, when the proper consistency has been reached, either run 3-16ths of an inch thick on waxed-paper covered trays, dry, and cut out into lozenges with a small ellipse-shaped cutter, and dry and crystallise, or run into shapes, moulded in starch trays, using fine pulverised sugar sifted very light instead of starch, covering the shapes entirely with sifted sugar after filling. Dry in the warm room, and sift away the sugar when set. The shapes should be thin lozenge shape.

Another plan is to run the paste into starch impressions, and when dry wash the starch off the surface in water and roll in fine castor. But, unless carefully dried afterwards, the surface sugar is apt to be damp, if not wet, and the lozenges quickly get out of condition.

DAMSON CHEESE PASTE.

This paste was once a great favourite, and can easily again become so. It is best made f om fruit preserved in bottles, without water (*see* Preserved Fruits). The fruit should be turned out, passed through a hair sieve or eight-mesh brass sieve, to remove both stones and skins, and to each 1 lb. of pulp add 1 lb. 2 ozs. of fine crushed sugar or the same weight of unblued pulverised sugar. If crushed sugar be used, add sufficient water to dissolve it, and boil to the soft ball. Add the sugar to the heated pulp, and evaporate over a warm bath until the proper consistency is obtained.

Have ready the necessary moulds (small new heart shapes or dariole moulds are suitable), lightly oil them with sweet olive oil, and fill in with the paste. When set they will easily turn out, and must be rinsed in warm water to remove all trace of the oil. The surface will soon dry, and remain bright and glossy. These little shapes can be arranged to sell at any set price from 6d. per lb. upwards, and can be filled daily as required if the paste be made in quantities of, say, a week's supply, after testing the sales for a time. It

All about Ices.

is only necessary to melt the paste slowly in a hot-water bath. These little moulds of paste are pretty certain to show a good return to the first man who starts making them in any district, and if he does not make them from his stored fruit until after the fruit season is over, no rival can start until the following season, the first man having by that time obtained some measure of reputation if he does the thing at all well.

FRUIT PULPS FOR JAM MAKING.

There are two forms of packing fruit pulps for jam making, One, the better, being in one, two, or three gallon stone jars, the other in casks. The cask form is seldom resorted to except when fruit is arriving in unusual quantities, is very cheap, and when jars are scarce, and it is not recommended for the following reasons :—

1. Great bulk generally means loss of colour.
2. Casks are unmanageable, must not be moved, even if they could be easily shifted, because a mould plant always forms on top of good pulp, and shifting or rolling means mixing this with the pulp to its detriment.
3. When a cask is opened the whole of it contents must be used at once.
4. Casks must be tightly bunged whilst the fruit is hot, and the decrease of bulk as the pulp cools is very marked, leaving a large area over which the mould plant spreads, necessitating the taking off of the cask head for its removal, and also leaving at least one-fifth of the cask to dry and leak. Jars are therefore advised.

The jars must be quite clean and dry, and each one must have its cork ready fitted before the filling commences.

The corks must be cut across the grain, otherwise percolation is almost certain. It is well to choose the jars with 2-in. necks, and to have the corks cut to fit. Any large cork-cutter will supply fruit shives to the required size, from 8s. to 10s. per gross, if ordered some time before the fruit season begins.

Fumigation of Jars.—This is an absolute necessity if the pulp is to be kept in good condition. Each package, whether jar or cask, must be well filled with sulphur fumes, for two reasons. The first is that the package is thus sterilised, and the second that the fumes being heavier than the ordinary atmosphere, outside air cannot enter as long as the sulphur fumes are there, and these are only driven out as the pulp expels them.

There are several ways of filling jars with these fumes. The usual plan is quick, effective, but not over nice. It is to cut short 12-in. lengths of canvas or sizal rope, dip half their length into methylated spirit, and roll in pulverised sulphur, light, and hang the lighted end inside the jars, and hold in position with the cork at an angle. In five minutes this should be removed and the cork fitted to the neck until the jar is wanted. This is to avoid an influx of air as the fumes cool and contract. Occasionally pieces of the burnt canvas or rope fall inside the jar, and for this reason the plan has objections. With care, however, this objection may be overcome. The better plan, if many jars have to be treated is to have a small box, tin, zinc, or felt lined, the front to hinge and fasten with a button, and with cork fitted tubes standing up on top. Sulphur can be burned inside in a shallow tin or saucer, the corks removed, and jars inverted over the tubes. This method of filling the jars takes rather longer, as the fumes rise slowly, so fifteen minutes should be allowed for each jar, which can then be removed and corked as before, and another substituted for the one removed. When jars are not on top the corks should be placed in the tubes, as the sulphur fumes are not pleasant to breath.

Jams and Conserves.

The proper way to fill the jars is with a wide spout copper funnel with a shut-off stick, so that the funnel may be lifted to observe the nearness of filling without the danger of overfilling or waste of pulp.

Each jar should be filled right to the top of the neck, allowed to subside a quarter of an inch, not more, a small square of well-washed and dried unbleached calico placed on top, the cork pressed slightly in to get a grip and exclude the air, and a few minutes later driven home with a wooden mallet.

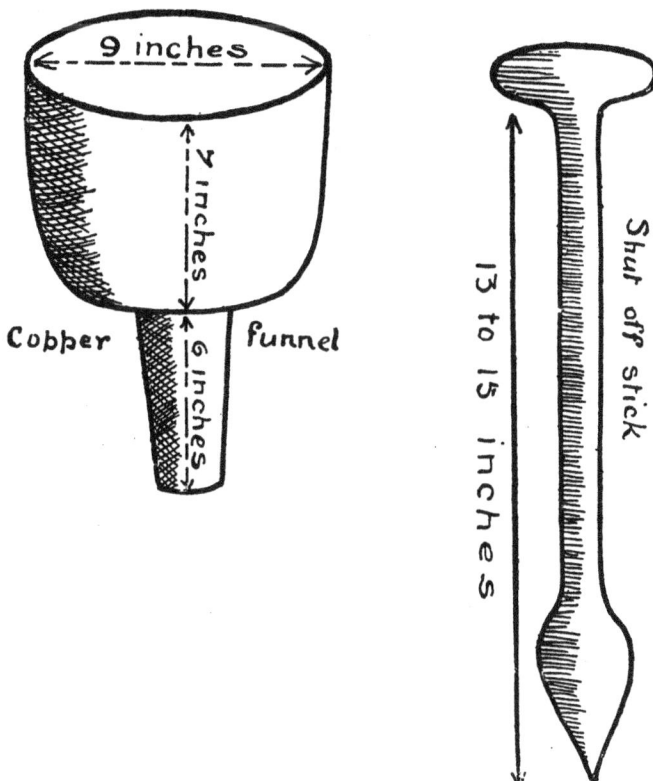

As soon as possible afterwards run a sharp knife across the neck of each jar, cutting off cleanly the top edge of the cork and the edges of the calico. Melt some bottle wax and pour a little over each cork and edges. Label the jars, and stock in cold, dry store, upright, in tiers, with wooden frames between, or on shelves.

The jars must not be laid on their sides, because on top of the pulp in each jar a thick leathery mould plant will form, which must be removed before the pulp is poured out. This mould plant is the hall-mark of good condition, and is never there when from any cause the pulp has fermented. If the jars be laid on their sides there will be a greater surface covered in this way, and it will be impossible to remove without mixing with the pulp, to its great detriment.

RASPBERRY PULP

These must be pulped as soon as possible after received. Use no water, but turn into the pan, bring to a boil as quickly as possible, and boil for a few moments, stirring con-

All about Ices.

tinuously, and turn into the jars all properly sulphured, and store as directed. No pulping through a sieve is necessary, as this will be done before making into jam.

RED OR WHITE CURRANT PULP.

If the fruit be picked from the stalks (not often practicable), turn into the pan with one quart of water for every 10 lbs., bring to the boil, and boil for a few minutes, stirring continuously. Turn into the jars, and store as directed. If not picked, rub through a six-mesh sieve or an equally coarse cane sieve into the pan, rinse the stalks in a little water, squeeze them out dry, add the water to the pulp, and treat as for picked fruit.

GREENGAGE PULP.

Pick the stalks off the fruit, wash them, turn into the pan, add one quart of water to each 10 lbs. of fruit, bring to the boil, stir constantly, and boil until the whole of the fruit is well broken down, then turn into the jars, stones and all, and store as previously directed.

HARD GREEN PLUM PULP.

Treat these exactly as for greengages, allowing a little more water, as they may need boiling a little longer to break them down.

RIPE PLUMS OF ALL SORTS.

Pick off the stalks, wash the fruit, add one quart of water to each 10 lbs. of fruit, boil until quite broken down, stirring continuously. Turn into jars, and store as previously directed.

GREEN GOOSEBERRY PULP.

Well wash the fruit, add one quart of water to each 9 lbs. of fruit, boil until well broken down. Turn into jars, and store as previously directed.

RED GOOSEBERRY.

Well wash the fruit in lots of water, and pick out the leaves (there will be many), add one quart of water to each 10 lbs. of fruit, boil until thoroughly broken down. Jar and store as previously directed.

The green berries are fairly certain to be sound, but there is always danger with over-ripe fruit, and care must be taken to sort out any that is over-ripe or unsound, unless later trouble is desired. Ripe berries are very often dirty from rain and mud splashing, so use great care in washing. If possible, choose Warringtons or Crown Bobs, both hairy varieties.

APPLE PULP.

For ordinary apple pulp that is to be used to tone up red fruit jams the colour is not of great moment. These should be washed, quartered, and thrown into cold water to prevent undue discoloration, and when put in the pan have sufficient water added to cover them when pressed down. Bring to the boil, covered, without stirring, then simmer

Jams and Conserves.

slowly stirring continuously, until well broken down. Turn at once into jars, seal and store as previously directed.

If the apple pulp be desired white, and white pulp is far more valuable than the discoloured, be careful to choose soft white-fleshed apples (see Jams), peel and core with a machine, throw at once into cold water, afterwards boiling and storing as described.

The peel and cores need not be wasted. Do not allow them to discolour, but throw into sufficient cold water to keep them covered, and as soon as may be, boil them in the water without stirring, and turn into a flannel bag for the juice to run through, and boil into second grade apple jelly by using 12 ozs. of fine crushed sugar to each pint of juice. Thus will carefulness be rewarded.

APRICOT PULP.

This fruit is never sufficiently low in price in this country to make it worth while to put down in pulp form. The French, Spanish, Italian, Californian, and latterly the Australian canned apricot pulps are available at prices far below those at which they could be preserved here, and are almost universally used

STRAWBERRY PULP.

This pulp is of little value alone, owing to its want of mucilaginous matter, but the fruit is often so low in price for about one week in the season that it may be worth while to store some of it only for blending with the more mucilaginous pulps.

It must be picked. If boiled with the hulls on, not only is the colour very bad, but the flavour is worse. After picking, turn into the pan as quickly as possible without water, slowly bring to the boil, stirring continually, and boil gently for at least ten minutes. Quickly run into the jars, and seal down as hot as possible, and store as previously described.

BLACK CURRANT PULP.

This has been left until the last, not because it is the least important, but because it is not advised to be pulped at all. The black currant makes one of the very best jams, but does not pulp well. The skins have a tendency to become hard and leathery when stored. If desired they can be treated as red currants, but our advice is to boil the fruit whilst fresh into jam, instead of storing the pulp.

FRUITS BOTTLED IN WATER FOR TARTS, ETC.

All tart fruits can be satisfactorily bottled in water, and under special conditions some can be bottled without water. The advantage of using water is that much less care is needed, and the percentage of loss by breakage and fermentation or mould is reduced to a minimum. The disadvantage is that a portion of the flavour is taken up by the water and unless this can be utilised with the fruit the flavour of the fruit must suffer to some extent. If, however, the water be used reduced to jelly form (see Jellies), and used as a covering, the loss of flavour is infinitesimal. Bottled in this way fruits retain their form, whilst by the other method they are more or less pulped.

All about Ices.

Water.—The water used should be cold spring. Failing this, distilled water will give fine results, but if this be considered too expensive, then it will be necessary to sterilise it by some plan. A perfectly effective plan is to use ordinary town water, place it in a large earthenware pan, and to each 10 gallons add one teaspoonful of powdered alum. Mix thoroughly, cover the pan, and allow to stand for two hours or more, when the water, slightly milky from the admixture, will be almost clear, with a very slight iridescence, and the bulk of the alum showing as a precipitate. The clear water must then be decanted, leaving the precipitated alum in the pan along with, of course, a certain portion of the water. Keep the clear water covered until required for use to avoid contamination from the atmosphere.

Bottles.—Ordinary fruit bottles, six to the gallon, preferably curved to the neck (the ones with sharply-defined shoulders do not empty so freely), and with fairly wide necks, say 1¼ in. to 1¾ in. These should be all the same size in the neck, so that only one size cork is needed. The large-necked ones need longer and more expensive corks, but have the great advantage of removing contents with little breakage.

Clamps.—These are an absolute necessity to effective and economical fruit packing. They are made from hoop steel 1 in. wide, and at least 1-12 in. thick, cut to the shape shown to fit the necks of the bottles to be used, the inbent ends fitting under the second ridge of the neck of the bottles. As the steel has a little spring, they can be pushed into position, but must not fit too tightly, or the pressure will break the glass. After the corks have been driven home, the clamps should be fixed in position accurately in the middle of each cork. This method is much more effective than tying with string, and is fixed in a fraction of the time required for tying.

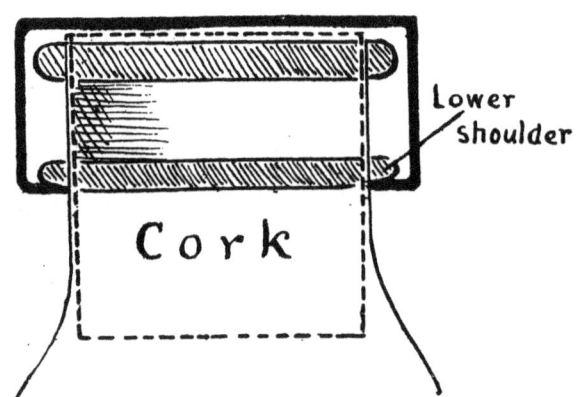

Corks.—Properly-cut fruit shives must be used, the same size their entire length, cut across the grain, and 1¾ in. to 2 ins. long. These will cost from 8s. to 10s. per gross, according to quantity bought and the individual views of the cutter. In all cases they should be bought, like the bottles, some time before the actual season commences.

Bottling Needle.—This is an ingenious little tool that saves much time and many broken bottles and wasted fruit. Any bottler will supply one for a shilling, and it will save its cost many times over in one season. It consists of a pear-shaped handle, to which the needle is hinged so that it can be folded when not in use. The needle itself is from 3 ins. to 4 ins. long, is pointed at the end, rounded on the outside, and on the inside has a grooved channel. In use the channel side is placed against the inside of the bottle neck about 2 ins. down, the bottle being filled to the top of the neck. The cork is pressed in and driven home with a small wooden mallet. The pressure of the cork on the water drives the superfluous water up the channel of the needle so that the cork rests on the water with no air space intervening. If the work be properly done, and the corks good, the bottles are practically full after the scalding is completed. Without the needle the driving in of the cork compresses the water dangerously if quite filled, and if a space be

Jams and Conserves.

left the water is still more or less compressed with an air space between cork and water, and breakages are frequent, and when the fruit has cooled the bottles are never full.

Scalding.—This is best done in some sort of a flat tank with a steam inlet, especially if many bottles are being done at one time. The bottles can then rest flat on a sack or a layer of straw, be covered in the same way, and layer after layer set on top to within a few inches of the top, and again be well covered down. Should the tank be wide enough, more than one row may be set necks facing one another, but with a piece of sacking or a whisk of hay or straw between. The tank should then be filled with cold water, the steam turned on, and heated as afterwards according to the character of the fruit. Should a tank not be available, and only a few bottles required to be treated at once, a large pot over the open fire will answer, or even an ordinary kitchen boiler, but they must be well packed to avoid the danger of moving and breaking.

GREEN GOOSEBERRIES

must be small and hard, the harder the better will be the colour. Snuff and stalk, fill the bottles to half-way up the neck; tap the bottles a little so that the fruit settles into position, fill up with the prepared water, cork as directed, fit on the clamps, arrange in the tank, and fill with water, and slowly heat up to 180 deg. F. Keep them at this heat for 20 minutes, then bring up to the boil, turn off the steam, and let them gradually get cold. Do not touch for two hours, then run the water off, and when cool enough to handle easily (next morning if the boiling has been done late at night), lift out and examine each bottle. A few of the corks may require driving home again. When quite cold stack all those in which the corks are sound and firm in rows, flat, in a cold, dry warehouse. If there are plenty of clamps, they may be left on the bottles, but if the corks are a close fit this should not be necessary. It is essential that the bottles be packed on their sides so that the water keeps the corks swollen and tight. If the corks get dry they will shrink, and the fruit be spoiled.

RASPBERRIES.

These must be very fresh, carefully picked from the hulls, the bottles filled without breaking the fruit, filled up to the brim with water, corked and clamped, set in the tank as described, and the water slowly raised to 180 deg. F., and kept at that temperature for 20 minutes, then slowly raised to 212 deg. F., the steam turned off, and then the fruit must be left untouched for 30 minutes, when the water must be run off and the bottles be left untouched until cold. Examine, and store as previously directed

RASPBERRIES AND CURRANTS.

Treat as for raspberries, except that the fruit is best put in the bottles in layers, currants being both top and bottom.

BLACK CURRANTS

must be firm and dry. Strip carefully from the stalks, fill into bottles, fill up with spring water (the alum water will make them hard and milky), cork, clamp, and heat slowly in tank to 180 deg. F. Rest for 20 minutes, slowly bring up to 212 deg. F., turn off steam, allow to stand for one hour, then run off water. Do not disturb until cold. Carefully examine corks, and store as previously directed.

All about Ices.

MULBERRIES.

Treat these as black currants.

GREENGAGES.

Choose small, hard, unripe fruit. Pick the stalks off, fill into bottles, tapping them a little to settle, fill up with the prepared water, cork, clamp, and heat slowly in tank to 180 deg. F. Rest for 20 minutes, slowly raise to 212 deg. F. Let rest for one hour, then draw off the water, and do not disturb until cold. Examine, and store as previously directed.

All other types of hard green plums may be treated in the same way.

MIRABEL PLUMS (YELLOW).

Pick off the stalk, bottle, fill up with spring water, cork, clamp, and slowly heat in tank to 180 deg. F. Rest for 15 minutes only, then slowly raise to 212 deg. F. Let rest for half an hour only, then run off the water, and do not disturb until cold. Examine, and store as previously directed.

CHERRY PLUMS (RED).

Treat as for mirabels, except that they must not be raised above 200 deg. F., and after standing at this temperature for 15 minutes, the water must be run off. Do not disturb until cold.

ORLEANS PLUMS (EARLY).

Treat as for greengages..

ORLEANS PLUMS (LATE).

Treat as for mirabels.

Gisbon plums, Victoria plums, Pond's Seedling, Magnum Bonum, and most other red or purple plums can be treated exactly as for mirabels.

Washington gages, the late bush plums (purple), and all other types of prune plums can be treated exactly as greengages.

DAMSONS.

These are best when fully coloured and matured, but quite hard. Pick off the stalks, bottle, fill up with spring water, cork, clamp, and heat slowly in the tank up to 180 deg. F. Let rest for half an hour, slowly raise to 212 deg. F., rest for half an hour, then run off the water, and do not disturb them until cold. Carefully examine, and store as previously directed.

BULLACE AND SLOWS

can be treated as for damsons.

Jams and Conserves.

FORCED RHUBARB

must be washed, trimmed, cut into 1¼-in. lengths, carefully packed in bottles on ends, with the aid of a bottling stick, filled up with the prepared water, corked and clamped and boiled exactly as for cherry plums.

GREEN RHUBARB.

The large champagne variety should be chosen whilst still green, trimmed, peeled, and cut into 1¼-in. lengths, packed on ends in bottles, and boiled exactly as for mirabels.

BOTTLED CHERRIES IN WATER.

On the Continent, where open cherry tarts are largely made, the cherries are always stoned before bottling, but in the United Kingdom this plan seldom obtains, because the bulk of the fruit is used for covered tarts, and the flavour of the fruit is certainly better when left intact. Large numbers of the French bottles of stoned fruit are, however, sold here, and there is no reason why the stoned fruit as well as the unstoned should not be put up by the confectioner for his own use, instead of buying what he needs. The cherries must be of the right kind, and in perfect condition. Of the early sorts the bright red transparent Kentish, Flemish, and May Dukes and the late Morellas are all suitable, the latter being much deeper in colour.

Pick the fruit when not quite ripe, but fully matured. Pick off the stalks and at once fill into clean dry bottles (for unstoned), fill up with spring water to the top of the necks, cork with the bottling needle, set on the clamps, and slowly heat in the boiler to 180 deg. Fahr. Keep them at this temperature for half an hour, then slowly raise to 212 deg. Fahr., and keep the water at a gentle ebullition for fifteen minutes, then run away the water and let rest until cool. Carefully examine each cork to see that all are sound and none leaking. Dip corks and 1 in. of the necks into melted bottle wax, mixed as before with beeswax or hard paraffin wax, and store on their sides in racks in a cool, dry cellar.

STONED CHERRIES IN WATER.

The stones must be removed (if no machine be available) either with tiny ivory spoon scoops, or hairpins or bent wires fitted into small wooden or cork handles—girls rapidly become expert with a hairpin—and the fruit dropped into a pan of cold water. Care must be used not to bruise the fruit at all by finger pressure, as every mark will show in the finished product. Fill into dry, clean bottles, and finish exactly as for unstoned cherries, except that the heat of the bath must be slightly different. Raise up to 180 deg. Fahr., and keep there for forty minutes, then slowly raise to 200 deg. only; keep there for ten minutes, and at once run off the water and allow to rest until cool. Examine, seal with wax, and store as previously directed.

FRUITS IN BOTTLES WITHOUT WATER.

All of the foregoing fruits, except rhubarb, can be preserved without water by simply filling the bottles with fruit as full as they will hold, exhausting the air by means of one of the small vacuum exhausts, and corking, clamping, and heating as before directed, but there are several very necessary rules that must be observed. These are given below.

All about Ices.

A partial vacuum may also be obtained by rarification. If the bottles after filling be stood firmly in a hot-water bottle for 15 minutes the air inside will be rarified, and a portion of it expelled. If as each bottle is corked the flame of a spirit lamp be held over the open neck for a few seconds, a further portion will be withdrawn. In any case the following rules must be observed:—

The fruit must be perfectly dry and freshly picked.

The bottles must be perfectly dry.

The corks must be dry and made pliable by squeezing.

The clamps must be firmly fixed, and the bottles stood upright in a water bath with hay packed between them, and water half-way up the necks.

The time allowed for heating in each case must be increased by one-half, as the fruit will not have the assistance of the inside water, and the bottles must remain in the water bath until almost cold.

When the clamps are removed and each cork examined, there must be a tin of bottling wax melted and mixed in the proportion of 3 ozs. of beeswax or hard paraffin wax to each pound of bottle wax ready, and as each, corked, is passed as sound it must be dipped into the hot wax, covering the cork and 1 in. of the bottle neck to seal it. This is absolutely necessary, as there will be no water inside the bottle to keep the cork swollen and tight. Care must be taken to have both the surface of the cork and the bottle neck quite dry. All these fruits can be stored as previously directed, but they must be periodically examined, as mould is apt to supervene. Any bottles that show signs of mould or other deterioration must be earmarked for earliest use.

Although fruit so preserved has the advantage in flavour over that bottled by the water process, it is always more or less pulped, and on that account of less utility to the confectioner. The one exception to this rule is the damson, for in this form it answers admirably for making damson cheese, and it is advised that damsons be so preserved for this purpose.

FRUITS PRESERVED FOR ICES.

Pride of place must be given to the strawberry, for it is by far the greatest favourite. Every confectioner who makes ices during the season when fresh strawberries are not obtainable will know that preserved fruit in some form is very desirable, and should not miss the opportunity of providing for his needs at the proper time.

All sorts of plans for bottling have been tried during the last thirty or forty years with more or less success or failure. The peculiarity of the strawberry is that its distinctive flavour disappears when it is cooked, and therefore nearly all experiments have been made with the object of packing in the raw state.

Without traversing the long series of experiments that have occupied the time and attention of confectioners for so many years, it will be sufficient for our purpose here to deal with those methods that survive. Although there are variants of each of them, there are only four distinctive types that need be noticed. They are given not in the order of merit—for each confectioner must decide which plan he likes best—but in chronological order.

No. 1.—Pulped fruit without sugar, the whole of the pulp being used (when it happens to be fit to use).

No. 2.—Pulped fruit with sugar, the whole of the pulp being used (sometimes).

No. 3.—The juice of pulped fruit with sugar, automatically separated from the pulp by slight fermentation.

Jams and Conserves.

No. 4.—The juice of the fruit separated by slight fermentation from the pulp, without sugar.

No. 1.—STRAWBERRIES PULPED WITHOUT SUGAR.

The fruit should be picked on a perfectly dry day, and be treated as near as possible to the place of growth. Pick the hulls from the fruit and pass through a coarse hair sieve, using a large wooden spoon to press through into a basin underneath. As fast as a few pounds are through fill into soda-water bottles or small champagne bottles, which must be quite clean and perfectly dry. Cork at once with the corking needle, tie down tightly, and dip the corks and an inch of the necks into melted bottle wax mixed with one-fifth its weight of beeswax or hard paraffin wax. Store at once in a cold, dry place. This pulp is never a good colour, even when it does not ferment sufficiently to burst the bottles, as it often does.

No. 2.—STRAWBERRIES PULPED WITH SUGAR.

This must be treated under the same conditions as No. 1, as to picking and pressing, but before bottling add $1\frac{1}{2}$ lb. of fine sifted sugar to each pound of pulp. Then bottle, cork, tie down, and seal, and pack away in exactly the same manner. Both Nos. 1 and 2 will be found after a time to have the juice and pulp quite separate in the bottles, and whilst the juice will be of good colour the pulp will be otherwise. It was this curious separation that led up to the method of preparing Nos. 3 and 4.

No. 3.—THE JUICE OF PULPED STRAWBERRIES WITH SUGAR.

In establishments where large quantities are needed it is sometimes considered easier to put pulp down in brandy or sherry casks, and this plan answers admirably if sufficient care be used. The casks must have one head removed and the bung-hole made secure. A hole must be bored 3 ins. from the bottom of the cask as it stands open end uppermost. Fit this hole with a wine cork quite securely. This is to admit of a wooden tap being driven in when it is necessary to withdraw the syrup.

Choose the fruit carefully. Wild Scarletts are best, but Paxtons, Dr. Hoggs, British Queens, or Royal Sovereigns are all suitable. They must be ripe, quite fresh, and dry. Pick from the hulls, press through a coarse hair or wicker sieve, or an eight-mesh brass sieve, using the back of a wooden spoon for crushing through. As fast as the pulp is passed weigh it and pour into the cask, stood open end uppermost on a stand a foot from the floor in a cold, dry cellar. Complete the operation as quickly as possible, and when the cask is rather more than half full add $1\frac{3}{4}$ lb. of fine sifted sugar to every pound of pulp, and stir occasionally with a large wooden spattle until the sugar is dissolved and ceases to settle at the bottom. Complete each cask the same day that it is started, and even if there be still room for more do not add to or interfere with it. After the first day cover the top with a clean linen cloth and a thin piece of canvas. By the following day a slight fermentation will be set up, and the whole of the pulp will gradually rise to the top, leaving the clear syrup below. When the fermentation subsides a rather dingy, unpleasant looking and smelling crust will form over the whole. This must on no account be broken or interfered with, or more pronounced fermentation will set in and spoil the whole.

All about Ices.

When the syrup is wanted for use carefully drive in a wooden tap at the corked hole near the bottom, and draw off just the quantity and no more than required. This syrup will be as bright as wine and will make admirable ices, both cream and water, but must be used as soon as it is drawn, and not allowed to stand, or it will quickly ferment. As the syrup is gradualy withdrawn the top crust will, of course, sink in the cask, and will form a protective covering as long as there is any syrup remaining. When any of the crust comes away with the syrup, if slight it should be strained, but if thick it is time to throw away what is left and clean the cask for another season.

This syrup has so fine a flavour that it is a great temptation to use it for flavouring fondant centres for chocolates, but be warned by the experience of those who have tried and do not give way to temptation. The slight first fermentation will have in no way interfered with the fresh fruit flavour, and although it can be traced in the syrup, there will be no detrimental flavour either in cream or water ices made from it.

In establishments where comparatively small quantities are required it is advised to use stone jars with taps at the bottom, treating the fruit as for the casks. Even 7-lb. jam jars are sometimes used, but there is always a little trouble to separate the syrup from the incrusting pulp, and when disturbed it is essential that the whole of the syrup in the jar be used at once.

No. 4.—THE JUICE OF PULPED STRAWBERRIES WITHOUT SUGAR.

This juice is most useful for making summer drinks. It can be put down either uncooked or cooked. A little natural effervescence occasionally develops in the uncooked juice, which renders it unfit for cream ice making, but is no detriment for iced drinks. It is then practically strawberry wine, and very good wine, too, and makes admirable strawberry cup, one of the iced cups too seldom met with.

The fruit must be fresh and dry. Pick off the hulls and pass through a coarse hair sieve into a large bowl. Cover with a piece of thin paper pricked with holes here and there, and set in a cool cellar for from two to three days. In a temperature of 65 to 70 degrees in 24 hours it should be in full ebullition, and in forty-eight hours should have subsided, with the pulp on top and the juice underneath. Skim away the thickest of the pulp, and pass the juice through a thin flannel bag until it runs quite bright and clear. At once fill into small champagne bottles, cork with the corking needle, and if intended to be unheated tie down the corks and seal with bottle wax. Store at once on their sides in a cool, dry cellar, and avoid moving until required for use. If the syrup be desired heated, do not wax until afterwards, but tie down and place in the tank, separating carefully with whisps of hay, turn on the water to cover, and then heat up to 180 deg., and keep at that temperature for half an hour; cool down, remove the bottles, examine each one, wax the corks and necks, and store in a cool cellar. All these bottles should be labelled before being stored, so that the contents and the date of putting down may be known. Both these syrups are suitable for water ices and iced drinks, and the heated one will make good cream ices, but without the freshness of the uncooked syrup.

BOTTLED CHERRIES FOR ICE MAKING.

Kentish, Flemish May Dukes, or Morella cherries are the best, and practically the only sorts worth bottling. Whichever sort be used, they must be sound. Well rinse in a hair sieve under a running stream of cold water, pick from the stalks, and pound a few

Jams and Conserves.

at a time in a perfectly clean mortar, breaking up the stones and kernels as well as the fruit. Lift out with a horn scoop into a basin or enamelled pan, and fill into ordinary fruit bottles, nearly reaching the top. Cork with sound corks, using the corking needle, fix on the clamps, set in the tank, and heat up to 180 deg. Fahr. slowly. Rest for half an hour, then raise gradually to 212 deg. Fahr. and keep them at this temperature for fifteen minutes. Then run off the water and let them remain until cool. Examine each cork to see that it is sound, and store on their sides in a cool, dry cellar until wanted. This pulp will make cherry-water ice or cherryade, as fresh in flavour as the new fruit, and with a far stronger noyeau flavour than fresh fruit will give.

RED CURRANT JUICE FOR ICES.

The fruit should be fresh and dry and fully ripe. Pick from the stalk, crush through either a cane or eight-mesh brass sieve into a stone pan, cover with a perforated paper, and set in a cool place for two days to ferment. Pass through a jelly-bag until bright, bottle in champagne bottles, cork, and clamp or tie down, and heat in the tank up to 180 deg. Fahr. Let them rest for half an hour, then slowly raise to 212 deg., and at once run off the water. When cool examine each carefully. Seal all the sound ones with bottle wax, and store on their sides in a cool cellar. This syrup will make admirable water ices or iced drinks, and will be as fresh and bright as fresh fruit.

If desired, the fruit may be simply strained without fermenting, then bottled and heated in the same way, but it will have a heavy sediment, and the taste will not be so crisp.

RASPBERRY JUICE FOR ICES.

Prepare these in the same way as for red currants. The fermented plan is by far the best, although some folks prefer not to so treat them. Another plan is to add $\frac{3}{4}$ lb. of fine sifted loaf sugar to each pint of strained juice, bottle, and heat as before, but this has a totally different flavour, and is not so suitable either for water ices or for drinks.

White and black currants can be treated exactly as for red. Two-thirds black and one-third red or white will make a splendid juice if fermented and stored exactly as for red currants.

PRESERVED FRUITS—WET AND DRY.

GLACE CHERRIES.

This fruit is used by practically every confectioner in the country, but it is the exception to find one who preserves his own. The process is rather lengthy, something like fourteen days being taken from start to finish.

The acid fruit, such as the Kentish, Flemish, and May Duke cherries, give the best flavour, what little there is, but although when raw they are very transparent, when finished they are not nearly so bright in colour or so transparent as the white Bigarreau types. Whichever sort be used, they must be fully matured, but firm and slightly under-ripe. They must be used quite fresh and sound, and no two sorts must ever be mixed together.

Decoloration.—The fruit on the stalks must be set thinly on wooden trays, with latticed or slotted bottoms. Cane or wicker will answer equally well. Place them on racks in a cupboard built on purpose, so that pans of sulphur may be burned below them, and with a

All about Ices.

flue above through which the heavy fumes may be slowly carried into the open. One open pan with 1 lb. of powdered sulphur loosely spread over it, and lighted by making a little depression and pouring in and lighting a tablespoonful of methylated spirits of wine, will be sufficient for each ten trays, one above the other and a few inches apart. The cupboard must be tightly closed, the flue opened, and the whole left for at least three hours, when the fruit will be found to be almost colourless. Throw at once into a clean galvanised or copper tank, filled with cold water and arranged for a continuous stream to enter at the bottom at one end and leave by a waste overflow at the other. In this way all taste of sulphur will be washed out in from three to four hours. Failing this arrangement, the water must be changed four times—once every three hours—and left in the last water all night. The reason for this decoloration is the necessity of starting with a neutral colour base, so that the even desired colour may be given to the whole of the fruit alike.

Picking.—The cherries may be lifted, free from water, into wooden or enamelled pails, the stalks picked off, and the cherries thrown into pails of clean cold water. In France and Italy the stalks are dried and tied up in small bundles, and sold for making a kind of medicinal tea.

Stoning.—Unless some small machine be available—at present there is only one machine that satisfactorily does the work, and that is not on the market—the stoning must be done by hand as already explained for bottled cherries. During the whole of this part of the work the fruit must be out of the water as little as possible; that is, it must be lifted from one pail of water to be stoned and thrown into another pail of water at once.

Boiling.—When a sufficient quantity have been stoned place them in a steam pan, or for small quantities into a copper preserving pan. Cover with cold water, and bring slowly up to the boil. Simmer slowly until the pulp feels soft to the fingers when pinched. Turn off the steam or lift off the fire, throw in a little cold water, and let the fruit sink from the top. Let it rest a minute or two, and once more bring to the boil, and again let it sink, this time running in as much cold water as possible to cool the fruit. Reduce with cold water to 65° or 70°, then lift from the water with a perforated hand bowl, drain as dry as may be, and put into each enamelled bowl rather more than half as many as would fill it.

These bowls and the copper bowls for finishing must be in sequence for size, as they almost alone are used in the finishing process. The proper relative sizes should be copper egg bowls one-third larger than the enamelled bowls.

Have ready prepared a sufficient quantity of hot syrup made with fine small crushed sugar and water boiled together, and registering 25 deg. by the saccharometer and coloured a deep red with liquid carmine. Pour this over the cherries in the pans in sufficient quantity to float them. Press well under the syrup, and although they will at first stand out above the syrup, in a few hours, when the syrup begins to permeate them, they will gradually sink. This syrup must be hot—say 200 deg.—when used, but the cherries must not exceed 70 deg., or they will shrivel.

Pile the pans one above the other, with two wooden battens between each. In this way they will occupy very little floor space. Let them stand until next day, by which time some of the water in the fruit will have been expelled and some of the sugar will have been taken up in its place. This will leave the syrup lighter, and it will be necessary to thicken it a little beyond its original density. This is done by adding sugar and boiling all together as follows:—

Assuming that each bowl holds about 10 lbs. of fruit and about the same weight of syrup, to avoid the necessity of weighing each addition of sugar use a scoop that will hold about 2 lbs. of fine small crushed sugar and make your additions with this.

Jams and Conserves.

Turn a bowl of cherries and syrup carefully into a perfectly clean copper egg bowl, add a scoop of sugar, and place on the open stove. Bring to the boil without stirring, but ensure homogeneity by shaking the pan from side to side. Boil for about half a minute only, and then turn back into the original pan. When all are finished, pile up in the same way as before. Before this first boiling it is well to judge the colour, and bearing in mind that this will deepen a little by future boilings, add a little extra colour if it be needed. Boiling will make the skin of the fruit harder, and the colour must be put into the fruit before this hardening renders it difficult, if not impossible.

The following day add another scoop of sugar, and bring to the boil as before, and repeat the process on the third day. Then miss a day, and on the fifth day repeat the process, but instead of sugar use 2 lbs. of liquid glucose, which can for convenience also be measured with a small copper sugar-boiler. Again rest, missing a day, and on the seventh day repeat the boiling with a second 2 lbs. of glucose.

Allow the bowls to stand for three days, then drain each bowl on concave perforated trays over pans; turn the whole of the syrup into a large steam pan, bring it to the boil, and test with the saccharometer. If less than 35 deg. boil it down until it reaches that density. If over 35 deg., which is not likely, add a little water to reduce it. For the sake of obtaining as near perfect uniformity of the entire batch, turn the whole of the drained cherries into the syrup, and again bring the whole up to the boil, by which time the syrup should register 36 deg. by the saccharometer.

The fruit is preferably stored in syrup in tins with spring-on lids, and should be filled into these whilst hot and piled a little above the tops to allow for shrinkage as they cool.

If it be desired to obtain the exact weight in each tin the fruit must be drained whilst hot, the tins tared and filled in, weighed, hot syrup poured over to fill the tins, and again weighed to be certain of the gross and nett weights of fruit and syrup.

Glucose.—This is very difficult to measure in its cold state, and it is advised that previous to boiling the fruit on the days that glucose must be added that a pan of glucose be slowly melted and stood handy for measuring liquid into the pans as required. The glucose is used not so much to cheapen the cost of production as a safeguard against crystallisation.

Packed in this way the cherries will keep in good condition for at least one year; after that time the colour will gradually deteriorate. When required for use or for boxing they will need to be drained, and if for crystallising must be surface dry.

For counter sale these fruits are sometimes crystallised, and very occasionally glacéd, but for confectioners' use are always drained only, although they are called glacé, which is an inaccurate trade term. The syrup in which the cherries are preserved is generally saved and used in the next year's work for the first syrup, in which case it must be strained, boiled, skimmed, and reduced to the lower degree of density; and as glucose is then present in a certain proportion, sugar is substituted on the fifth and glucose added on the seventh day.

PEEL PRESERVING (DRAINED).

Orange, lemon, and citron peels are largely used by confectioners, and can upon occasion be advantageously preserved by them. All these peels, however, are to be bought at such comparatively low prices that except for occasionally using up peels that would otherwise be wasted it is scarcely ever worth while to bother with them. The wholesale houses utilise space and labour at a time when they have both to spare, and even then, except in very few cases, they do not make much money at it. Their one

All about Ices.

considerable advantage lies in selling cut peel, which is often the broken caps and small pulpy pieces from which the sound caps have been sorted. This is generally overloaded with syrup, and cakes together in masses that are not easily separated. It is, however, low in price, and there is a ready sale for it.

Large quantities of orange and lemon, and all the citron that is preserved in this country, reach here packed in brine in large pipes, the fruit being cut in halves and the pulp remaining intact, sometimes less the juice. The best-coloured orange and lemon, however, is made from the fresh fruit, which from January 1st onwards for two months or more is, as a rule, fairly cheap. The treatment is as follows:—

LEMON PEEL.

The plant necessary will depend upon the quantity to be handled, but in an ordinary business this being small the plant will generally be available. A low cutting table is useful for fresh fruit, sufficiently heavy to withstand a little leverage. The size is of no importance, provided it is either bolted to the floor or is heavy enough not to be easily shifted. Two feet or not more than 2 ft. 3 ins. in height will be suitable. In the middle have a square hole cut 4 ins. each way, then mark a larger square of 5 ins., but only cut out the front and back sides $\frac{1}{4}$ in. deep, leaving on those two sides a shoulder $\frac{1}{2}$ in. wide. In the shoulders cut up channels so that four or six square brass bars, each 5-16 in., may be set, equally spaced. Then take a piece of 3-in. quartering about 3 ft. or 3 ft. 6 ins. long; shave one end of it into a rounded handle, sink a flat steel blade $3\frac{3}{4}$ ins. long and $4\frac{1}{2}$ ins. wide $1\frac{1}{2}$ ins. into the middle of one flat side, exactly fitting the middle of the 4-in. opening when the uncut square end is flush with the inside edge of the table. Hinge the uncut end with a well screwed on 3-in. butt to the inner side of the table, and the rod will then lift up by the handle and 3 ins. of the blade (well sharpened) fit exactly between the two middle bars of the 4-in. opening. This will give you a cutting table upon which when the lemons are set on the bars the knife will cut through from end to end, and the square sides will squeeze the juice through the bars into a pan placed underneath to catch it. The squeezed halves must be thrown into a tub of salt and water, in which they will need to remain for two or three days, according to the strength of the brine.

As fast as the juice accumulates it should be passed through a jelly-bag and filled into dry one or two gallon jars, previously sulphured, and to each gallon $\frac{1}{2}$ oz. of powdered sulphur added. The jars can be corked and sealed as described for fruit pulps, and stored for use, and very useful this fine white clear juice will be for many purposes.

When the peels have stood in the brine sufficiently long to reduce their bitterness pass through running cold water to remove all traces of salt, and then boil in plenty of water until a straw will easily pass through them or until the pulp can be removed by running the thumb round. Throw out into plenty of cold water, and pulp by inserting the thumb between the rind and the inner pulp and forcing it round, and again throw into cold water until all are done. Then drain and arrange neatly but loosely in small tubs or pans, and pour hot syrup 25 deg. by the saccharometer over to cover. The syrup can be made from granulated sugar, and is best used at about 200 deg. Fahr. Each tub or pan should be provided with a round lid or cover smaller than the top of the pan, so that its weight will serve to keep the peel under the syrup, whilst its covering will keep out dust and dirt.

Jams and Conserves.

The tubs or pans should each have an opening near the bottom in which a plug or cork is fitted, so that the syrup may be drawn off, for this must be done several times.

Next day draw off the syrup from all the pans, boil and add sugar to bring it up to 28 deg. by the saccharometer. Repeat this for three days, then leave for three days and again boil the syrup, adding sugar and glucose to reach 30 deg. After a further three days draw off the syrup, strain it, and reduce it by boiling to 35 deg., add about one-eighth of its weight of glucose; drain the peel as dry as possible, pack it in compact rings fitted closely together in perfectly dry tubs or pans, pour over it sufficient of the finished syrup quite hot to well cover it, set the wooden covers on the top, and store in a dry, cold place until needed.

If small quantities only be done at a time, say one or two hundredweight, or even less, the remaining syrup can be used in sequence, always remembering to adjust the glucose according to what has been previously used.

The syrups will darken considerably, and if really fine-coloured peel be wanted fresh syrup should be used each year, the old syrups being utilised for making gingerbreads, or they can be strained and clarified with animal charcoal, but this is messy and troublesome to those who have had little or no experience. The writers have always been able to utilise the syrup without waste, but this is not a universal experience.

ORANGE PEEL.

This is treated in every particular exactly as lemon peel, with the proviso that it will need far less boiling to soften it. If Seville oranges be used they will need longer in the brine, or the bitter flavour will be too marked. The juice of the orange is not so readily usable as that of the lemon, except on the day of squeezing, but if strained through a fine cane sieve and 12 ozs. of sugar added to each pint, measured first and reduced on the fire before adding the sugar, it will make an admirable orange jelly that can be used for sandwiching, etc. Also, if 3 lbs. of sugar be added to each strained gallon of juice it can be readily fermented into a really good wine; so it should never be wasted.

CITRON PEEL.

Citron peel when it reaches this country unpreserved is always in halves in the brine, and only needs soaking in running water to remove the salt before treating in practically the same way as lemons and oranges. In France they are often stabbed with the point of a knife to assist the sugar permeation. This plan certainly has the desired effect, but the peel cannot afterwards be cut in strips for Madeira tops, etc. The English method is to allow the sugar to enter from the pulp side only, and this gives more solid peel. The writers, however, prefer the plan of pricking the caps with the needle prick used for greengages and other firm-skinned fruits, as it greatly assists the entry of the sugar without hurting the fruit for after use. This needle is easily made by cutting a sound wine cork to half its length, pushing a dozen small darning-needles through so that the eye ends are flush with the top of the cork and the points equi-distant at the other end, and then with some strong adhesive fastening a small wooden or tin disc on the top to prevent the pressure pushing the ends back.

Citron peels should be carefully assorted into sizes and colours into different pans or tubs, and before boiling it is advisable to differentiate between the hard unripe caps and the soft overripe ones, so that the mistake of over-boiling some be not made. This sorting will minimise waste appreciably.

All about Ices.

MARRONS GLACE.

Marrons glacé are in great demand on the Continent, and fully deserve their popularity, for they are, when in condition, a most delicious confection. Most of them that are sold in this country are too high in price to make for very large sales, but under the ordinary conditions it is not possible to reduce the price without sacrificing most of the necessary profit. Whilst the nuts are kept in syrup, and glacéd only as required, they will keep, if carefully stored, through the entire season, but after being dried and glacéd they soon get hard and unsaleable. Small quantities are shipped over here in syrup in both bottles and cans, but mostly they are glacéd abroad, and travel by grande vitesse, a costly method of transit, but even then taking from two to three days out of their short life. The fact that the loss by waste owing to the short time they remain in prime condition is very considerable materially affects the price at which they must be sold to cover the loss.

The bulk of the trade here is in the hands of the high-class Italian warehouses, instead of the confectioners, although a few of the latter do every year preserve large quantities, and make good profits thereby.

It is a great advantage to put these confections freshly glacéd on the sales counter every day, and to be able to avoid all waste, except that of breakage. It is in the hope that one more source of profit may be opened to British confectioners, as well as in response to many requests for information on the subject, that full instructions by which British confectioners may profit are given here.

The Nuts Themselves.—It is an almost universal mistake to assume that the nuts are the same as those known here as chestnuts. They are not. It is true they belong to the same family, but there are several distinct points of difference. Whence the origin of the term "chestnut" we know not, but hope it is not Bohemian In Italy, where it is grown in immense quantities, and called "castagna," it enters very largely into the food of the people, the marrana being used almost exclusively for preserving in sugar. The burr of the castagna (chestnut) generally contains three, and sometimes four, nuts, which vary in form, the middle one having generally two flat sides. The burr of the marrana nearly always holds two nuts only, each having a flat and a rounded side. It is also very seldom that the inner covering of the castagna does not in places run into the nuts, occasionally even dividing the kernel into two or more distinct sections. Whilst this skin seldom pierces the marrana nut at all, but envelopes it as a whole, this is not an absolute rule but is sufficiently general to make a distinct variety. The marrana also is a much larger nut than the castagna.

There are several varieties of the marrana, but this is apparently a question chiefly of locality. The best of all, although not the largest, are those grown at or around Cuneo, near Turin, which are so highly esteemed that large dealers from other parts of Italy and from France endeavour to secure the pick of the crops. When gathered they are carefully assorted into sizes, and the contract stipulates the approximate number to the kilo. For marketing they are generally packed in bags of 50 kilos, equal to 1 cwt. avoirdupois.

The marrana that can be bought in the English markets in November are packed in the same packages, and are nearly always the Neapolitan nuts, larger but not nearly so good in shape, flatter in form, especially on one side, not so good in fibre or flavour, and very seldom assorted.

Just a hint to those confectioners who would like to obtain the very best. Make inquiries in October through the British Consulate at Turin as to a dependable house or houses to negotiate with for supplies; get the fruit as soon as possible after the harvest

Jams and Conserves.

and deal with it at once. The results from freshly-gathered nuts are far and away superior to those from fruit that is dry and shrivelled.

Boiling the Fruit.—There are two distincts plans for rendering the fruit fit for preserving in syrup, and each plan has its votaries. The old-fashioned way is to remove the thick outer skin and boil in the thinner inner covering only. This plan has the great advantage of conserving the colour, as well as that of being able more nearly to judge the degree of softness reached. The disadvantage is the supposed greater liability to breakage, with consequent waste. The newer and more usual plan is to boil with both the outer and inner skin on, for the alleged reason that fewer nuts are broken. The writers are of opinion that the supposed advantage of this newer method has never been clearly demonstrated, whilst its disadvantages are admitted and clearly demonstrable. So the earlier method is here recommended and described. Whatever plan be adopted, there will be breakage, averaging from 25 to 30 per cent. of the whole, but this need not mean even 1 per cent. of waste, for every scrap of the broken nut can be utilised. It comes at a time when the unsweetened nuts can be used for many savouries. Turkey stuffing, galantines, purées, and sauces of various sorts will occur to the chef, and even if not usable for such purposes, preserved in syrup in the same way as the whole nuts it makes, pounded and mixed in various ways, splendid centres for chocolates and bonbons and fillings for gateaux and fancy pastries.

Small linen bags will be needed for the boiling, bags made with a round bottom like the end of a bolster case and holding about one gallon. The bags should be widely hemmed at the tops, each one having two looped cords or tapes threaded through, so that the mouths can be closed by drawing the cords tight. The ideal plan is to have a shallow boiling pan, preferably with a steam pipe or coil at the bottom, and for each bag use a small basket the same shape as the bag, but a trifle larger, with swinging handles, and suspend the baskets on a rod through the handles, the rod resting on the top of the pan.

Lightly score each nut with a sharp knife, fill a biscuit wire, or, better still, a galvanised wire, with the nuts, and pass into a warm oven for a few minutes. The outer skin will open out a little where the nuts were scored, and can easily be removed without breaking the inner skin at all. Fill into the bags, about 3 lbs. to 4 lbs. in each, close the tops, set in the baskets, hang them on the rod, and slowly bring the water up to 210 deg. It must never be allowed to boil fast, as there will be considerable breakage, and the outer portion of the nuts will be too soft. Keep the water just at the simmering point for about five hours, being sure that the bags are always covered with water. As this evaporates it must be added to, but always with boiling, or nearly boiling, water.

When the nuts are sufficiently cooked for a coarse needle to easily penetrate they must be lifted one at a time from the opened bag, the brown skin quickly peeled away, and the nuts thrown into a pan of cold water. This is the time that plenty of girl help is useful and necessary. All nuts that are broken should be kept separate from the whole ones to save unnecessary sorting and handling as the syruping proceeds.

When all are peeled and whitened in the cold water drain them on hair sieves, and half fill flat round enamelled pans. Prepare sufficient syrup from fine bright loaf or crushed sugar to cover the nuts well. The best density for the first syrup is 18 deg. by the saccharometer. Pour sufficient syrup into each pan to cover the nuts well, and assuming that each pan will hold 5 lbs. of nuts, cut a number of 6-in. vanilla beans in halves and add four pieces to each pan. This first syrup must not be too hot, or it will harden the nuts. From 70 deg. to 75 deg. Fahr. is recommended.

Unless the pans are to stand day by day in a place that is dust free, it is a good plan

All about Ices.

to cover each with a round of vegetable parchment as a protection. The pans can be stacked in piles, with two wooden battens between each. Leave for twenty-four hours. The following day the syrup will be much thinner, and must be thickened by one of two plans. The ideal way is to set them on a warm stove and raise the temperature to 200 deg. Fahr., and keep it there for three hours, adding a little fresh syrup as evaporation reduces the quantity. If this plan be followed it will be necessary to repeat the heating on the third, the fifth, and the seventh day, by which time the density should be increased to 28 deg. by the saccharometer.

The above plan, although the better one, is very tedious without a specially adapted stove, therefore an alternative one is suggested that will give almost the same results with less trouble. But care must be used to avoid breaking the nuts. On the second day carefully drain the nuts one pan at a time on a drainer or hair sieve over another pan. Place the syrup in a copper preserving pan (if each panful of syrup is to be dealt with in detail, or in a steam-jacketed pan if as a whole), and add sufficient fine sugar to bring the syrup when boiling to 22 deg. by the saccharometer; skim, and pour boiling hot over the drained nut returned to their original pans. Be careful to keep the proper proportion of vanilla to each pan. Repeat this draining and boiling on the third, the fifth, and the seventh days, gradually increasing the density of the syrup up to 28 deg. On the ninth day, whichever plan has been adopted, the treatment will be the same. Carefully drain the fruit, place the syrup in the steam pan, and boil it down to 32 deg.; then, having kept a record of the sugar used, add one-fourth its entire weight of liquid glucose, and again boil down to 34 deg. Skim, and pour boiling hot over the nuts as before.

On the Continent a large proportion of the marrons are sold at Christmas and the New Year, and it is customary to store these in the original pans until required to be drained and glacéd for sale, the balance being packed in cans or short wide bottles for later use. Those to be left in the pans must on the tenth or twelfth day be heated on the stove to the boil, covered, and stored in a cool, dry, dark place, and left entirely undisturbed. The ones to be bottled or canned should be drained, carefully placed in packages with the pieces of vanilla, filled up with the syrup, sealed, if possible, with a vacuum sealing machine, and before storing carefully heated up to 212 deg. in a water bath.

Glaceing for Sale.—Well drain the nuts and dry the surface only in a warm room. Boil a little plain syrup to the blow, rub a little on the side of the pan until it shows white. Scrape this down into the bulk, stir together until the surface is a little opaque, then dip the drained nuts with a dipping fork into the syrup; lift out on to a draining wire, rounded side uppermost, and in a few minutes they will be ready for the sales counter, and can be dished in rows on a silver dish or set in small paper cases. Should any be left unsold long enough to become white and grained, they can be revived by slowly simmering for a minute or two in very thin syrup, and drained as before. They will not be quite so transparent on the surface as when first glacéd, but quite fit for sale.

To be in perfect condition the marrons must be quite soft, thoroughly permeated with the syrup, retain their internal moisture, with a rich, delicate vanilla flavour. They are retailed variously from 3s. to 5s. per lb., but if made in quantity could easily be sold at a good profit at 2s. per lb., especially if the waste be minimised as suggested.

There are few confections so delicious as marrons glacé, and the main reason that they are less popular in Britain than elsewhere is the infrequency in which they are obtainable in perfect condition. When to this is added the abnormally high price charged here for the imported goods it is not difficult to account for small sales.

Jams and Conserves.

ANGELICA.

Preserved angelica is used by practically every confectioner for decoration of cakes and fancy pastries, and by many for blending with other fruits in ices, jellies, and creams. It is one of the numerous umbelliferous family of plants having tubular stalks that radiate from centres along the main stems. The particular one used for preserving is known as "arcangelica officinalis," and can readily be distinguished from its relations by its curious but appetising aroma. Its leaves, as well as the very young shoots, are largely used in the making of liqueurs, as well as many herbal medicines. It is easily grown from seed in rich loam, and should be cut whilst green and tender before the main stalks have become yellow and woody. Whilst large stalks are chosen for commercial packing, these have neither the colour nor flavour of the smaller ones, which are quite as useful to the confectioner and much more delicious. When packed for sale all the stalks must be cut to fit the boxes, and the cost is greatly increased by the percentage of débris (small pieces which have to be sold at a lower price). The consumer who preserves for home use can avoid this loss, for the length of the stalks is not of great moment. It is suggested that a small experimental batch be tried one season, and its cost per pound compared with the nett weight and cost of the imported goods, allowance being made for the sugar that must be washed off before using, whether the stalks be glacéd or crystallised.

Cut or procure the plants whilst quite green and tender, but of full size. Let them be delivered at the preserving house as whole as possible to avoid bleeding. Cut away the leaves and divide lengths, each stalk intact, but cutting away the umbels where the side stalks radiate. Place in a copper pan in cold water, in which 1 lb. of salt to each 10 gallons of water has been dissolved. Bring up to the boil slowly, and keep near the boiling point for ten minutes, then at once lift out into cold water, preferably running, to cool as quickly as possible, and also to wash away the slight taste of salt. The coarse stringy fibres on the outside of the larger stalks must now be peeled away and the stalks again turned into fresh cold water. Rubbing or slightly scraping will be sufficient with the small finger pieces. It is well at this stage to sort the different sizes (not lengths) into separate pans. When all are cleaned (it will be noticed that the stalks will be rather more yellow than green) and assorted, place in the copper pan, filled with cold water, to which ½ per cent. (½ lb. to each 10 gallons of water) of powdered alum has been added, bring to the boil, and simmer slowly until a pointed match will easily penetrate. At once add cold water, or lift into cold water and cool as quickly as possible. When quite cold lift on to drainers or hair sieves, and drain as dry as possible. Arrange the stalks neatly in small tubs or earthenware pans, with a tap or plug-hole at the bottom, and prepare the syrup. This must be made from fine crushed sugar, and should be 20 deg. by the saccharometer. Pour this at 80 deg. Fahr. over the angelica, well covering the stalks. Place clean wooden covers, cut to fit the inside of the pans, on top of the stalks to keep them under the syrup and to keep out any dust or dirt, and leave until the next day. On the second day draw off the syrup, put it in the copper pan, and, adding sufficient sugar to bring it up to 24 deg., boil, skim, and pour boiling over the angelica. On the third day repeat the process, bringing the syrup up to 26 deg.; on the fifth day repeat, and bring the syrup up to 28 deg.; and on the seventh bring up to 30 deg. Leave now for three days, then on the tenth day draw off the syrup, drain the angelica on drainers or hair sieves, and, having kept a record of the sugar used in the syrup, add to it 25 per cent. of its weight of liquid glucose. Boil the whole down to 33 deg. by the saccharometer, carefully skim, and add the angelica, and gently simmer together for ten to fifteen minutes, when the syrup should register 35 deg. Lift the angelica carefully into the cleaned dry pans, arrange

All about Ices.

it carefully so that all the stalks are straight, with no waste room, pour over it the hot syrup, and when cold cover each pan down carefully and store in a cool, dry place until required for use.

There are various opinions as to the relative values of alum, burnt alum, acetic acid, etc., for fixing the green colour, but the writers prefer the plan as above. Of late years aniline greens have sometimes been used in the blanching water, but if the stalks be young and fresh none will be needed.

At one time also it was customary to cover the pans day by day with fresh green vine leaves, under the impression that a deeper green was secured. The plan was quite nice, quite pretty, and very nearly almost quite idyllic, but it served no useful purpose. The adding of green dye to the alum water is distinctly effective, but is best done without if possible.

GREEN ALMONDS.

Green almonds are seldom used in any quantity in this country, although they might with advantage be utilised, both whole and cut, for decorative work, especially as the bulk of the fruit produced by the numbers of trees all over the country is almost entirely wasted. The trees appear to be grown for decorating gardens chiefly, and very decorative indeed are these, the earliest spring flowering trees, with their lovely pink blossoms showing before the leaves appear.

Choose and pick the nuts fully grown, but before the inner shell begins to harden; pick off any stalks that may remain, put the nuts in a small hair sieve and plunge them into a copper pan of boiling water in which a sufficient quantity of wood ashes to make a strong lye has been mixed.

A 5 per cent. solution of ordinary carbonate of soda (washing soda) or a 3 per cent. solution of caustic soda will be more effective in freeing the rough coats, but both, especially the latter, are very unpleasant for fingers and nails. Let the water boil barely half a minute, lift out the sieve and quickly clean off the fur-like coats either by brushing in hot water with a small hard nailbrush or in the more usual way of shooting into a small sack and shaking from end to end, allowing friction to do the work. Neither of these plans is so general as peeling thinly with a sharp knife in straight cuts from end to end. This, of course, removes the skin and reduces the weight, as well as taking away what little green there is, but the almonds are far nicer to eat when peeled.

Whichever plan be adopted, throw the nuts at once into cold water, and when all are ready turn them into a copper pan of cold water to which has been added $\frac{1}{2}$ per cent. of powdered alum (nearly 1 oz. for each gallon), place on a slow fire and gradually raise to the boil, then gently simmer until all are sufficiently soft to easily pierce with a large needle. The time necessary will vary with the condition of the almonds, but should not exceed five minutes. There will be a slight effervescence, as the acid neutralises any of the soda that may remain if the skins have not been peeled away. Skim away the scum as it rises, and if it is desired add a little liquid apple greening, gently stirring to ensure thorough and equal tinting. Be careful to lift away the nuts that soften first, whether on the surface or not, and when soft enough lift out with a copper skimmer or perforated ladle into a pan of cold water. Let them stand for an hour, by which time the taste of the alum will be imperceptible, and the green shade a little paler. Drain as dry as possible and half-fill flat enamelled pans, and cover with cold syrup that when boiling registered 20 deg. to 22 deg. by the saccharometer.

Jams and Conserves.

On the second day drain the fruit, add sufficient sugar to bring it up to 25 deg. of density, and when nearly cold again pour over the fruit. The third day repeat, bringing the syrup up to 28 deg. On the fifth day bring the syrup up to 30 deg. On the seventh day drain, and add one-fourth the total weight of sugar of liquid glucose, test up to 32 deg., and on the ninth day drain, boil the syrup up to 32 deg., carefully add the whole of the fruit, bring up to the boil and slowly simmer together for a few minutes only, by which time the syrup should be between 33 deg. and 34 deg. Fill the fruit into large open-mouthed glass jars with screw-on metal lids, with a round of cork in each, fill up to the neck with syrup, cover with a round of waxed paper, and as soon as cold screw the tops on tightly.

APRICOTS (GREEN).

Apricots seldom ripen very well in this country, and much of the fruit is therefore wasted. Gathered when quite green and before the stone has hardened, they make when preserved a useful addition to the too few green fruits available for decorative work. In the hard green state there will be a rough furry coat on the fruit, which can be removed by immersion in the lye or soda hot bath exactly as for green almonds, turning into cold water, and afterwards rubbing either individually with a small nailbrush in hot water or collectively in a small bag with some rough salt. In the latter case the salt must be thoroughly washed away afterwards.

Set the coatless fruit in a copper pan with cold water to which has been added a bare one-third per cent. of powdered alum, say ½ oz. to each gallon of water used. Slowly heat the water up to 210 deg., but do not let it boil. Reduce the heat so that the water remains just below boiling point, and let the fruit slowly simmer to get soft through without breaking. When they begin to rise to the top of the water examine them, and as soon as a large needle can be easily passed through them lift from the pan into cold water. When cold, drain them and half-fill enamelled pans, and cover with hot syrup of 18 deg. density. The second day drain the fruit, each pan separately, boil up the syrup separately in a copper pan, adding sugar to make up to 22 deg., and pour hot on to the fruit. The third day repeat, making the syrup 26 deg. On the fifth day bring the syrup up to 30 deg., using glucose instead of sugar, turn in the fruit, again bring to the boil, simmer slowly for a few moments, and return to the pans. On the seventh day turn each pan of fruit and syrup together into a copper pan, add sufficient glucose to make up to 32 deg., boil up once or twice, and return to the pans as before. On the ninth day repeat the boiling without any addition, when the syrup should register 34 deg. when tested. Store the fruit at once in small jars or tins, fill up with the hot syrup, and when cold cover down with rounds of waxed paper or vegetable parchment, and tie or cover down. Store in a cool, dry, dark place. It is not suggested that this fruit should be crystallised or glacéd for sale, but should be used drained for cutting up for decorative work. For this it is particularly suitable, as there will be shades of colour from the outer green inwards.

APRICOTS (RIPE).

Ripe apricots suitable for preserving for the fine crystallised or glacé fruit are never obtainable in this country at a price that will allow of saving upon the imported goods, but small pale French and Italian "cots" are often on sale in June and July at prices that will show a good margin of profit, and the fruit preserved and stored in syrup is very useful for many purposes. When fine fruit is put up for boxing in glacé or crystallised

All about Ices.

form it is split on the indented side, the stone removed, and when drained and dried for final treatment pieces of the smaller fruit packed in the stone hollow. This gives plumpness to the large fruit, and ensures the higher price for the débris and smaller fruit. This plan is unnecessary when only small fruit is put up for use in the kitchen or workshop.

The fruit must be firm and slightly under-ripe. With a sharp plated knife cut from the middle of the side depression to the stalk end, and with a bent wire (or hairpin) pushed into a cork or wooden handle prise out the stone.

Have ready a copper pan of water nearly boiling, put in the stoned fruit and carefully blanch them. Avoid over-cooking, or the fruit will fall to pieces. As fast as they soften and expand the fruit should rise, but this does not always happen, so care must be taken to lift out with a skimmer or perforated ladle those that are ready. Lift into cold water, and as soon as cooled drain and lift into a pan of hot syrup of 18 deg. density. On the second day drain, put syrup into a copper pan, add sugar, and boil up to 22 deg. Add the fruit carefully and bring all up to the boil, and then return to pans. On the third day repeat, bringing the syrup up to 26 deg.; on the fifth day up to 30 deg., using glucose only. On the seventh day drain, reduce the syrup by boiling to 32 deg., add the fruit, bring up to the boil three times, resting a minute between each boil up, carefully skim, pack the fruit carefully in jars, pour over the hot syrup, cover, and when cold tie down and store in a cool, dry, dark place until wanted for use, when they can be lifted out and drained.

Do not allow fingers to handle the fruit in the syrup, and avoid drops of water falling in, or fermentation will ensue.

GREENGAGES.

This fruit is always available, and a certain quantity should be put down for winter use. Choose large fruit, quite green and hard, and leave the stalks on. Before blanching it will need to be pricked all over with the needle pricker. Do not attempt to deal with large quantities at a time unless there is plenty of help. A few pounds in a small pan at one time will receive more careful attention than a larger quantity could. As fast as the fruit is stabbed throw into a bright copper pan of cold water, sufficient to float the fruit freely. Put on a slow fire, and gradually bring up to 200 deg. F. At first the fruit will sink, but will gradually begin to lift in the water. At once lift from the fire, and lift out the fruit with a perforated copper skimmer into an enamelled pan of cold water to which $\frac{1}{4}$ oz. of powdered alum has been added to each gallon of water. The fruit will now be slightly yellow, but if each pan be covered with spinach leaves and allowed to stand for five or six hours, the fruit will regain its green colour. It must now be again slowly brought to the boil in the same water, spinach leaves and all, and as soon as the fruit begins to rise and is sufficiently soft (synonymous conditions) it must be at once lifted out into cold water (running if possible) and quickly cooled. When cold, drain and place in the enamelled pans, cover it with cold syrup 18 deg. (when boiling), and allow to stand until next day. On the second day carefully drain, reboil the syrup, adding fine crushed sugar to bring it up to 22 deg., and pour boiling hot over the fruit. On the third day repeat the process, bringing the syrup up to 26 deg. On the fifth day repeat, and bring the syrup up to 30 deg., turn in the fruit, and just bring it up to the boil in the syrup. On the seventh day add one-fourth the total weight of the sugar used of glucose, boil the whole up to 30 deg., turn in the fruit, and give it a boil up, after which it can be packed in pans or jars for use as required, carefully covered, and stored in a cool, dry, dark place.

Jams and Conserves.

If the fruit is to be used for manufacturing purposes it will be only necessary to drain and partially dry for use, but if to be glacéd or crystallised it must be drained and well dried on the outside before coating with glacé or crystals.

The method of glacéing has already been dealt with, and as the treatment is the same for all fruits, it is not necessary to repeat it here.

For the sake of extra brightness it is sometimes considered advisable to coat the upper surface of glacé fruits (especially Metz fruits) with a saturated solution of gum arabic, put on hot with a soft brush after the fruits are packed for show.

Crystallising.—If it be desired, any of the fruits preserved in syrup can be crystallised instead of glacé, the process being practically the same for all varieties. For this purpose deep tinned pans of almost any size, preferably with slightly sloping sides, with one or more holes ½ in. in diameter at the bottom of one end, and fitted with two or more very fine wire trays according to the depth of the pans. The holes are for the purpose of draining off the syrup from the fruits at the proper time, and must be either corked or covered on the insides with strips of stout paper tightly fastened with white of egg or other adhesive. Formerly small tubes were fastened outside the holes, but they were liable to be badly battered in use, and were frequently filled with crystallised sugar The simple holes will answer all requirements.

Set one of the wire trays in the bottom, and arrange the fruit to be crystallised on the tray not too close together. The fruit must be well drained and lightly passed through hot water to remove the surface syrup, or the crystals will not adhere. Set another tray on top of the fruit, and cover with fruit as before, and assuming the depth of the tray to allow of the two layers, place a third tray on the second layer. Weight the top tray at both ends to prevent the fruit lifting in the syrup, set the trays one above another crossways in a warm room, and completely fill with the prepared syrup, and leave from six to twelve hours according to the deposit desired.

The syrup must be prepared from fine bright crushed sugar melted in water and boiled without acid until it registers when boiling 36 deg. by the saccharometer, and must be poured over the fruit whilst still hot. The crystals to be deposited on fruits must be larger and bolder than required for fine bonbons, therefore the greater heat at which it is used. It may be taken as a rule that the density of the syrup being equal, the higher the temperature of the syrup when used, the greater the size of the crystal deposit, and vice versa. Thus for very fine fondant bonbons the syrup is used almost cold.

When the crystallisation is heavy enough the syrup must be drawn off by removing the corks or piercing the paper covering the holes and tilting the pans over a receiver. Allow the pans to remain in the hot room until quite dry, when their contents can be emptied by reversing them and tapping over a coarse sieve or marble slab. The deposited crystallised sugar débris can be utilised for syrup or other purposes, but fresh syrup should always be made for each batch. Absolute cleanliness of all utensils is of the utmost importance.

GREEN FIGS.

The method of preserving these is the same as for greengages, and they also must be hard and unripe. Figs are not very largely grown in England, but those that are grown never ripen in the open, and are therefore entirely wasted. If picked when fully formed, but hard and green, they are in splendid condition for preserving, and should be utilised whenever possible.

All about Ices.

GREEN WALNUTS.

Select the nuts as soon as fully formed, but before the shell has begun to harden. Throw them into a copper pan of cold water, add a handful of salt, and gradually bring up to the boil. Remove from the stove, and ladle out the nuts into cold water. With a sharp silver or plated knife peel off the green outer skin in straight cuts from end to end, and throw the nuts into a copper pan of cold water to which ½ oz. of powdered alum has been added to each gallon. Add a handful of fresh spinach leaves, and slowly bring to the boil. Simmer slowly until they begin to rise in the pan, test them to see if a large steel pin will easily pass through them, remove from the fire, and allow them to stand in an earthen or enamelled pan in the spinach water until cold. Drain them as dry as possible, half fill the enamelled pans, and cover with cool, not cold, syrup of 18 deg. To finish, treat them in all respects as for green almonds.

GREEN CHINOIS.

Choose the small round Chinese oranges, Mandarines (not Tangerines, which are flatter in shape) when quite green. These are largely grown in Italy and the South of France, and can easily be obtained by previous arrangement. Put them in a copper pan of cold water with ½ oz. of alum to each gallon. Slowly bring them to the boil, and gently simmer until the rinds are soft, but not broken. Lift them out into cold water, and when quite cold drain them, half fill the pans with the fruit, and cover with cold syrup 18 deg. by the saccharometer. Cover each pan with spinach leaves, and finish on the successive days as for greengages. For trade use drain only, but for sale either glacé or crystallise.

CHINOIS D'OR.

These are the same variety of orange, but fully ripened to golden colour. Treat these as for the green chinois, but leaving out both alum and spinach. For trade use drain only, but for sale either glacé or crystallise.

GREEN GOOSEBERRIES.

This is a much neglected fruit, neglected without reason, for it is easily preserved. When carefully done, a really good light green colour, very useful for decorative work, obtainable everywhere, and always reasonable in price.

Choose hard green fruit as near one size as possible. Cut off the snuffs and stalks, and throw the fruit into a pan of cold water, adding a small quantity of salt. This will make the water a little heavier, help to keep the fruit suspended, and save pressure, and at the same time remove the surface must. When the snuffing and tailing is completed, lightly stab the fruit with the needle pricker, and throw into fresh cold water. When all are done, lift out into a copper pan of cold water, adding ½ oz. of powdered alum to each gallon of water. Slowly bring up to 200 deg. F., then add a handful of spinach leaves, gently simmer until the fruit begins to rise in the water, when it should be easily pierceable with a pointed wooden match, but not at all broken. Ladle out into cold water, cover the pans with a few fresh spinach leaves, and allow it to stand for a few hours. The fruit, which will turn out a little yellowish during the blanching, will recover its green colour, and be ready for draining and covering with cool syrup 18 deg. by the saccharometer. Finish on the successive days as for greengages.

Jams and Conserves.

WHITE PEARS.

The most suitable pears for preserving are those with greenish white flesh and a russet green skin. They are rather small in size, even in shape, and have stalks that are thick in proportion to the fruit. They are grown in nearly all the Continental countries and are less general here. Failing these any pears of a like character and size may be used. They must be quite hard and unripe. Throw them into a copper pan of cold water and slowly raise to 200 deg. F. Turn them into a pan of cold water, remove the snuff with a tiny vegetable scoop, and carefully pare them with a silver or plated knife by taking off thin slices from the snuff to the stalk. Cut off all but ¾ in. of stalk and drop each pear into a pan of cold water, and when sufficient are ready return the pan to the fire, slowly bring up to boiling point, draw back, and slowly simmer until a sharpened match will easily penetrate them. Great care must be used not to overcook them, but they must be soft right through. When ready, remove with a perforated ladle into cold water. When cold, drain them, half fill enamelled pans, and cover with cool syrup 18 deg. by the saccharometer. On the succeeding days finish exactly as for ripe apricots. For trade use they will only need to be drained, but for sale can be either glacé or crystallised.

RED PEARS.

These are preserved as for white, but the first syrup must be deeply coloured with liquid carmine. After the first day's steeping, should the colour absorbed not be deep enough, a little more carmine must be added when the syrup is boiled up.

MIRABELS.

The yellow mirabel is one of the best flavoured of all the preserved plums. It is common to all European countries, and although it is grown in Great Britain it is less general than elsewhere. It should be gathered as soon as the green colour changes to yellow whilst still hard. In the ripe state, whilst its flavour is richer, it is difficult to blanch, because its thin tissue-paper like skin is apt to split and curl up on the fruit. For this reason much of the fruit is lightly scored with a sharp knife, blanched as usual, and when the skin curls away at the scored part lifted out into cold water, the skin peeled off, the fruit dropped into cold water to prevent breaking, and afterwards drained, carefully filled into wide-necked bottles, filled up with syrup of 18 deg., corked or stoppered, and finished in a tank or bain marie exactly as for fruit bottled in water. It is then a most richly-flavoured compote fruit. (See Compotes.)

Prick the hard fruit lightly all over with the needle pricker, put into a pan of cold water and slowly heat up to 200 deg. It will very quickly soften, so great care is necessary. When the fruit begins to rise in the water lift out with a perforated ladle into cold water. When cold, drain, and afterwards finish as for ripe apricots. For sale this fruit is most effective when crystallised, but can be used either drained or glacé. If glacé a saturated solution of gum arabic should be added in the proportion of 10 per cent. to the glacéing syrup.

VICTORIA PLUMS.

Choose fruit that is fully coloured, but not at all soft. If too unripe the stones will not come away, and if too soft the fruit will pulp too readily. Split the fruit half its length along the depressed side down to the stalk end, and with a hairpin or bent wire remove the stone. Put into a copper pan of cold water and slowly heat up to 200 deg. Fahr.

All about Ices.

Do not allow the water to boil, but slowly simmer until soft enough, when at once lift out into cold water. When cold, drain, put in pans, and cover with cool syrup 18 deg. by the saccharometer, and on successive days, finish exactly as for ripe apricots. Drain, glacé, or crystallise as desired.

PINEAPPLE.

This is a most useful fruit, and can be used in so many ways that it should always form part of the confectioner's stock. Peeled whole pines in water can be bought very cheaply, and this form is recommended as being the most economical. Open the cans, lift out the pines, drain them, and carefully cut into slices ⅜ in. thick. If intended to be used solely for decorative work, the slices can be preserved entire, as the difference in diameter will not matter at all. It is, however, advised that each slice be cut to one size with a round cutter 2½ ins. in diameter. The rings cut away can then be divided into cubes and preserved separately. In the drained form they will be useful for many forms of gateaux, petit fours, or Genoese work, or they can be glacéd and sold as fruit bonbons at a remunerative price.

Place the rounds neatly in enamelled bowls and cover with hot syrup at 22 deg. by the saccharometer. The strained liquor from the cans can be used in making this syrup, and will add to its flavour. On succeeding days finish this fruit exactly as for ripe apricots. For sale glacéing is the most effective for the rounds and the most profitable for the cubes. These must be well drained, rinsed in warm water, and when the syrup is ready and rubbed white turn in the dried cubes; stir all together and turn on to an upturned open-mesh brass sieve set over a pan to receive the syrup. Spread the cubes apart and stand in a warm room to dry, when the cubes can be dished for sale.

It will be noticed that with this fruit the first covering syrup is heavier than usual. That is because the fruit is heavily charged with water, which will quickly reduce the density of the syrup.

RASPBERRIES.

This fruit is too soft for preserving in the ordinary way in syrup, but in the following form will be greatly appreciated as a whole fruit conserve.

Use very dry unstalked raspberries, and for every pound weight to be preserved put one pint of syrup 36 deg. by the saccharometer into a copper bowl and bring it up to the boil. Carefully pick the fruit into this (off the fire) without breaking. When all are in, lift syrup from the sides with a copper ladle and pour over so that the fruit is covered, but do not stir. Return the pan to the fire and quickly bring up to the boil, lift from the fire, and let it subside, then repeat the boiling up seven or eight times. Gently pour into an enamelled bowl and stand in a cool place until next day. Drain the syrup away, turning the whole on an upturned hair sieve and leaving until as dry as possible. With a dessertspoon fill the fruit into small glass jars. Measure the syrup into a copper bowl, and for every pint of it add three-quarters of a pint of bright strained red currant juice, and boil until it reaches the webbing point. Carefully fill up each glass with this jelly, tapping them gently to ensure every portion being filled. When set and cold, cover down in the usual way.

GREEN FRENCH BEANS

French beans preserved in this way are very useful for decorative work only, as they are a beautiful colour, and being soft are easily curved when cut, into almost any

Jams and Conserves.

graceful form. Select young thin beans, very fresh. If the seeds are fully formed they must be removed, but if taken at the earlier stage this will not be necessary. Cut off the points and stalks and put in a copper pan of cold water to which has been added a good handful of salt. Heat slowly up to the boil, then turn at once into a large pan of cold water and let cold water run in and over until quite cold and all trace of the salt is washed out. Have ready the copper pan filled with cold water to every gallon of which $\frac{1}{2}$ oz. of powdered alum has been added. Turn in the beans, slowly heat up to the boiling point, and gently simmer until the beans are soft enough to break easily, but not too soft. Turn into cold water, and cool as quickly as possible with running water. Drain well, arrange in rows in enamelled bowls, and pour over sufficient cool syrup at 20 deg. density to cover them. Finish on successive days exactly as for greengages. In each day's draining care must be used that the beans lie in straight rows to avoid breakage.

COMPOTES OF FRUIT.

COMPOTES, OLD AND NEW.

Compotes in some one or other form, and under their correct or incorrect name, will always have a certain place in bills of fare. When it was customary to display the whole or nearly the whole of the second course on the set table, compotes were an important and decorative part of the scheme. Compotiers still survive, and are largely used for the display of dessert fruits and flowers.

The more plebeian stewed fruits (the poor relations of compotes) are far better known to the average caterer than the aristocratic compotes, which are simply fruits cooked in light syrups without being pulped, with or without additions in the form of spirits, liqueurs, etc., etc. Compotes can be served in plain and decorative form, and examples of both kinds will be found in the following pages.

At one time it was customary to not only decorate the dishes with flowers, and even cut vegetables, but to cover each compote with sheets of apple and other fruit jellies, these being sometimes separately decorated. Since, however, this course so seldom figures in the scheme of table decoration, we propose not to waste time with obsolete forms, and to confine the examples of decorative compotes to forms that lend increased value to the dishes as sweets only.

STRAWBERRY COMPOTE.

Pick ripe dry strawberries into a shallow earthenware pan. Pour over them sufficient plain syrup, 18 deg. by the saccharometer and boiling hot, to float them. Leave until cold, dish up carefully in the compotier, and pour the syrup over them. If boiled red or white currant juice, prepared for ices either with or without sugar, be available, use this at the same saccharine strength instead of the simple syrup. Serve with slightly sweetened whipped cream in a separate dish.

RASPBERRY COMPOTE.

Prepare simple syrup of fine crushed sugar and water, well skimmed, and if necessary clarified, and boiled in a copper egg bowl up to 16 deg. by the saccharometer. Pick fine dry raspberries from the stalks and throw in as many as the syrup will float easily, bring up to the boil quickly and let the syrup boil up over the fruit twice, resting a short time

All about Ices.

between. Pour the whole gently into an earthenware pan, and when cold arrange the fruit in the compotier and pour the syrup over it. Serve with whipped cream, or, better still, Devonshire clotted cream, in a separate dish.

RASPBERRY AND RED CURRANT COMPOTE.

Treat as for raspberries alone, except that the red currants should be boiled up once before adding the raspberries. Serve with clotted cream.

RED CURRANT COMPOTE.

Prepare simple syrup boiled to 18 deg. by the saccharometer, add half its weight of previously made red currant jelly or apple jelly, tint it a pale red with liquid carmine, and put in sufficient carefully picked red currants to just float; boil them up three times, pour into an earthenware pan, and when cold dish up in compotiers and serve with crystallised red or white currants and clotted cream. The syrup should be of thin jelly consistency.

CRYSTALLISED RED OR WHITE CURRANTS.

Select large bunches of fine dry fruit. Break one or more whites of eggs, whisk it with an equal quantity of water, strain through a fine strainer or skim off the froth, dip each bunch of fruit into the liquid, drain for a minute, then lightly cover with fine caster sugar, and hang each bunch over a thread in a warm room until quite dry. These currants are delicious alone, with compotes, or with cream.

BLACK CURRANT COMPOTE.

Treat as for red currants, using the red currant jelly, or failing this, add in its place, after the syrup has cooled, half a pint of cassis, but previously boil the syrup to 20 deg. by the saccharometer. Serve in either case alone.

RED AND BLACK CURRANT COMPOTE.

Use equal parts of the red and black fruit, add the red currant jelly to the syrup or use in its place apple jelly, adding a little cassis when cold. Serve without cream or other addition.

LOGAN COMPOTE.

This is the fruit obtained by crossing raspberries and blackberries. It is slightly darker in colour than raspberries, large and of fine flavour. Treat as for raspberries, except that it will bear boiling up the third time, and will be the better for the addition of a little lemon juice; it will make a delicious compote. Serve either with or without cream.

MULBERRY COMPOTE.

Treat as for Logan, but leave out the lemon juice. Boil up three times, and when cold add to the syrup a little kirsch. Serve without cream.

Jams and Conserves.

APPLE COMPOTE.

Choose good white-fleshed cooking apples, pare them carefully; if very small core them with a corer, if larger halve or quarter them, taking out the cores; throw them into cold water until all are ready. Prepare some simple syrup, boil up to 18 deg. by the saccharometer, add a piece of cinnamon, turn in the apples, and gently simmer until soft but unbroken. When cold, drain the apples, dish up in the compotiers, strain the syrup through a fine hair sieve, boil it up to 22 deg., and when nearly cold add it to the dished apples. Serve without cream.

COMPOTE OF PEARS.

Choose hard white-fleshed pears of medium size, turn them into a copper pan of hot water and simmer for a few minutes until they can be easily pared. Turn into cold water directly the peel is taken off to prevent them changing colour. Have ready some simple syrup at 18 deg., add a little lemon juice and a small piece of cinnamon, and slowly simmer until the pears are quite soft but unbroken. When cold, dish up in the compotiers, boil the syrup up to 22 deg., and when cold pour over the fruit. Serve alone. If desired, the pears can be tinted pink by adding a little liquid carmine to the syrup before putting in the fruit. In this case keep out the lemon juice, or the carmine will be apt to precipitate, as it is an alkaline solution. Large pears can be halved or even quartered, but the small whole fruit has a better appearance. Serve without cream.

COMPOTE OF CHERRIES (MORELLA)

Choose large ripe fruit, pick off the stalks, throw the fruit into simple syrup 18 deg. by the saccharometer, slowly bring to the boil, then boil up five times, letting them subside between each boiling. Pour into an earthenware pan, when cold, drain, and reboil the syrup, adding one-fourth its weight of apple jelly; boil up to 24 deg., and when nearly cold dish up the fruit and pour the reduced syrup over it. It should be a rich red colour, but can be deepened in tint with liquid carmine if desired. Serve without cream.

COMPOTE OF CHERRIES (FLEMISH).

This fruit is not so deep in colour or quite so rich in flavour. It should be treated in all respects as for Morella cherries, but when the syrup is cooled after the last boiling add a little kirsch to tone up the flavour.

COMPOTE OF MELON.

Select either the green or yellow Spanish melons, not too ripe, cut into slices nearly an inch thick (if too long divide into two), turn them into hot syrup 18 deg., and slowly simmer until transparent and soft, but unbroken; lift out into compotiers, reboil the syrup with a little apple jelly up to 24 deg., and when nearly cold add sufficient kirsch to give a nice flavour, and pour over the fruit. Serve without cream.

BANANA COMPOTE.

Remove the skins from firm fruit, cut into inch lengths, put in an earthenware pan, pour over sufficient syrup at 18 deg. boiling hot to float them, and allow to stand for six hours. Drain off the syrup, strain it, add a little apple jelly and lemon juice, boil up to 24 deg., and when cold add a little yellow chartreuse and pour over the dished fruit. Serve without cream.

All about Ices.

GREENGAGE COMPOTE.

Choose hard green fruit, prick all over with the needle pricker, throw into cold water in which a little alum has been dissolved When all are done, drain and throw into a copper pan of water and slowly bring up to 200 degrees. At once lift out into cold water, and when cold drain and turn into a pan of cold syrup at 18 deg. Slowly bring up to the boil, by which time they should be soft, but unbroken; boil them up twice, subsiding between, then remove from the fire, pour into an earthenware pan, cover with spinach leaves, and let them rest until quite cold, then drain them from the syrup, dish them up in compotiers, strain and reboil the syrup up to 22 deg., and when nearly cold add a little maraschino or prunella to flavour, and pour over the fruit.

COMPOTE OF VICTORIA PLUMS.

Choose large ripe fruit, cut in halves with a silver knife and remove the stones. Have ready simple syrup at 18 deg., throw in the stones and bring to the boil, then turn in the fruit; boil up three times. Turn out into an earthenware pan and stand until cold. Drain the fruit, dish up in compotiers, strain and reboil the syrup up to 22 deg., add when cold a little kirsch, and pour the syrup over the dished fruit. Serve without cream.

COMPOTE OF MIRABELS.

Choose fully-formed but hard unripe fruit. Make an incision in the skin of each fruit and throw into a pan of hot water (a few dozen at a time in a small hair sieve is the better plan). In a few minutes the fruit will rise and the skin begin to peel away from the incision. At once throw into cold water, and the skin will easily peel away. As they are peeled again throw them into cold water to keep them unbroken. When all are done, turn them into a copper pan of hot syrup 18 deg. by the saccharometer. Slowly bring up to the boil, then boil up twice, letting the syrup subside between the boilings. Turn into an earthenware pan, and when cold, drain, pile up the fruit in the compotiers, reboil the syrup up to 22 deg., and when cold add a little noyeau and pour over the fruit. Serve either with or without whipped cream.

COMPOTE OF GREEN APRICOTS.

Use the fruit whilst still hard and green, blanch them in the lye or soda bath (see Green Apricots in "Preserved Fruit"), turn them into a copper pan of cold water, and when the rough, furry coats have been removed prick them lightly with the needle pricker, bring them slowly to the boil, and as soon as the fruit begins to soften lift from the fire, cover with spinach leaves, and leave in the water until cold. Carefully drain, pour cold syrup of 18 deg. density over them, again cover with spinach leaves, and let them stand until next day. Drain away the syrup, bring it up to the boil, reduce to 22 degrees, turn in the fruit, and give a boil up twice, allowing it to subside between. In a few hours the fruit will be sufficiently impregnated with sugar to be lifted out into compotiers, when the syrup should be strained through a fine hair sieve, and sufficient of it to cover the fruit reboiled up to 24 deg., a little fresh lemon juice added, and when almost cold strongly flavoured with maraschino and poured over the fruits. If kept in a cool place this compote may be kept for two or even three days, but each second day must be strained and the syrup reboiled, or it is certain to ferment. Do not add either lemon juice or liqueur until preparing to serve. Serve with cream.

Jams and Conserves.

COMPOTE OF RIPE APRICOTS.

If very large fruit be used it must be halved, but the small fruit is more suitable. If the fruit be quite ripe, prick lightly with the needle pricker, make an incision on the depressed side half the length only from the stalk end, and remove the stone. Place the fruit in a copper pan of cold water and slowly bring up to the boil, using plenty of water to float the fruit. As soon as slightly soft lift out into cold water, and when cool drain thoroughly, and throw into a pan of syrup of 18 deg. density. Boil up three times, allowing the syrup to subside between each boiling. Pour into a pan to cool. Arrange the drained fruit in compotiers, strain the syrup, add a little lemon juice to the quantity required, boil up to 22 deg., and when cool flavour strongly with maraschino, and pour over the fruit.

Canned apricots can be finished exactly the same way, draining them and adding to the syrup, strained and brought up to the proper density.

Large fruit, halved and stoned when finished, can be dished with the flat sides uppermost, and after the syrup has been carefully poured over, each apricot half can be filled with a teaspoonful of firmly whipped cream, dropped in spoon meringue shape.

COMPOTE OF PEACHES.

If fine, fresh, ripe peaches be used they should be carefully peeled in cold water, halved with a silver knife, the stone removed, drained dry, and dished up in the compotiers. Syrup of 22 deg. should be richly flavoured with kirsch and poured over the fruit quite cold. Serve as cold as possible with clotted cream or junket.

If the canned peaches be used the white free stone should be chosen, as they are much more tender than the yellow cling stone variety.

COMPOTE OF NECTARINES.

This is one of the most delicious of the compotes, but is so very expensive that it is seldom used except in the macedoines.

Drop the fruit, one or two at a time, into boiling water for not more than a few seconds, lift out into cold water, and with a silver knife remove the rind. Drop them into hot syrup at 18 deg. of density, tinted pink, and boil them up twice very quickly, allowing the sryup to subside between the boilings. Let them stand in the syrup until cool, lift out and drain, and set in the compotiers whole. Strain sufficient of the syrup to cover them, boil it up to 22 deg., add a little kirsch and mandarine when nearly cold, and pour over the fruit. Serve very cold with whipped or clotted cream separately.

COMPOTE OF PEARS WITH SAUTERNE.

Almost any of the various soft-fleshed dessert pears in their season are suitable for this compote. Select those that are slightly under-ripe, and carefully remove the rind with a silver knife. If at all hard, blanch them in boiling water before peeling them. Cut in halves, or if very large in quarters, leaving a small piece only of the scraped stalk on them. Set them in a small copper pan with sufficient sauterne to just cover them, and for each half-pint of the wine a half-pound of small loaf sugar and 1 in. of cinnamon. Let them steep for half an hour, then slowly raise to the boil, and simmer gently until soft, but not broken. Boil up twice, then carefully turn into an earthenware pan. When cold, drain, strain the syrup, and boil up to 22 deg., tint it a pale pink, and when cold add a little pale brandy and pour over the fruit in the compotiers. Serve alone.

All about Ices.

COMPOTE OF QUINCE.

Blanch the fruit in boiling water, turn into cold water, and quickly remove the outer rind. Cut into quarters, remove the cores, drop into cold water until all are done, drain, and put in a copper pan with sufficient syrup at 15 deg. of density, slowly bring to the boil, and simmer gently until soft, then turn ont into an earthenware pan, and let them stand until cold. Drain away the syrup, strain it, add a little lemon juice, and boil up to 22 deg., turn in the fruit, boil up twice, skim carefully, and dish up in the compotiers. Serve with clotted cream in a separate bowl.

COMPOTE OF PINEAPPLE.

Use a canned Singapore pineapple, drain free from liquor, cut into rounds nearly $\frac{1}{2}$ in. thick, divide these into halves or quarters, turn into sufficient cold syrup of 18 deg. density to cover the fruit, add the liquor from the can, slowly bring to the boil, and boil up well six or seven times, skim well, and turn into an earthenware pan to cool. Drain and dish up symmetrically in the compotiers, reboil sufficient of the syrup up to 22 deg., add a little lemon juice, and, when cold, a small quantity of fine Jamacia rum, and pour over the fruit. Serve alone

COMPOTE OF PINEAPPLE AND APPLE JELLY.

Prepare the pineapple in the same way as for pineapple compote, except that the slices must be cut rather thinner, and all cut to a uniform size with a small round cutter, say, 2 ins. in diameter, or into half circles all one size. Fill small dome-shaped petit fours moulds, round or crescent shape for the half circles with melted pink apple jelly, or run into impressions in the starch tray, the shapes being suitable to the pineapple basis. When set, turn out of the moulds, or wash free from starch, and set in position on the pieces of pineapple, and arrange symmetrically in the compotiers. Use sufficient of the syrup to cover the bases, boil it with a little lemon juice up to 22 deg., and when cold, add a little fine Jamaica rum, and pour over, covering the base well, but leaving the apple jelly upstanding above the syrup.

COMPOTE OF APPLES AND CRANBERRIES.

Use the Michigan cranberries about the size of small cherries. Sort them carefully, picking out those that are soft or discoloured. Soak them in very cold water for an hour, and then lightly prick with the needle pricker to prevent them bursting and collapsing. For each pound of apples used one-fourth of a pound of cranberries will be sufficient.

The apples must be cut in quarters or less according to size, and must be carefully simmered as for apple compote, separately from the cranberries. Have ready a little syrup at 18 deg., taken from that used to cook the apples, and reduced to the proper saccharine strength, turn in the cranberries, slowly bring up to the boil, and then boil up twice. Skin carefully, and when cold drain the fruit, add it to the apples in the compotiers, and cover with the cold apple syrup at 24 deg. of density. Serve with thin, sweet, unwhipped cream in a cream jug.

COMPOTE OF CRANBERRIES.

Prepare as above, except that the cranberries are served with their own syrup boiled to 24 deg. of strength, and when cold slightly flavoured with kirsch. The syrup should be a pale red.

Jams and Conserves.

COMPOTE OF GREEN GOOSEBERRIES. (1).

Use the hard unripe fruit, remove the snuffs and stalks, prick them all over with the needle pricker, throw them into cold water, and slowly bring them to 200 deg. F. Lift out into cold water to cool, and cover them with two or three cloths, and leave them to recover their colour. When quite cold, drain them, lift into syrup of 15 deg. by the saccharometer, and slowly bring them up to the boil and gently simmer until soft but unbroken, by which time they should be quite green. Turn into an earthenware pan, and if not sufficiently green cover with spinach leaves until cold. Drain, dish up in the compotiers, strain the syrup, and boil up to 24 deg., by which time it should show signs of jelly-like consistency. When nearly cold, add a little noyeau, and pour over the fruit. Serve with thin sweet cream.

COMPOTE OF GREEN GOOSEBERRIES. (2).

Choose large almost ripe green berries, snuff and stalk, very lightly prick with the needle pricker, and throw at once into syrup 18 deg. by the saccharometer. Slowly bring to the boil, let it subside for a few minutes, then boil up twice. Finish in exactly the same way as for No. 1, but flavour the syrup with a little maraschino. Serve with thin sweet cream.

Almost ripe yellow gooseberries should be treated exactly as for green No. 2, but flavoured with kirsch.

COMPOTE OF DAMSONS.

Select the fruit when fully matured, but not soft. Pick off the stalks, prick all over with the needle pricker, throw into cold water, and slowly bring up to 200 deg. F. Lift out into cold water, and when cold drain and turn into syrup 15 deg. by the saccharometer. Slowly bring up to the boil, and boil up three times, allowing the syrup to subside between each boiling. Let them stand in the syrup until cold, drain, dish up in the compotiers, take sufficient of the strained syrup, add one-sixth its bulk of apple jelly, boil up to 24 deg., by which time it will show signs of jellying, and when nearly cold add a little pale brandy and pour over the fruit. Serve alone.

COMPOTE OF MACEDOINE.

This is the best known of all the compotes, because it can be made up from a number of open tins of canned fruits. It consists of almost anything available, such as slices of apple, pear, pieces of apricot, peach, banana, greengage, pineapple, glacé cherries, green and black grapes, nectarines, etc., all cut somewhat alike in size, and covered with syrup of 20 or 22 deg. of strength strongly flavoured with kirsch or manderine, or both. The fruits that need cooking are afterwards indiscriminately mixed with those that do not, but the blend of colours should be effective, and the whole should be served as cold as possble.

COMPOTE OF ORANGE.

Use fully ripe sweet oranges, remove the rind and every particle of white pith, divide the orange through the middle, and take away the pith from between the sections. Cut into $\frac{1}{4}$ in. thick slices, and remove every pip. Arrange the cut slices in overlapping concentric rings in the compotiers, boil a little pineapple or simple syrup up to 22 deg., and when cold, flavour it strongly with orange curacoa, and pour it over the fruit in the compotiers.

All about Ices.

COMPOTE OF ORANGES (TANGERINE).

Prepare this in the same way as for the sweet oranges, except that the syrup must be strongly flavoured with mandarine and slightly with fine pale Jamaica rum.

COMPOTE OF CHESTNUTS (MARRONS).

Use the large Italian marrons. Score them on both sides with a sharp knife, put them on a wire in a very hot oven to roast, testing them occasionally so that they may be taken as soon as ready. If allowed to over-bake the outsides will get hard and the syrup will not perpetrate them. They should be soft and floury. If at all old soak them in warm water for an hour or two before roasting them. When ready peel away both outer and inner skins, and whilst still hot press them a little flat with the hand. Have ready a little syrup 15 deg. density, add a little lemon juice and a piece of a vanilla bean, turn in the nuts, slowly raise the syrup up to 200 deg., and slowly simmer for half an hour, then pour into an earthenware pan and stand until cold. Drain, pile up in the compotiers, strain the syrup, boil it up to 22 deg., and when nearly cold add a little noyeau and pour over the nuts. Serve with plain whipped cream.

COMPOTE OF CHESTNUTS AND ORANGES.

Use Italian marrons, score them and put in a very hot oven for a few minutes to free the outer skin. Tie them loosely in a small linen bag and boil them in plenty of water until getting soft. The time will vary according to the size and age of the nuts, but will not be less than two hours. When nearly done, pour away a portion of the water and make it up with hot milk to improve the colour of the nuts. When soft enough peel off the inner skin quickly, and throw into cold water. When quite cold drain them, weigh, and pound in a marble mortar into a smooth, floury paste, flavour with vanilla sugar, and to every pound add half a pound of loaf sugar boiled to the hard ball, working the whole well together into a smooth paste. Whilst still hot pass the whole through a twelve-mesh brass sieve, rubbing the paste through with the back of a wooden spoon on to a sheet of manilla paper. Fill the centre of a compotier with the marron paste roughly piled up, border it with whipped cream flavoured with curacoa, and surround the whole with slices of sweet orange prepared as for orange compote, pouring the orange syrup over the fruit and the marrons, and very lightly over the cream to avoid its running down, or the cream may be served separately.

COMPOTE BORDEAUX.

Pick the hulls from 2 lbs. of fine ripe strawberries into a deep basin, place ½ lb. of fine loaf sugar in another basin, and pour over this a pint bottle of good red or white claret. When the sugar is dissolved strain the wine through a fine hair sieve, add a wineglassful of pale brandy, and pour the whole over the strawberries. Place in the refrigerator for an hour or two to get thoroughly cold, then dish up in compotiers and pour the wine over. Serve alone.

COMPOTE OF GREEN FIGS.

Blanch the ripe green figs in boiling water for two minutes, after pricking the outer skins with the needle pricker. Lift out into cold water, and when cold drain, pass into syrup at 18 deg. by the saccharometer, slowly bring to the boil, boil up twice, turn into an

Jams and Conserves.

earthenware pan with the syrup, and let stand until quite cold. Next day, drain, strain and re-boil the syrup up to 22 deg., and when nearly cold add a little old Jamaica rum and pour over the fruit, dished up in the compotiers.

Should the fruit be at all hard and unripe, the rind after blanching may be peeled away in long straight cuts from top to stem. Finish as before. Serve with plain sweet cream.

COMPOTE OF CHERRY APPLES.

This pretty little fruit is not so generally grown, or when grown used as it might be. It must be quite ripe and free from blemish. Pick off the stalks, core them by using a very tiny gouge or $\frac{1}{4}$-tube cutter and twirling the fruit on the half-round or round edge, thus cutting out a small cylindrical hole through the fruit. Throw them into cold syrup 15 deg. of saccharine strength and slowly bring up to the boil, and simmer until soft but unbroken. Turn out, drain, re-boil a portion of the syrup with one-third its bulk of clear apple jelly up to 22 deg., turn in the fruit, boil up twice, and when cold pile up symmetrically in the compotiers. Add a little brandy and kirsch to the jelly-like syrup and pour over the fruit. Serve with plain whipped or clotted cream.

COMPOTE OF WINTER STRAWBERRIES.

This fruit is the product of the abutilon tree that grows freely in all semi-tropical countries, and almost as well in some of the southern counties of Great Britain. It is not half as well known as it deserves to be.

Place 2 lbs. of the fruit in a deep basin, pour a pint of chablis over $\frac{1}{2}$ lb. of small loaf sugar, and when the sugar is dissolved strain through a fine hair sieve; add the juice of one lemon and a wineglassful of mandarine, and pour over the fruit. Keep it in the refrigerator until very cold, then dish up the fruit in a pile in the compotiers and pour the syrup over. Serve alone.

COMPOTE OF MEDLARS.

Select fruit of an even size when perfectly mellow and soft. It is customary to say that medlars are only fit to eat when they are rotten. Needless to say that no fruit is eatable when in that state. Medlars when gathered are always hard and uneatable, but they quickly become mellow if kept at a moderate temperature on hay or straw. Their chief objections are the coarse leathery skins, the large snuffs, and the large bean-like seeds, the first two of which cannot conveniently be removed, and the last only at the expense of a goodly portion of the pulp-like flesh. If the fruit is very large it is a good plan to divide into halves and try and get away the stones. Have ready a little syrup of 18 deg. density, add a little lemon-juice (freshly squeezed), throw in the medlars, slowly bring up to the boil, and boil up once only. Let the fruit remain in the syrup until cold, then drain it. Dish up the fruit in the compotiers. Strain sufficient of the syrup to well cover the fruit, with a little added clear apple jelly; reboil it to 22 deg., and when nearly cold flavour strongly with brandy and kirsch and pour over the fruit. Serve alone.

COMPOTE OF MUSCAT GRAPES.

Choose ripe grapes just turning yellow. Prick them lightly with the needle pricker, set them in a basin, and cover with white muscat wine or with Sauterne, previously mixed with $\frac{1}{2}$ lb. of small loaf sugar to each pint bottle. Let them steep for two hours, then drain.

All about Ices.

Strain the syrup through a fine hair sieve and reduce it on the fire to 20 deg. by the saccharometer. When nearly cold, add to each pint a tablespoonful each of kirsch and pale brandy and pour over the grapes. Keep them in the refrigerator until very cold, then dish up in small cups or glasses, with a teaspoonful of lemon or orange water ice on top of each.

COMPOTE OF MUSCATELS.

Pick large muscatel raisins from their stalks, set them in a basin in even layers and cover with chablis or sauterne, and let them steep until they have become swollen, and have absorbed almost all the wine. Have ready a little syrup at 18 deg. and half the quantity of red currant jelly. Melt and warm this together and turn the swollen fruit into it. Slowly raise to the boil and give one good boil to entirely cover the fruit. Turn out, and when cold drain the fruit, dish it up in small cups or glasses, flavour the syrup with orange curacoa, and fill up the glasses nearly to the top. Cool in the refrigerator, and when serving cover the top of each glass with a little orange-water ice.

GOOSEBERRY FOOL.

Use hard green berries, set them in an untinned copper pan with a little water, slowly bring to the boil and simmer gently until the fruit is quite soft and easily broken. Break up thoroughly with the spattle against the side of the pan, and see that the whole is reduced to a pulp and free from any pieces. Remove from the fire and turn into a basin, cover with a clean cloth, and allow it to get quite cold in the refrigerator. When wanted to serve, add just sufficient pulverised sugar to take off the edge of the sourness, say one-fourth of its weight, and then very gradually one-fourth of its bulk of thin sweet unwhipped cream, or thick cream reduced with milk. At the last moment stir in to each quart a dessertspoonful of kirsch, and dish up in small pony tumblers.

RASPBERRY FOOL.

Use very fine ripe fruit, pick them into a basin, break up with a silver fork, add sufficient pulverised sugar to make only pleasantly sweet, to each pint a dessertspoonful of mandarine and nearly half a pint of thin unwhipped cream, and well mix, but do not beat at all. Serve in small custard glasses, very cold.

STRAWBERRY FOOL.

Make this as for raspberry fool, flavouring with a dessertspoonful of fine old Jamaica rum to each pint of the puree before adding the thin cream. Serve very cold in small custard cups of glasses, with half a strawberry on each.

SECTION VII.
WINE CUPS & FRUIT BEVERAGES.

Amongst the most popular beverages for large gatherings, such as balls, receptions, and other occasions covering a length of time are the various wine cups. If one may judge by the frequency of its use, it would be correct to place claret cup as the favourite; but there are other reasons than popularity for this almost universal choice. One is that most caterers can make claret cup of a sort, and it may be that there are many like unto the one who wrote to the writer for a recipe for "champagne cup," and admitted that he was unaware of any but "claret cup." Probably, however, the low prices at which this wine is obtainable and its blendable acidity have been helpful factors to its use.

Claret is essentially a British title; and in the early part of the eighteenth century, when the more wealthy of our fighting ancestors delighted in mulled, spiced, and buttered claret, the term covered most of the lighter red wines (even those from Oporto), but to-day applies chiefly to the dark red (and white) Bordeaux wines, and various brands of red ink.

Wine cups at one time consisted of wines thoroughly iced and strengthened or flavoured with spirits or liqueurs, sweetened or soured, or both, according to their character, and were not at all like the semi-temperance drinks of to-day. Their present form—reduced with mineral waters, sweetened, soured, flavoured, and thoroughly iced—is greatly preferable as a beverage taken at intervals during an evening function, and, although not actually free from alcohol, practically innocuous.

Wine cups are at their best when crisp and sparkling, and their worst when flat and dead. It is therefore advisable to have them as freshly made as possible, icing both wine and mineral waters beforehand.

A very general plan is to serve in a large bowl with a ladle, and to place a good-sized lump of ice in the bowl. This effectively ices the drink and increases its bulk, but at the expense of reducing the quality, which must constantly vary as the ice dissolves.

No. 1.— CLARET CUP.

1 large bottle of claret.
1 bottle of soda water.
1 bottle of seltzer water.
5 ozs. of loaf sugar.
2 lemons.
1 orange.
$\frac{1}{6}$ of a pint of pale brandy.
Small bunch of borage or 2-inch piece of cucumber.

Cut the rind in thin pieces from one of the lemons, peel away the white, pithy portion from both, cut into thin slices, remove the pips, slice the orange (peel and all) in the same way, and place the zest and slices of orange and lemon, with the sugar, in a large deep jug.

All about Ices.

Pour the wine over, tie the borage in a little bunch (or slice the cucumber thin) and add to the wine. Ice the whole for two hours, and to finish strain through a fine hair sieve, add the brandy and the iced mineral waters. Keep in ice, and serve in small pony tumblers.

No. 2.—BURGUNDY CUP—RED.

1 large bottle of still Burgundy.
1 bottle of soda water.
1 bottle of seltzer water.
4 ozs. of loaf sugar.
3 lemons (cut zest of 1, squeezed juice of 2, 1 peeled and sliced).

1 orange (sliced, and pips removed).
2 bay leaves.
$\frac{1}{8}$ of a pint of orange Curacoa.
Small wineglassful of pale brandy.

Make and ice as for claret cup.

No. 3.—CHABLIS CUP.

1 large bottle of Chablis.
1 bottle of lemonade.
1 bottle of soda water.
5 ozs. of loaf sugar.
2 lemons (1 squeezed, one peeled and sliced).

2 oranges (one squeezed, 1 sliced).
2 fresh-green mint leaves.
$\frac{1}{8}$ of a pint of kirsch.
1 small wineglassful of pale brandy.

Mix and ice as for claret cup.

No. 4.—SAUTERNE CUP.

1 bottle dry Sauterne or Graves.
1 large bottle of Apollinaris water.
1 small bottle of seltzer water.
5 ozs. of brown sugar candy (crushed fine).
3 lemons (1 peeled and sliced, 2 squeezed).

2 Tangerine oranges peeled and sliced.
1 inch of stick cinnamon.
1 oz. of shred angelica.
$\frac{1}{8}$ of a pint of mandarine.

Tear the peel f   angerine oranges and let it steep in the wine with the fruit, sugar candy, cinnamo   ..ngelica. Strain, mix, and ice as for No. 1.

No. 5.—HOCK CUP.

1 large bottle of still hock.
1 bottle of soda water.
1 bottle of seltzer water.
4 ozs. of brown sugar candy (crushed fine).
3 lemons, peeled and sliced.

2 oranges (sliced zest of 1, strained juice of 2).
1 bay leaf.
1 wineglassful of orange Curacoa.
1 wineglass of mandarine.

1   eglassful of orange bitters.

Mix, strain, and ice as for No. 1.

Wine Cups and Fruit Beverages.

No. 6.—MOSELLE CUP.

1 large bottle of still Moselle.
1 large bottle of Apollinaris water.
1 small bottle of seltzer water.
4 ozs. of loaf sugar.

3 lemons (cut zest of 1, 3 peeled and sliced).
2 inches of cucumber (finely sliced).
$\frac{1}{8}$ of a pint of yellow Chartreuse.

1 small wineglassful of pale brandy.

Mix, steep, strain, and ice as for No. 1.

No. 7.—MOSELLE CUP.

1 quart bottle of sparkling Moselle.
1 large bottle of Apollinaris.
1 small bottle of seltzer water.
$\frac{1}{8}$ pint of simple syrup.

3 lemons (cut zest of 1, 3 peeled and sliced).
2 ozs. of shred angelica.
$\frac{1}{8}$ of a pint of green Chartreuse.

1 small wineglassful of pale brandy.

In this cup syrup is used instead of sugar, to avoid agitation as much as possible, thus conserving the effervescent condition of the wine. Mix, steep, strain, and ice as for No. 1.

No. 8.—CHAMPAGNE CUP.

1 quart bottle of Champagne.
1 large bottle of Apollinaris water.
1 small bottle of seltzer water.
$\frac{1}{8}$ pint of simple syrup.

3 lemons (peeled and sliced).
1 orange (cut zest of, and sliced).
$\frac{1}{4}$ pint of kirsch.
1 small wineglassful of mandarine.

To be steeped all together except the wine, which must be iced and added after straining.

No. 9.—SAUMUR CUP.

Make this cup as for champagne, substituting a bottle of dry Saumur or Sillery for the champagne. In practice this is pretty general, but it is not so usual to use the correct title. It is generally called champagne. If champagne be used it is not necessary to choose high-priced cuvées, but it is necessary to avoid low-grade brands.

No. 10—CHIANTI CUP.

This is an Italian wine of the Bordeaux character, but of greater body, and makes a really first-class cup, treated as for claret cup, or with the following slightly altered formula:—

1 large flask of Chianti (red).
1 bottle of seltzer water.
1 large bottle of Apollinaris.
6 ozs. of loaf sugar.
3 lemons (cut zest of 1, 2 peeled and sliced).

2 oranges (sliced).
2 ozs. of shred angelica
$\frac{1}{8}$ of a pint of kirsch.
$\frac{1}{8}$ of a pint of orange Curacoa.

Mixed, steeped, strained, and iced as for claret cup.

All about Ices.

No. 11.—MARSALA CUP.

1 large bottle of Marsala.
1 large bottle of Apollinaris water.
1 small bottle of seltzer water.
4 ozs. of brown sugar candy (bruised fine).
4 oranges (2 sliced, 2 squeezed).
2 lemons peeled and sliced.
$\frac{1}{8}$ of a pint of mandarine.
1 small wineglassful of orange bitters.

Mixed, steeped, strained, and iced as for No. 1.

No. 12.—MUSCATEL CUP.

1 large bottle of Muscato.
1 bottle of soda water.
1 bottle of seltzer water.
4 ozs. of loaf sugar.
8 ozs. of Muscat grapes (crushed).
3 lemons peeled and sliced
$\frac{1}{4}$ pint of pale brandy.

1 small wineglassful of orange-flower water (triple).

If Muscat grapes be not available, or too dear (the same thing), Muscatel raisins may be substituted, and must be split before steeping; or a further alternative is $\frac{1}{2}$ oz. of Darjeeling tea infused in $\frac{1}{4}$ pint of boiling water for three minutes only, cooled, and added to the bulk before icing, or a second alternative, a small bunch of elderflowers, may be used with good effect.

Both port and sherry cups are occasionally made, but neither of them is fit for human beings to drink, and, as this is not intended to be a temperance lecture, possible arguments are not to be advanced.

No. 13.—PUNCH CUP.

$\frac{1}{4}$ pint of brown brandy.
$\frac{1}{4}$ pint of old Jamaica rum.
$\frac{1}{4}$ pint of kirsch.
1 quart of seltzer water.
3 ozs. of brown sugar candy (bruised fine).
2 lemons (zest of 1, 2 squeezed).
2 oranges (zest of 1, 2 squeezed).

Steep the oranges, lemons, and sugar candy n the spirits and liquerfor four hours, strain, add the seltzer and ice as for claret cup.

No. 14.—GIN CUP.

$\frac{1}{2}$ pint of Hollands.
1 small wineglassful of mandarine.
1 small wineglassful of kirsch.
3 ozs. of loaf sugar.
2 lemons (zest of 1, 2 squeezed).
1 Tangarine orange (sliced, and the pips removed).
1 large bottle of Apollinaris water.

Steep the rind of the orange, the zest of the lemon in the spirit, liqueurs, and the juice for four hours, strain, and add the mineral water and ice as for No. 1.

No. 15.—CIDER CUP

1 quart bottle of cider.
1 quart bottle of seltzer water.
4 ozs. of loaf sugar.
3 lemons (zest of 1, peel and slice 3).
1 orange (sliced).
6 cloves (whole).

1 small wineglassful of maraschino.

Mix, steep, strain, and ice as for No. 1.

Wine Cups and Fruit Beverages.

No. 16.—PERRY CUP.

1 quart bottle of perry.
1 quart bottle of seltzer water.
4 ozs. of loaf sugar.
3 lemons peeled and sliced.
2 oranges (cut zest of 1, 2 sliced).

1 inch of stick cinnamon
1 wineglassful of kirsch.
1 wineglassful of Benedictine.
1 wineglassful of orange-flower water (triple).

Mix, steep, strain, and ice as for No. 1.

LEMONADE.

This is the most popular of all the still temperance drinks, and if properly made is deliciously refreshing. As a rule, it is far too strong of the water, and sweetly insipid. It is not possible to give proportions that will be always accurate, because the size of the lemons, as well as the amount and acidity of the juice, vary considerably; the following proportions are therefore only approximately correct.

10 lemons.   1 pint of simple syrup.
3 quarts of cold spring water.

Take the zest off half tne lemons with a razing knife, place in a large basin, cut and squeeze the lemons into another basin, and before adding to the zest remove the pips. Add the syrup, and let the whole steep for the syrup to extract the oil from the zest. Add the water, mix well, taste, and if too sweet or sour adjust to taste. If sufficiently strong of the zest, strain through a fine hair sieve, or better still, a thin jelly bag, and set on ice. Serve very cold. If desired, less water may be used, and a piece or pieces of ice, the equivalent of the deleted water, added.

It is usual to pour boiling water over sugar and juice, and to cut slices of lemon or peel to flavour, but the result is never quite saitisfactory. The cold method is the only one that will give the beautiful fresh flavour.

It is worthy of note that lemon juice quickly loses its fresh crisp character, and must therefore be squeezed only when wanted for use.

LIMEADE.

Limes have much of the lemon character, but are smaller, thinner skinned, and have a quite distinct flavour of their own. Most folks associate limes with the slightly mouldy flavour of so-called lime juice and cordials, but these are entirely free from the distinguishing flavour and aroma that belong to the fresh fruit. Use sufficient limes to squeeze out

1 pint of juice $1\frac{1}{4}$ pint of simple syrup
3 quarts of cold spring water.

Take off the zest of eight or ten, and finish as for lemonade. Serve very cold.

ORANGEADE.

10 fine ripe oranges.   1 pint of simple syrup.
4 large lemons.   3 quarts of cold spring water.

Take the zest from five of the oranges, cut and squeeze both oranges and lemons, finish and cool as for lemonade.

All about Ices.

TANGERINE ORANGEADE.

12 Tangerine oranges.
4 large Denia oranges.
4 lemons.
1¼ pint of simple syrup.
3 quarts of cold spring water.

Strip the loose rind from the Tangerine oranges, and pound half of it to pulp in a marble mortar, lift out into basin, cut the fruit in halves, and remove the pips, and then pound to a pulp in the mortar. Add to the rind, cut and squeeze the Denia oranges and the lemons, remove the pips, and add with the syrup to the pounded pulp. Let all steep for an hour, then add the water, mix well, and strain through a thin jelly bag, and ice very thoroughly.

CHERRYADE (1).

3 lbs. of cherries.
1¼ pint of simple syrup.
The juice of 2 lemons.
2½ quarts of cold spring water.

Choose the transparent Kentish, Flemish, or Duke cherries, pick them from the stalks, and pound the stones and all to a pulp in a marble mortar. Lift out into a copper sugar-boiler and simmer until reduced to a pulp, add the syrup and simmer for a few minutes together. When nearly cold, add the water and the strained lemon juice, and, if desired, a few drops of liquid carmine. Strain through a thin jelly bag, and ice thoroughly.

CHERRYADE (2).

3 lbs. of Morella cherries.
1¼ pint of simple syrup.
2½ quarts of cold spring water.
1 tablespoonful of kirsch.

Prepare in the same way as for No. 1, adding the kirsch after straining. No colour will be needed.

RASPBERRYADE.

3 lbs. of picked raspberries.
1½ pint of simple syrup.
½ lb. of picked red currants.
2½ quarts of cold spring water.

Crush the raspberries and currants in a deep basin, and let them stand in a warm place, say 70 deg., for at least two days to ferment. Skim the scum from the top, and pass through a jelly bag until quite clear. Add the syrup and the cold water, and, if desired, a little liquid carmine; strain again through a thin bag, and ice thoroughly. The red currants may be left out, and the juice of two lemons added instead, but the liquor will not be so bright. If the process of fermenting be too long, the fresh fruit may be strained, but it is certain to be more or less cloudy, and not so crisp as by the above method.

STRAWBERRYADE.

3 lbs. picked strawberries.
1½ pint of simple syrup.
Juice of 2 lemons.
2 quarts of cold spring water
1 tablespoonful of Jamaica rum.

Ferment the fruit as for raspberryade, adding the lemon juice before the final straining, and the rum afterwards. Fresh fruit may, if desired, be broken down and strained without fermenting, but the drink will be insipid as well as cloudy, and entirely lack the crispness given by the above plan. It will also deteriorate much more rapidly and successfully.

Wine Cups and Fruit Beverages.

PINEADE.

- 1 No. 3-sized can Singapore pine.
- 3 oranges.
- 2 lemons.
- 1 tablespoonful of Jamaica rum.
- 1¼ pint of simple syrup.
- 2 quarts of cold spring water.
- 1 tablespoonful of kirsch.

Lift the pine from the can, drain the liquor into a large basin, cut the pine in slices, and pound to pulp in a marble mortar. Lift out into the basin, add the strained juice of the oranges and lemons and the syrup, let it steep for an hour, then add the water, stand awhile and strain through a thin jelly bag until quite bright. Last of all add the kirsch and rum, and ice thoroughly.

MILLE FRUITADE.

- 6 lemons.
- 6 Denia oranges.
- 3 Tangerine oranges.
- 50 large whole raspberries.
- 25 strawberries (cut in halves).
- 20 small Muscat grapes.
- 1 tablespoonful of green Chartreuse.
- A pony tumbler each red and white currants.
- 1¼ pint of simple syrup.
- 2½ quarts of cold spring water.
- 1 tablespoonful of kirsch.
- 1 tablespoonful of mandarine.

Prepare and blend the oranges and lemons as previously described, add the syrup and water, and strain into a large bowl or deep jug. Add the liqueurs and mix well, then turn in the various fruits, place a small board on top to keep the fruits under, and ice thoroughly. Serve with a small ladle, and let some of the fruits be placed in each small tumbler. If liked, a few Morella cherries may be added, but they are apt to stain the liquor in their immediate neighbourhood. This drink is delicious and unique.

ORGEAT WATER.

- 1 lb. of sweet Sicily almonds.
- 2 ozs. of bitter almonds.
- 1 lemon (juice only).
- 1½ pint of simple syrup.
- ⅛ of a pint of orange-flower water.
- 2½ quarts of cold spring water.
- Small wineglassful of rum or pale brandy.

Blanch the almonds and throw them into cold water to whiten them. Pound them in a marble mortar, using the orange-flower water to prevent them oiling. When thoroughly pounded into a paste lift out into a basin. Mix in the strained lemon juice, the syrup, and a portion of the water, and strain through a silk tammy cloth, two persons twisting up the ends tightly. Any of the almonds still remaining in the cloth must be repounded and mixed with some of the remaining water and again passed. Add the rest of the water and the spirit, and ice thoroughly. The liquid should be quite white, like milk, and of fine flavour. Care must be taken not to oil the almonds when pounding, and to use very cold water, otherwise the liquid will be apt to disintegrate, like curds and whey. A very satisfactory orgeat water may be made from the commercial marzipan (two-thirds being almonds, and one-third sugar), adjusting the proportions accordingly.

ICED COFFEE.

- 8 ozs. of freshly-ground coffee (⅓ Mocha, ⅓ peaberry, ⅓ plantation).
- 4 pints of water.
- A pinch of salt.
- 1¼ pint of simple syrup.
- 1 pint of double cream.
- 2 pints of new milk.
- ½ oz. of vanilla sugar.

All about Ices.

Boil the water, throw in the salt and coffee, boil up once, strain quite clear through a small jelly bag, add the syrup and vanilla sugar, heat the milk and cream to 150 deg. F., and add to the strained coffee. Mix well, pour in a porcelain freezer or a large jar, and set up in ice and a little salt, and ice thoroughly, but without freezing hard. Serve in tiny coffee cups or small glasses.

Note.—When fresh strawberries, raspberries, or cherries are not available almost equally satisfactory "ades" may be made from the fruit preserved for ices. (See "Fruits for Ices.")

THE END.

INDEX.

ALEXANDRA PUDDING, 53
Almond Praline Cream (Brown), 112
,, ,, ,, (Mottled Brown), 112
,, ,, ,, Ice (Custard) 49
,, ,, and Pistachio Bombe, 69
Almonds (Green), 162
Ambassador Cream, 113
Angelica, 161
Apple Compote, 171
Apple Conserve for Masking, 128
Apple Jelly (Cherry Apples), 135
,, ,, (Fresh Fruit), 135
,, Paste, 139
,, Pulp, 144, 145
,, Water Ice, 14
Apricots (Green), 163
,, (Ripe), 163
,, Charlotte, 95
,, ,, Cream for, 95
,, Cream, 102
,, ,, Ice, 35
,, Jam, 128
,, ,, (Blended), 128
,, ,, (Fresh), 123
,, ,, (from Pulp), 128
,, Jelly, 89
,, Paste, 139
,, Water Ice, 13
Aspic Jelly, 90, 92
Aveline Praline Cream Ice (Custard), 49
,, ,, and Vanilla Bombe, 69

BANANA COMPOTE, 171
,, Cream, 104
,, Charlotte, 96
,, ,, Cream for, 96
,, Water Ice, 19
Barberry Jelly, 90
Belgrave Jelly, 82
Benedictine Cream (White), 111
Black Currant Compote, 170
,, ,, Jam (Blended), 130
,, ,, ,, (Fresh), 120
,, ,, ,, (Pure), 130
,, ,, Jelly, 132
,, ,, Paste, 141
,, ,, Pulp, 145
,, ,, Water Ice, 12
Black Currants, 147

Biscuit Glacé, 39
,, ,, Caramelled, 40
,, ,, Macaroon, 41
,, ,, Marasquin, 41
,, ,, Vanilla, 40
Blancmange (White), 115, 116
Brown Bread Cream, 114
,, ,, or Digestive Iced Pudding, 56
,, ,, Iced Souffle, 63
,, ,, Cream Ice, 39
,, ,, and Vanilla Bombe, 70
Bullace and Slows, 148
Burgundy Cup—Red, 180

CALVES' FEET JELLY STOCK, 73
Canteloup Melon Cream, 105
Caramel Cream, 115
,, Souffle, 64
Carmine, Liquid, for Colouring, 123
Cassis Cream (Pale Purple), 111
,, Jelly, 80
,, Water Ice, 21
Cedrati Water Ice, 8
Chablis Cup, 180
Champagne Cup, 181
Champagne Jelly, 84
,, Water Ice, 22
Charlotte a la Russe 93
,, ,, Cream for, 93
Charlottes of Cream, 93
Cherryade, 183, 184
Cherries, Bottled, for Ice Making, 152
,, ,, in water, 149
,, Stoned, in water, 149
Cherry Charlotte, 94
,, ,, Cream for, 95
,, Cream, 101, 102
,, ,, Ice (Fresh Medoc), 37
,, ,, ,, (Fresh Morella), 37
,, ,, ,, (Preserved Cherries), 37
,, Water Ice, 13
,, Jelly, 88
,, and Maraschino Bombe, 71
,, and Pistachio Bombe, 68
,, Plums (Red), 148
,, Plum Jam (Fresh), 124
Chestnut Cream (Pale Brown), 114
Chianti Cup, 181
Chocolate and Vanilla Bombe, 71

Index.

Chinois (Green), 166
,,   D'Or, 166
Chocolate Cream, 109, 110
,,   ,,   Bombe, 67
,,   ,,   Ice (Custard), 45, 46
,,   Souffle, 66
Christmas Pudding (Iced), 53
Cider Cup, 182
Cider Granito, 30
Cinnamon Cream Ice, 4
Citron Peel, 157
Claret Cup, 179
Claret Granito, 29
Clear Orange Marmalade, 130
Coffee Cream, 109
,,   ,,   Ice, 38
,,   ,,   ,,   (Custard), 45
,,   and Green Coffee Bombe, 70
,,   and Pistachio Bombe, 68
,,   Souffle, 66
,,   Jelly, 81
Colouring Jellies Pink, 85
Compote of Green Gooseberries, 175
,,   of Damsons, 175
,,   of Macedoine, 175
,,   of Orange, 175
,,   of Oranges (Tangerine), 176
,,   of Chestnuts (Marrons), 176
,,   ,,   and Oranges, 176
,,   Bordeaux, 176
,,   of Green Figs, 176
,,   of Cherry Apples, 177
,,   of Winter Strawberries, 177
,,   of Medlars, 177
,,   of Muscat Grapes, 177
,,   of Muscatels, 178
,,   of Ripe Apricots, 173
,,   of Peaches, 173
,,   of Nectarines, 173
,,   of Pears with Sauterne, 173
,,   of Quince, 174
,,   of Pineapple, 174
,,   ,,   and Apple Jelly, 174
,,   of Apples and Cranberries, 174
,,   of Cranberries, 174
,,   of Pears, 171
,,   of Cherries (Morella), 171
,,   ,,   (Flemish), 171
,,   of Melon, 171
,,   of Victoria Plums, 172
,,   of Mirabels, 172
,,   of Green Apricots, 172
Compotes of Fruit, 169
Conservators, 4
Cranberry Jelly, 90
,,   ,,   (Fresh Fruit), 134
Cranberry Water Ice, 18

Cream Des Anges, 115
Creams, 92
Creme de Menthe Granito, 30
Crystallised Red or White Currants, 170
Curacoa Cream (White), 10
Custard Ices, 41

DAMSONS, 148
Damson Cheese Paste, 141
Damson Jam (Blended), 131
,,   ,,   (Fresh), 126
,,   ,,   (Pure), 131
,,   Water Ice, 18
Decorated Moulds, 76
Dessert Ices, 57
Digestive or Brown Bread Pudding Iced, **56**

ELDERBERRY WATER ICE, 24

FLORENTINE GRANITO, 27
Freezers, 2
Fruit Jellies, 86
,,   Pastes, 137
,,   ,,   Boiling the Pulp, 137
,,   ,,   Boiling the Pulp into Pastes 137
,,   Pulps for Jam Making, 142
Fruits, Bottled in Water for Tarts, 145
,,   in Bottles without Water, 149
,,   Preserved for Ices, 150

GELATINE, TO MELT, 86
Gelatine and Isinglass, 74
,,   Jelly Stock, 74
Gelee a la Durer, 81
,,   a la Russe, 83
Gin Cup, 182
Ginger Water Ice, 21
Gisbon Plum Jam (Blended), 131
,,   ,,   ,,   (Fresh), 126
,,   ,,   ,,   (Pure), 130
Glacé Cherries, 153
Gooseberry Fool, 178
Granita or Granito, 24
Grape Jelly, 89
Green Coffee Cream Ice, 3
,,   ,,   and Coffee Bombe, 70
,,   ,,   Souffle, 65
,,   ,,   Jelly, 82
Green Chartreuse Cream, 111
Green Figs, 165
Greengage Compote, 172
Greengages, 148
,,   164
Greengage Cream, 106
,,   ,,   Ice, 37
,,   Jam (Fresh), 123

Index.

Greengage Jam (Blended), 129
,, ,, from Pulp, 129
,, Pulp, 144
Greengage Water Ice, 17
Green Gooseberries, 147
,, Gooseberry Jam (Fresh), 124
,, ,, from Bottled Fruit, 133
,, ,, Pulp, 129, 144
Green Tea Cream Ice, 38
,, Victoria Plum Jam, 125
,, ,, ,, Pulp, 129
,, Almonds, 162
Green Walnuts, 166
,, Chinois, 166
,, Gooseberries, 166
,, French Beans, 168

Hard Green Plum Pulp, 144
Harlequin Bombe, 70
Hock Cup, 180

Ice, 1
Ice Caves, 62
Iced Bombes, 67
,, Puddings, 51
,, Souffle, 61
Iced Coffee, 185
Iceland Moss Jelly, 86
Ices (Freezing), 6
Imperial Charlotte, 97
,, ,, Cream for 98
Isinglass and Gelatine, 74
,, To Clarify, 76
Italian Cream Ice (Custard), 49
,, ,, (Pale Yellow), 113
,, Cream and Maraschino Bombe, 71
,, Souffle, 67

Jams from Pulped Fruit, 127
Jellies, 131
Jelly Bags, 73

Kirsch Cream (Pale Pink), 112
Kummel Cream (Pale Yellow), 111

Lemon and Strawberry Bombe, 68
Lemon Cream, 108
,, Jelly, 78
,, Marmalade, 137
,, Paste, 140
,, Peel, 156
,, Sponge Jelly, 7
,, Water Ice, 85
Lemonade, 182
Limeade, 183
Lime Water Ice, 6
Logan Compote, 170
Lombard Granito, 27

Macedoine of Jelly, 83
Mandarine Cream (Yellow), 119
Maraschino and Cherry Bombe, 71
,, ,, Italian Cream Bombe, 71
,, ,, Orange Bombe, 68
,, Cream (Pale Pink), 110
,, Granito, 26
,, Jelly, 80
,, Water Ice, 23
Marmalade, 135
,, Preparation of Peel and Pulp, 136
Marrons Glacé, 158
Marsala Cup, 181
Melon Cream, 104
,, Iced Pudding, 55
,, Mould Dessert Ice, 61
,, Pear Water Ice, 24
,, Water Ice, 16
Melting Isinglass and Gelatine, 93
Mikado Charlotte, 99
,, ,, Cream for, 100
Milan Cream, 114
Mille Fleur Cream, 108
,, ,, Water Ice, 10
,, Fruit Cream, 107
,, ,, Granito, 31
,, ,, Water Ice, 10
,, Fruitade, 184
Mint Cream, 115
Mirabel Cream, 105
,, Jam (Fresh), 12
,, ,, (Pure), 130
,, Plums (Yellow), 148
Mirabelle Water Ice, 19
Mirabels, 167
Morella Cherry Jelly, 88
Morella Cherry Water Ice, 13
Mosaic Neapolitan Ice, 60
Moselle Cup, 180, 181
Moselle Granito, 30
Muffin Iced Pudding, 57
Mulberries, 148
Mulberry Compote, 170
Mulberry Cream, 106
,, Water Ice, 18
Muscatel Cup, 181
Muscat Water Ice, 10

Neapolitan Cream, 114
,, Dessert Ices, 58
,, Ices a la Russe, 60
,, Souffle, 65
,, Ice, Mosaic, 60
,, Ices, Tutti-Frutti, 59
Nectarine Cream, 103
,, Water Ice, 20

Index.

Nesselrode Pudding, 51
Noyeau Cream (Pale Pink), 112
  ,,   Jelly, 84
ORANGE CURACOA WATER ICE, 9
    ,, Curacoa Jelly, 79
    ,, Cream, 107
    ,, Flower Cream Ice (Custard), 50
    ,, Flower Jelly, 79
    ,, Jelly, 78
    ,, and Maraschino Bombe, 68
    ,, Paste, 140
    ,, Peel, 157
    ,, Puree, 137
    ,, Sections Iced, 61
    ,, Sponge, 85
    ,, Water Ice, 8
Orangeade, 183
Orgeat Water, 185
Orgeat Water Ice, 21
Orleans Plum Cream Ice, 36
    ,, Plums (Early), 148
    ,,   ,, (Late), 148
    ,, Plum Jam (Fresh), 125
    ,,   ,, Cream, 106
    ,, Plum Water Ice, 16

PANACHEE JELLY, 84
Pastes, Crystallising the, 140
Peach Cream Ice, 36
  ,,   ,,   ,, (De Luxe), 36
  ,,   ,,   102
  ,, Jelly, 89
  ,, Paste, 139
  ,, Water Ice, 14
Pear Water Ice, 15
  ,, Paste, 139
Pears (White), 167
  ,, (Reed), 167
Peel Preserving (Drained), 155
Perry Cup, 182
Perry Water Ice, 22
Pineade, 184
Pineapple, 168
Pineapple Charlotte, 97
    ,,   ,, Cream for, 97
    ,, Cream Ice, 35
    ,, Water Ice, 15
    ,, Cream, 103
    ,, Jelly, 89
    ,, Cream Ice (Custard), 48
Pistachio Water Ice, 23
    ,, Cream Ice, 48
    ,,   ,,   ,, (Custard), 47
    ,, Cream (Pale Green), 112
    ,, and Coffee Bombe, 68
    ,, Souffle, 65
    ,, and Almond Praline Bombe, 69

Pistachio and Cherry Bombe, 69
Plombiere Iced Pudding, 54
Pomegranate Water Ice, 20
Pompadour Cream, 113
Pompadour Jelly, 80
    ,,   Bombe, 69
Praline Charlotte, 97
  ,,   ,, Cream for, 98
  ,,   ,, Praline for, 98
Preserved Fruits, Wet or Dry, 153
Princess Charlotte, 98
  ,,   ,, Cream for, 99
Pruneau Cream (White), 112
Punch Cup, 182
Punch Water Ice, 22

Quirnale Granito, 26
QUINCE AND APPLE PASTA, 139
  ,, Paste, 138

RASPBERRIES, 168
Raspberries, 147
  ,, and Currants, 147
Raspberry Water Ice, 11
  ,, and Red Currant Water Ice
  ,, Granito, 28
  ,, Cream Ice (Fresh Fruit),
  ,, Cream Ice (Preserved Fruit)
  ,, and Red Currant Cream Ice
  ,, Jelly, 87
  ,, and Red Currant Jelly, 88
  ,, Juice for Ices, 153
  ,, Jelly (Fresh Fruit), 133
  ,,   ,, (from Pulp), 134
  ,, Pulp, 143
  ,, Jam (Blended), 127
  ,,   ,, (Pure), 127
  ,, and Red Currant, 128
  ,,   ,,   ,,   ,, Jam, 1
  ,, Jam (Fresh), 119
  ,, Cream, 100, 101
  ,, and Red Currant Cream, 10
Raspberryade, 184
Raspberry Compote, 169
  ,, and Red Currant Compote, 1
Raspberry Fool, 178
Red Currant Compote, 170
  ,, and Black Currant Compote, 170
Red Currant Jelly, 87
  ,,   ,, Water Ice, 12
  ,,   ,, Juice for Ices, 153
  ,, or White Currant Pulp, 144
  ,, Gooseberry Jam from Pulp, 129
  ,, Currant Jam (Pure), 130
  ,,   ,, Jelly (Fresh Fruit), 131
  ,,   ,,   ,, (Pulped Fruit), 132
  ,,   ,,   ,, (from Bottled Fruit)
  ,, Gooseberry Jelly (Fresh Fruit), 1

Index.

Red Gooseberry Jelly (from Pulp), 133
  ,,   ,,   144
,, Currant Jam (Fresh), 120
,, Gooseberry Jam (Fresh), 125
Red Pears, 167
Rhubarb (Forced), 149
,, (Green), 149
Ripe Plums of all Sorts, 144
Rock Melon Cream, 105
Roman Cream (Pale Pink), 114
,, Punch Granito, 25
Rose Jelly, 85
Rum Jelly, 84
,, Punch Jelly, 82
,, ,, Granito, 25

SALT, 2
Samur Cup, 181
Sauterne Cup, 180
Seville Orange Marmalade, 136
Shaddock Water Ice, 15
Sherry Granito, 29
Small Tangerines Iced, 61
Souffle, Iced, 61
,, Dishes or Moulds, 62
,, Syrup, 63
,, Brown Bread, 63
,, Strawberry Cream, 63
,, Victoria, 64
,, Caramel, 64
,, Pistachio, 65
,, Neapolitan Green Coffee, 65
,, Coffee, 66
,, Chocolate, 66
,, Des Anges, 66
,, Italian, 67
Spinach Mould Cream Ice, 61
Strawberries Pulped without Sugar, 151
,, ,, with Sugar, 151
,, Juice Pulped with Sugar, 151
,, Juice Pulped without Sugar, 152
Strawberryade, 184
Strawberry Compote, 16
,, Fool, 178
Strawberry Water Ice, 12
,, Granito, 28
,, Cream Ice 32
,, ,, ,, (Fresh Fruit), 32
,, ,, ,, (Preserved Fruit), 33
,, ,, Souffle, 63
,, and Lemon Bombe, 68
,, and Tangerine Orange Bombe, 68
,, Jelly, 87
,, Charlotte, 94
,, ,, Cream for, 94
,, Cream, 100

Strawberry Jam, 121
,, ,, (Whole Fruit), 121, 122
,, ,, (Pulped Fruit), 123
,, Jelly (Fresh Fruit), 134
,, Pulp, 145
Syrup (Simple), 7, 87

TANGERINES (SMALL) ICED, 61
Tangerine Orange Water Ice, 9
,, ,, and Strawberry Bombe, 68
,, ,, Jelly, 79
,, ,, Charlotte, 95
,, ,, ,, Cream for, 96
,, ,, and Grape Charlotte, 96
,, ,, ,, ,, Cream for, ,, 96
,, ,, Cream, 107
,, ,, Marmalade, 137
Tangerine Orangeade, 183
Tart Fruit Generally in Water, 133
Tea Cream Ice (Custard), 46
,, Jelly, 82
,, Infusion, 82

VANILLA CREAM ICE, 42, 43
,, Sugar, 44
,, Extract of, 44
,, and Aveline Praline Bombe, 69
,, and Brown Bread Bombe, 70
,, and Chocolate Bombe, 71
,, Jelly, 81
,, Cream, 108, 109
Victoria Plum Water Ice, 17
,, Pudding, 52
,, Souffle, 64
,, Jelly, 80
,, Plum Jam (Fresh), 125
,, Cream (White), 113
,, Plum Jam (Green), 125
,, ,, ,, 130
,, ,, ,, (Blended), 130
Victor Jelly, 80
Victoria Plums, 167

WALNUTS (Green), 166
Washington Gage Jam (Fresh), 126
Whipping Cream for Moulds, 92
White Coffee Cream Ice, 38
,, Currant Jelly, 88
,, ,, Water Ice, 12
,, Raspberry Water Ice, 11
White Pears, 167

YELLOW CHARTREUSE CREAM, 111

For Product Safety Concerns and Information please contact our EU representative GPSR@taylorandfrancis.com
Taylor & Francis Verlag GmbH, Kaufingerstraße 24, 80331 München, Germany

www.ingramcontent.com/pod-product-compliance
Lightning Source LLC
Chambersburg PA
CBHW080937300426
44115CB00017B/2855